I0091308

Abstracts
Of
Sampson County
North Carolina
Wills

1784-1895

By Cora Bass

Contents

Unprobated Wills 1-13

Recorded Wills 14-95

Deed Record Book II (Wills) 96-99

Unrecorded Wills (Loose) 100-118

Olds' N. C. Abstracts Of Wills (Sampson)............. 119

Index 120-175

Unprobated Wills

(BOOK A)

(D) date of will.

ADAMS, Mary - D. May 2, 1808
  Grandchildren: Edwin Adams, Sentha Adams, Murtilda Ivey,
                  Rebeckah Wall, Rebekah Adams, Colon Adams
  Exec: Nathan Godwin, Lewis Adams
  Wit: Thinchen Adams, Wallis Mobley

AMMONS, Thomas - D. June 15, 1792
  Wife: Elizabeth Ammons
  Sons: Vaughn, Nowell, Joshua Ammons
  Exec: Sons, Joshua, Vaughn Ammons
  Wit: Jonathan Carr, Benj. Carr

AUGHTRY, Drury - D. 1808
  Sons: Raiford, Archibald Aughtry
  Daus: Sarah, Charlotte and Charity Aughtry, Milly
                  Faircloth
  Exec: Thomas Maxwell, Caleb Faircloth

BAREFOOT, Isabel - D. June 13, 1797
  Daus: Sarah Porter
  Son-in-law: William Porter
  Heirs: Sally Bryan (dau. of John Bryan, Sr.), John
                  Bryan, Sr., Friend
  Exec: Friend, John Bryan, Sr.
  Wit: Martha Thornton

BARKS, Joseph - D. Nov. 14, 1807
  Wife: Tamer Barks
  Sons: Henderson, Littleton Barks
  Exec: Wife, Tamer Barks, John Fleming
  Wit: Alex N. Benton, James Holly

BASS, Andrew - D. August 18, 1786
  Mother: Elizabeth Bass
  Exec: Burrell Bass, William Bass
  Wit: Lewis Bass, Ann Bass, James Mobley

Copyright 1958 by:

Cora Bass

All rights reserved. No part of this publication may be reproduced, stored in a retrieval system or transmitted in any form or by any means without the prior written permission of the publisher.

Please Direct All Correspondence and Book Orders to:
Southern Historical Press, Inc.
PO Box 1267
375 West Broad Street
Greenville, SC 29602-1267
or
southernhistoricalpress@gmail.com

ISBN #0-89308-897-8

Printed in the United States of America

CARR, Thomas - D. March 2, 1798
  Wife: Mary Carr
  Sons: Theophilus, Reddin, Joseph, Moab, Enoch,
             Patrick, Jonathan, Thomas, William Carr
  Daus: Betsey Carr, Thamer Carr, Mary Carr
  Exec: Wife, Mary Carr, Theophilus Carr
  Wit: Laban Taylor, Turner Carr, Elizabeth Gowry

CARR, Patience - D. May 13, 1818
  Son: Jesse Carr
  Heir: Janet Chesnutt
  Mentions part of estate of deceased brother John Turner.
  Exec: Aaron Hargrove
  Wit: John Sellers, Joel Britt

CARR, Patrick - D. July 6, 1825
  Wife: Tabitha
  Exec: Gary Toole
  Wit: John Sellers, Gainey Westbrook

CARRELL, Alexander - D. February 25, 1827
  Wife: Lucey
  Sons: Hardy, Wylie, Reason Carrell
  Daus: Rebekah Carrell, Phanney Bridges, Mary Ann
             Tedder, Betsey Ann Royal
  Exec: Wife, Lucey Carrell, Hardy Royal
  Wit: Daniel Williams, Nathan Williams, Thomas
             Maxwell

CARRELL, Jesse, Sr. - D. March 10, 1802
  Wife: Rachel Carrell
  Sons: Jesse, John, Thomas, Joseph Carrell
  Daus: Mary Hollingsworth, Priscilla Carrell,
             Rachel Carrell
  Exec: Sons, John, Jesse Carrell
  Wit: John Carrel, David Chesnutt, Alexander
             Chesnutt

CARRELL, John - D. May 22, 1814
  Sons: Raeford Carrell (other children mentioned
             but not named)
  Exec: Rashel Carrell
  Wit: Hiram Blackburn, Raiford Carrell

CARTER, Naaman - D. March 7, 1810
  Wife: Elizabeth
  Sons: John, Daniel Carter
  Daus: Charity Stevens, Seeney Carter, Elizabeth
                Carter, Sarahon Carter
  Exec: Daniel Carter, Richard Parker
  Wit: Payton A. Parker, Nicholas Parker

CHESNUTT, David - D. May 27, 1831
  Wife: Anny Chesnutt
  Sons: Mitchel, William, James, Daniel, Henry
  Daus: Peggy, Anney Jane, Asha, Polly
  Exec: Wife: Anny Chesnutt, William Chesnutt
  Wit: Asha, Edward C. Gavin, David Chesnutt

COGGINS, Thomas - D. February 12, 1797
  Wife: Martha Coggins
  Dau: Mary Coggins
  Heir: Unborn child
  Exec: Martha Coggins, William Robinson
  Wit: George Taylor, William Fryar, W. Robinson

COLE, William - D. December 1, 1807
  Wife: Sary Cole
  Son: William Cole
  Dau: Martha Cole
  Sons-in-law: George Hobbs, Thomas Hollingsworth
  Exec: John Fleming, Daniel Kinsey
  Wit: Thomas Hollingsworth, William Cole

COOK, James - D. June 3, 1786
  Sons: John, Cornelius Cook
  Daus: Jean Cook, Ann Watkins
  Exec: Ann Watkins
  Wit: Jon Parker, Cader Vann, George Bain

CRUMPLER, Jacob - D. January 22, 1817
  Sons: John, Owens, Evan Crumpler
  Daus: Nancy Peterson (wife of Babel Peterson),
                Rachel Spell (wife of Lewis Spell), Mary
                Wise (wife of Morris Wise), Molsey
                Honeycutt (wife of Willie Honeycutt),
                Colin Crumpler
  Exec: Son, John Crumpler, Redman Crumpler, Nephew
  Wit: Ben Phillips, Blackman Crumpler

CRUMPLER, John - D. February 17, 1782
  County: Duplin
  Sons: Jacob Crumpler, John, Cajiah Crumpler
  Daus: Rachel, Sarah, Nancy, Elizabeth, Grace
                 Crumpler
  Exec: Jacob, John Crumpler, Elisha Wiggins
  Wit: Arthur Coor, Daniel Coor, William Wiggs

DANIEL, Jonathan - D. March 2, 1811
  Wife: Susanna Daniel
  Sons: Raiford, Isaac Daniel
  Daus: Polly Daniel, Lydia Daniel
  Father, Isaac Daniel
  Exec: Josiah Blackman
  Wit: Josiah Powell, Furney Westbrook, Lenny
                 Daniel

DARDEN, Billy, Jr. - D. April 21, 1818
  Wife: Peggy Darden
  Sons: Henry, Reddick, John, William Jackson Darden
  Dau: Catharine Oats
  Son-in-law: Jesse Oats
  Exec: Peggy Darden, Henry Darden
  Wit: John Eliot, Sophia Bradshaw, Samuel Stanley

DAUGHTRY, Lydda - D. May 25, 1813
  Heirs: Friend, Nathan Boyt, David Darden, Edny
                 Standley
  Exec: Nathan Boyt, David Darden
  Wit: James Oates, Stephen Oates

DEVANE, George - D. February 10, 1810
  Wife: Miriam Devane
  Sons: Cornelius DeVane, John T., Felix DeVane
  Daus: Elizabeth, Catharine, Mary Ann, Tabitha,
                 Miriam DeVane
  Exec: Wife, Miriam DeVane, Alexander Cromartie
  Wit: John Herring, Stephen Herring, John
                 Treadwell, Jr.

DINKINS, Joseph John - D. July 3, 1810
  Wife: Seley Dinkins
  Daus: Ann Lewisar Denkins, Lettie Lucinder, Sally
                 Surreney Dinkins, Elanah Dinkins
  Exec: Wife, Seley Dinkins, Edward C. Gavin,

```
                        Elijah Gregory
        Wit:            Lott Gregory, Surrene Gregory


DREW, Alcy - D. September 13, 1825
    Son:                Huey Drew
    Bro:                Josiah Drew
    Sis:                Marry Stevens, Sary Drew
    Heirs:              William Drew's heirs, Willis's heirs, Wil-
                        son's heirs
    Exec:               Son, Huey Drew
    Wit:                John Brown, Z. Williamson, Nathan Boyett,
                        A. L. Brown


DUACH, Magdalene - D. May 14, 1785
    Sons:               William, Caleb, Henry Duach
    Daus:               Selah, Phoebe, Bettsy, Onece Duach, Sarah
                        Cammeron
    Exec:               Riner Blackman
    Wit:                Henry Faison, Henry Holland, Samuel Oates


DUDLEY, Levi - D. Jan. 11, 1808
    Sons:               Elam, Ely, Enoch, John Dudley
    Daus:               Nanney, Lydia, Hepzibak, Lilly, Jenet Dudley
    Bro:                Eden Dudley
    Exec:               Bro., Eden, Son, Elam Dudley
    Wit:                Nedham Dudley, Eleas Peters, Young Keen


FRYER, Jacob - June 26, 1785
    Wife:               Winneford Fryer
    Heirs:              Mary, Edy Fryar (children of brother Jona-
                        than and his present wife, Elizabeth)
    Exec:               Winneford Fryer, Jonathan Fryar
    Wit:                R. C. Clinton, Charles Murphy, Demcy Carroll


GAVIN, Samuel - November 30, 1807
    Wife:               Sarah Gavin
    Son:                Edward C. Gavin
    Dau:                Mary Chesnutt
    Exec:               Edward C. Gavin, John Chesnutt
    Wit:                Benjamin Warters, Asia Gregory, Elisha
                        Gregory


GENKINS, Thomas - D. July 6, 1809
    Wife:               Tabitha Genkins
    Bro:                Jonathan Genkins
```

```
Sis:            Nanny Parker, Mary Smith , Sealey Genkins
Exec:           Andrew Smith
Wit:            H. G. Morris, Abel Mate
```

HAIR, John - D. July 30, 1809
```
  Wife:           Elizabeth
  Sons:           Isaac, William, John, Thomas Hair
  Daus:           Zilpha, Sarah, Letha, Eady Hair
  Sons-in-law:    John Strickland, Joseph Lockamy
  Exec:           Odom Lockamy
  Wit:            Mark Porter, John Strickland
```

HAIR, William - D. March 21, 1825
```
  Sons:           William Hair, Arthur Hair, Felix Hair
  Grandson:       Guilford Hair
  Wit:            Raiford Coor, Blueford Hare
```

HALL, Armager - D. June 7, 1811
```
  Wife: (2nd)     Feby Hall
  Son:            William Hall
  Daus:           Hizziah, Zilper Hall

  Exec:           Son, William Hall
  Wit:            Simon Hobbs, Hester Hobbs, O. Mobley
```

HANEY, Sarah - D. July 12, 1814
```
  Sons:           Joseph John, Gabriel, Lalon, Joshua Haney
  Daus:           Elizabeth Register, Sarah Cooper, Penny
                  Hayes, Susanah Smith, Polly Spyvea
  Exec:           Son, John Joseph Haney
  Wit:            Lalon Laton, Hiram Blackburn
```

HARGROVE, Arthur - D. January 23, 1815
```
  Dau:            Feriby Drew, Abner Williams, Charity Carr
  Grandson:       Benjamin Hargrove
  Exec:           James Fredrick, Aaron Hargrove
  Wit:            James Fredrick, Jonathan Carr
```

HAY, Charles - D. 1789
```
  Wife:           Sarah Hay
  Son:            Peter Hay
  Daus:           Mary Rice, Winny Hay
  Grandson:       Solomon Hay
  Exec:           Wife, Sarah Hay, Son, Peter Hay
  Wit:            Thomas Goff, William Price
```

HERRING, B. M. - D. July 2, 1863
  Wife: Sarah Herring
  Heirs: Nancy Warren (wife of William H. Warren),
               Stephen B. Herring
  Exec: William H. Warren
  Wit: R. C. Lee, Elem Lee

HERRING, Jacob - D. September 13, 1796
  Wife: Betsy Herring
  Son: Stephen Herring
  Daus: Sarah, Mary, Betsy Herring
  Exec: Wife, Betsy, Bro., Uzzell Herring
  Wit: William Gamford, Thomas Vann

HERRING, Stephen - D. April 20, 1817
  Wife: Eleanor Herring
  Sons: Bright Middleton, Robert Nixon Herring
  Daus: Polly, Kitty, Sallyan, Eliza Herring
  Exec: Alexander Benton, Joab Blackmon
  Wit: Duncan McPhail, Allen Barbary

HERRING, Uzzill - D. March 6, 1803
  Wife: Ann Herring
  Sons: Joseph, Nathan, John, Benjamin, William
               Herring
  Dau: Nancy Herring
  Exec: Wife, Ann Herring, William Smith
  Wit: William Vann, Lewis Gavin, Benjamin Warters

HOLDER, George - D. August 25, 1799
  Wife: Mary Holder
  Sons: William, George Vincent, Thomas Holder
  Daus: Rachel Hodge, Mary Bell, Elizabeth Hair,
               Telitha Royal, Tabitha Wooten
  Nephew: Robert Saunders
  Exec: Mary Holder, George Vincent Holder, Thomas
               Holder
  Wit: Hardy Holmes, Gabriel Holmes

HOLDER, John - D. June 23, 1780
  Wife: Ann Holder
  Sons: Jese Holder, Nathan Holder
  Daus: Mary, Sally, Anna, Martha, Glada, Lilla
               Holder
  Exec: John Holly, Amos Runnels
  Wit: John Holly, Anna Holly, Betty Bass

HOLLAND, Thomas - D. October 21, 1819
```
  Wife:        Milly Holland
  Sons:        Henry Holland, John Holland
  Daus:        Mary Charity, Nancy Orpha, Milly Holland
  Heirs:       Thomas James Holland, Son, Willis Daniel
               Holland
  Exec:        Daniel Holland
  Wit:         Fleet Cooper, Ann Duffie
```

HOWARD, Thomas M. - D. June 4, 1862
```
  Bro:         Fleet H. Howard
  Sis:         Sarah A., Mary E. Howard, Rebecca M. Maxwell
  Exec:        J. R. Maxwell
  Wit:         Thomas A. Howard, J. C. Howard
```

JACKSON, James - D. March 31, 1825
```
  Wife:        Aney
  Sons:        Allen, Joel, Drew Jackson
  Daus:        Patty Jackson, Amy Jackson
  Exec:        John Jackson
  Wit:         Isaac Strickland, Alexander Tew, Bennett
               Jackson, Sr.
```

JACOB, Abraham - D. February 13, 1807
```
  Heir:        Susana Carter
  Exec:        Susana Carter
  Wit:         H. Holmes, Feriby Holmes
```

JOHNSON, Ephrian - D. December 8, 1818
```
  Sons:        Aaron Johnson, Jese Johnson, John Johnson,
               William Johnson
  Daus:        Nancy Elizabeth, Maurrisy Johnson
  Granddau:    Kitty Johnson
  Bro:         Solomon Johnson
  Exec:        John, William Johnson
  Wit:         W. Robinson
```

JOHNSON, William D. (?)
```
  Wife:        Betsey Johnson
  Sons:        Allen, Taylor, George, William, Nathan,
               Joel, Joab Johnson
  Daus:        Dorcas, Nancy, Betsey Johnson
  Granddaus:   Molsy Chappell Johnson, Nancy Jean Fryer
  Exec:        Wife, Betsey Johnson, Son, Joab Johnson
  Wit:         William Robinson
```

JOHNSTON, John - D. August 31, 1814
- Wife: Elizabeth Johnston
- Sons: John, Mark, Mathew Johnston
- Daus: Elizabeth Faircloth, Hannah Faircloth, Mary Hall, Milly Faircloth
- Granddaus: Mary (dau. of Isham Faircloth), Susannah Faircloth (dau. of James Faircloth)
- Exec: Wife, Elizabeth Johnston, John Johnston
- Wit: Salmon Sessoms, Robert Grice, James Faircloth

JOYNER, James - D. February 27, 1805

"To James Marley all of my estate in addition to what I have already deeded him in the estate of Benjamin Joyner (dec'd).
- Exec: James Marley
- Wit: Kedar Vann, James Aswell, Nancy Stanley

JONES, John - D. April 14, 1824
- Wife: Sally Jones
- Exec: Sally Jones, James Odom
- Wit: Thomas Sutton, Buthsdela Sutton, Milcoh Jones

JONES, Thadrick - D. December 19, 1802
- Wife: Mary Jones
- Sons: Reddick, Benjamin, Philip (dec'd) Jones
- Daus: Polly, Rachel, Thadrick Jones
- Sons-in-law: Thomas Wo---, Ambrose Simes, Jesey Cotton, Walas Mobley
- Exec: Son, Benjamin Jones
- Wit: William Killen, Thadrick Jones, Jr.

KEEN, John, Sr. - D. December 12, 1803
- Wife: Elizabeth Keen
- Sons: William, John Keen
- Exec: Wife, Elizabeth, Son, John Keen
- Wit: Sherwood Holly, Hillery Laton, Elam Dudley

KELLY, Joseph - D. January 1, 1795
- Wife: Elizabeth Kelly
- Sons: William, Jacob Kelly
- Daus: Mary Kelly, Gemimy Kelly
- Exec: Joshua Sikes, Jacob Kelly
- Wit: Joshua Sikes, Alexander Carroll

LOCKAMY, Eli - D. November 13, 1950
    Dau: Marjorie Jane Lockamy Hunter
    Exec: Marjorie Jane Lockamy Hunter
    Wit: R. J. Stewart, Wade, N. C.
                Wiley B. Barefoot, Dunn, N. C.

MARLEY, Frances - D. April 21, 1824
    Sons: Horatio, Rolland, Willie Marley
    Daus: Elizabeth Smith, Harriett Vail, Eliza
                Marley, Sally Ann Marley
    Exec: Ollen Mobley, Robert Marley
    Wit: Edward Vail, Ollen Mobley

MARTIN, Richard - D. April 19, 1810
    Wife: Mary Martin
    Son: Lewis Martin

    Dau: Sally Martin
    Exec: John Ingram, James Moore
    Wit: H. Holmes, Jacob Flowers, Stanley Davis

MATTHIS, Joel - D. June 1, 1821
    Wife: Kathern Matthis
    Mentions children but does not name them.
    Wit: Joel Mathis, John Johnston, Robert Williams,
                Alen Porter

MATTHIS, Zacheous - D. 1837
    Wife: Mary Matthis
    Sons: John C., Henry, Milton, Marshall Matthis
    Daus: Mahala Vail, Jenetty Matthis
    Exec: George W. Robinson
    Wit: Liza Matthis, Thomas Matthis

MERRITT, Nathaniel - August 18, 1819
    Sons: Gabriel, Patrick Merritt
    Daus: Treecy, Unity, Ann Merritt
    Exec: Patrick Merritt, John Bryan
    Wit: John Bryan, David Merritt, Lewis Bowden

MERRITT, Unity - D. December 1, 1873
    Son: James Merritt
    Sis: Teresy Merritt, Ann Merritt
    Bros: Patrick Merritt (son, Kilby Merritt)
                Gabriel Merritt (dau. Temperance)
    Exec: Dickson Sloan

```
Wit:            Dickson Sloan, Patrick Merritt
```

MOBLEY, Biggers - D. February 26, 1802
```
    Wife:       Elizabeth Mobley
    Sons:       Ollen, Willie Mobley
    Daus:       Betsey Mobley, Fanny Marley (wife of James
                Marley)
    Exec:       Ollen, Willie Mobley
    Wit:        Dan Coor, John Barnes, Gardner Keen
```

MACKLEMORE, West - D. January 22, 1818
```
    Wife:       Seley Macklemore
    Son:        Redick Macklemore
    Daus:       Zilpha Peters, Nanny Tew
    Exec:       Samuel Peters, Jonathan Godwin
    Wit:        George Lassiter, Jordan Coats
```

MCILWINER, John - D. March 14, 1792
```
    Wife:       Fannie McIlwiner
    Exec:       Fannie McIlwiner, John Hayard, Fayetteville,
                N. C.
    Wit:        Thomas Sewell, Thomas Ivey, Thomas Ivey, Jr.
```

MCLENDON, Lewis - D. August 6, 1778
```
    County:     Craven
    Wife:       Mary
    Sons:       Shadrick, Jule, James, Denes, John, Burrel
    Daus:       Zilpha, Mary, Sally, Patsy McLendon
    Exec:       Wife, Mary, Bro., Dunnes McLendon, Son,
                Shadrack McLendon

    Wit:        Jesse McLendon, Simon McLendon, L. W.
                McLendon
```

MCLEOD, Neill - D. July 21, 1818
```
    Wife:       Sarah
    Sons:       Angus, Neill, Jr., Malcom, John McLeod
    Daus:       Sarah McCorcudale, Polly McKinnen
    Son-in-law: Daniel McQueen
    Wit:        Neill Stewart, James Calhoun
```

OATS, Stephan - D. March 7, 1816
```
    Wife:       Fanny Oats
    Son:        John Olin Oats
    Exec:       Olin Mawbley, John Oates
    Wit:        Stephan Slocum, Kedar Vann, Robert Marley
```

ODOM, Sarah - D. April 24, 1787
```
  Heirs:        Cozzen Jacob Odom, Sarah Lockamy, Bethany
                Harris, Charity Smith, Richard Odom
  Son:          William Odom
  Exec:         Friend, William Odom
  Wit:          John Odom, Annie Hobbs, Jacob Odom
```

PARKER, Jonathan - January 22, 1806
```
  Sons:          Richard, Peyton Parker
  Daus:         Elizabeth Chesnutt, Tobitha Tucker,
                Bathsheba, Jimima Parker, Susannah Matthis
  Grandson:     Nicholas Parker
  Exec:         Richard Parker, John Bryan
  Wit:          Kedar Bryan, Micager Newsom, Felix Hines
```

PORTER, John - D. June 27, 1796
```
  Wife:         Not named
  Sons:         William, Absolom, Samuel Porter
  Daus:         Elesabeth Porter, Mary Autry, Jemima Coor,
                Delila Hair, Ann Hinson
  Grandsons:    John Porter, Samuel Porter
  Granddaus:    S. Porter
  Exec:         John Holly, Jacob Lockermon
  Wit:          Mark Porter, John Holly, Jacob Lockerman
```

Recorded Wills

(BOOKS 1, 2, 3)

(D) date of will. (P) date will was probated.

ALDERMAN, Amariah Biggs - D. Dec. 2, 1878 - P. July 4, 1890
    wife: Pennie Eliza Alderman
    Sons: Amariah Enoch, James Edwin, Leroy Walton,
                   John Thomas, Palmer, Julian, Jacob Oliver
    Daus: Lillean Isabella, Lena May, Pennie Ann,
                   Ella Jane Alderman
    Exec: Sons, John Thomas, Palmer Alderman
    Wit: Whitney Royal, W. L. Stevens

ALDERMAN, Daniel W. - D. Sept. 8, 1882 - P. Feb. 15, 1892
    Wife: Catherine E. Alderman
    Son: Livingston W. Alderman
    Daus: Mary P., wife of George Ward; Susan R., wife
                   of Casper Walker; Eliza J., wife of John
                   Tyler, Emma H., wife of H. J. Cooper; Laura
                   A., wife of C. C. Johnson; Catie F. Alderman
    Exec: Son, L. W. Alderman
    Wit: Frank P. Alderman, Henry Murphy

ANDERS, Nancy C. - D. Nov. 18, 1872 - P. Aug. 23, 1877
    Husband: James K. Anders
    Exec: Friend, Wm. R. Weeks
    wit: A. H. King, W. A. Anders

ANDREWS, Peter - D. Jan. 6, 1843 - P. May, 1844
    wife: Elizabeth Andrews
    Exec: Wife, Elizabeth Andrews
    wit: Gabriel Holmes, James C. Dobbin

ASHFORD, Elizabeth A. - D. May 3, 1875 - P. Aug. 23, 1877
    Sis: Mary B. Elliott
    Niece: Flora Griffith
    No identity: Dollie Griffith (dau. of Flora G.), Ida May
                   Shaver (dau. of P. A. Shaver), Jno. Ashford,
                   Margaret Elizabeth Shaver (wife of P. A.
                   Shaver)

```
Exec:        Jno Ashford, A. B. Chesnutt
Wit:         W. C. Blount, C. T. Murphy, J. I. Stewart
Codicil:     D. July 3, 1877
Wit:         A. A. McPhail, C. A. Oates
```

ASHFORD, Thomas - D. July 1, 1864 - P. Nov., 1865
```
  Wife:        Isabella Ashford
  Sons:        John, Thomas B. Ashford
  Dau:         Rebecca E. Hines
  Sis:         Rebecca Slocum
  Grandchild:  Kate Pender Ashford
  Exec:        Son, Thomas B. Ashford, Dr. Thomas Bunting,
               Amma B. Chesnutt, Allmand A. McKoy
  Wit:         W. A. Faison, B. F. Marable
```

AUTRY, Edney - D. March 6, 1834 - P. Feb., 1836
```
  Son:         George Autry
  Daus:        Edney Autry, Martha Lockamy, W. Autry
  Exec:        Son, George Autry
  Wit:         Dickson Jackson, Abraham Naylor, Sr.
```

AUTREY, Mary - D. Apr. 8, 1859 - P. Aug., 1859
```
  Husband:     George W. Autrey
  Exec:        Husband, George W. Autrey
  Wit:         John J. Highsmith, John W. Matthews
```

AUTRY, George -D. June 3, 1868 - P. June 19, 1869
```
  Sons:        Isham, Archibald, John Autry
  Dau:         Edney Williams
  Exec:        Blackman Autry
  Wit:         William C. Jackson, Joel Jackson
  Affidavit:   D. June 19, 1869
  Names:       Frances Autry and 4 children
```

BALKCUM, Hester - D. March 9, 1843 - P. May, 1843
```
  Daus:        Nancy, Mariah
  Granddau:    Mary Ellen Johnson
  Grandsons:   James Lucien Balkcum, John Balkcum, Harmon
               Balkcum, Lemuel B. Balkcum
  Exec:        William L. Robinson
  Wit:         Isaiah Robinson, Abner Robinson
```

BALKCUM, Nancy- D. Aug. 20, 1853 - P. Feb., 1854
```
  Son:         Harman Balkcum
  Daus:        Margaret, Eliza, Mary Balkcum
```

```
Exec:           Wm. L. Robinson
Wit:            Nathan Johnson, Joshua Rackley
```

BARBREY, A. B. - D. April 18, 1889 - P. June 12, 1889
```
  Sons:         Jesse, William, L., Edgar, Thaddeus Barbrey
  Daus:         Mamie Barbrey, Sarah McMillan, Lizzie Royal
  Exec:         Son, Thaddeus Barbrey
  Wit:          A. G. Barbrey, R. H. King
```

BARBARY, Allen - D. May 13, 1853 - P. Aug., 1853
```
  Sons:         Peter, William, Ollen, Gabriel, Allen B.
  Grandsons:    Peter B. Troublefield, Willie Troublefield
  Daus:         Jennett Cole, Nanny Barbary, Margaret Jane
                Hobbs, Mary I. Weeks, Susan A. Royal, Rhoda
                A. Beaman
  Granddau:     Rebecca Eliza (Troublefield) Hobbs
  Exec:         Sons, Gabriel, Allen B. Barbary
  Wit:          A. Monk, J. C. Monk
```

BARDEN, Ephraim - D. Jan. 3, 1837 - P. Feb., 1837
```
  Wife:         Nancy Barden
  Sons:         Sherwood, John, Woodward, Jesse, Everitt G.
  Daus:         Fanny Meriah, Zilphy, Polly, Peggey Waters,
                Nancy, Jane, Elizabeth
  Exec:         Sons, Jesse, Sherwood Barden
  Wit:          Edward C. Gavin, Henry Hollingsworth
```

BARDEN, John   D. April 8, 1884 - P. Feb. 5, 1894
```
  Wife:         Nancy Barden
  Son:          James J. Barden
  Daus:         Mary C. Murry, Nancy J. Windows, Virginia T.
                Orrell, Charlotte R. Smith, Rebecca M. Page,
                Rachel V. Herring, Minnie D. Blanchard, Ida
                C. Barden
  Exec:         Son, James J. Barden
  Wit:          Thomas L. Hubbard, M. C. Richardson
```

BARDEN, Woodard - D. Jan. 19, 1866 - P. Aug. 12, 1870
```
  Wife:         Patience Barden
  Sons:         Jesse E., Allen S., John, Killbee, Ephraim
  Daus:         Zilpha Ann, Margaret E., Elizabeth C., Mary
                J., Martha P., Frances, Sally A. Barden
  Exec:         Son, John Barden
  Wit:          Wm. S. Matthis, Archibald Matthis
```

BARFIELD, Granger G. - D. June 3, 1861 - P. Nov., 1861
    Bro: George, Blake Barfield
    Exec: Julius C. Eason
    Wit: J. C. Monk, G. R. Williams

BARFIELD, George - D. Dec. 8, 1862 - P. Feb., 1863
    Mother: Sarah Barfield
    Bros: Blake, John F. Barfield
    Nephews: Boswell Barfield, Allen B. Grantham (son of
                Bowdoin Godwin), George Barfield
    Exec: J. C. Eason
    Wit: J. C. Monk, A. Thornton

BARKSDALE, Sherod - D. May 26, 1876 - P. Sept. 30, 1889
    Wife: Hattie
    Children: Not named.
    Exec: Marsden C. Peterson, John H. Hill
    Wit: T. L. Hubbard, Josiah Robinson
    Codicil: D. Feb. 17, 1883
    Exec: Changed to A. F. Johnson, J. A. Ferrell
    Wit: Thomas L. Hubbard, Albert C. Garris

BASS, Felix - D. Aug. 22, 1835 - P. 1835
    Wife: Kiddy Bass
    Sons: Henderson, Traven, Hillory Bass
    Exec: Abraham Naylor, Senior
    Daus: Rebecca Bass, Roxy Bass
    Wit: Handy Warren, Sophiah Bass

BASS, John - D. Oct. 2, 1885 - P. Oct. 13, 1887
    Sons: Wm. Everett (dec'd), Amma, John I., Robert,
                Joshua Bass
    Daus: Angelina Warren, Virginia Barfield
    Grandson: John Bass
    Exec: Edwin W. Kerr
    Wit: E. W. Kerr, J. C. Slocumb

BASS, Joshua - D. Sept. 19, 1828 - P. Aug., 1829
    Wife: Priscilla Bass
    Son: Uriah Bass
    Daus: Ferebee Carr, Rebecca Lamb
    Grandson: Isaac Peterson
    Granddaus: Milly Jane Carr, Eliza Lamb, Nancy Jane Bass
    No identity: James Chesnutt
    Exec: Everitt Bass, John Lamb
    Wit: Samuel A. Bunting, Jonathan Carr

BASS, Rhoda - D. Aug. 28, 1851 - P. Feb., 1853
  Son: William Bass (dec'd)
  Daus: Catharine Ann Blount, Polly King, Mary
              Jane King , Rebecca Eliza King
  Grandchildren: William Bass, Mary Jane Blount, Sherman
              Blount, Michael Everett King, John William
              King, Stephen James King, Louis D. King,
              Sally Ann King, Mary Jane King, Thomas Wm.
              King, Cherry Catharine King
  Exec: Wm. Ashford, Benjamin Hargrove
  Wit: Thomas Ashford, James Moore

BASS, William - D. Jan. 24, 1853 - P. Aug., 1853
  For Services: Susan Standley
  Trustee: Thomas Ashford for Joel Britt, Robert Shipp,
              Mrs. Catharine Oates (wife of Jethro Oates)
  Exec: Thomas Ashford
  Wit: Joel Hines, John Boyett

BEAMAN, J. R. - D. March 20, 1890 - P. Feb., 1892
  Sons: Wm. K., J. R. Beaman
  Daus: Mariah Ruth, Lovic Worth, Charlotte, Vir-
              ginia Pigford
  Granddaus: Mary, Susan J.
  Exec: Mariah (Mittie) R. Beaman, Dau.
  Wit: In court, James M. Spell, R. C. Holmes,
              C. P. Johnson

BELL, Michael - D. Oct. 8, 1831 - P. Nov., 1831
  Bro: Robert Bell
  Sis: Clarrissa King
  No identity: E. Bell
  Exec: John Bell
  Wit: Bright S. Herring, James Bell

BELL, Robert - D. June 1, 1816 - P. --18--
  Wife: Katharine Bell
  Sons: James, John Bell
  Exec: Wife, Katharine, son, John Bell, Louis Peck
  Wit: Micajah Bell, Sr., Thos. Byrd, Richard Wolf,
              Levi Barden

BELL, William W. - D. July 17, 1884 - P. Jan. 14, 1885
  Wife: Sally Bell
  Sons: Jefferson, Wm. James, Luther, Charley Bell

```
Daus:           Shug, Sarah Jane Bell, Susan Anna Sutton
Exec:           Son, William James Bell, Wife, Sally Bell
Wit:            E. E. Johnson, A.M. Lee
```

BENNETT, Fleet S. - D. June 20, 1864 - P. Aug., 1864
```
Bros:           Hardy K., George W. Bennett
Sis:            Sarah E. Page
Exec:           Sis., Sarah E. Page
Wit:            John Fowler, John S. Crumpler
```

BENNETT, Hardy - D. Jan. 31, 1870 - P. (?)
```
Wife:           Penny Bennett
Sons:           George W., Robert Henry Bennett
Daus:           Harriet Cooper, Sarah E. Page
Grandchildren:  Mary Page, John Richard Page
No identity:    (Youth) Willy T. Stevens
Exec:           Jonathan L. Stewart
Wit:            G. W. Crumpler, Amos J. Cooper
```

BENNETT, James - D. Aug. 31, 1848 - P. (?)
```
Wife:           Nancy Bennett
Exec:           J. L. Boykin
Wit:            Robinson Boykin, John W. Brown
```

BENNETT, Sampson - D. April 2, 1862 - P. Feb., 1863
```
Sons:           Hardy, Thomas K., Henry, James R. Draughon
Daus:           Harriett Jones, Barella Alderman
Grandsons:      Fleet, Hardy, S. E. Bennett, Miles Sampson
                Draughon, Henry Sampson Alderman, Haywood
                Alderman
Exec:           Hardy Bennett, Owen Alderman
Wit:            Neill Watson, G. W. Crumpler
```

BENTON, Alexander - D. Sept. 20, 1836 - P. Aug., 1838
```
Sons:           John, Alexander, Jr.
Daus:           Polly Benton, Annie Blackman
Exec:           Sons, John, Alexander Benton
Wit:            Noel Williams, John Flemming
```

BIZZELL, James A. - D. March 16, 1878 - P. May 14, 1878
```
Widow of Bro. Henry:  Celestial P. Bizzell
Nephew:         Henry, James S. Bizzell
Wit:            J. R. Beaman, John C. Carroll
```

BIZZELL, Repsey - D. Sept. 16, 1871 - P. April 1, 1872
  Mother: Polly Bizzell
  Exec: Blackman Lee
  Wit: Joseph R. Westbrook, G. A. Tart

BLACKBURN, Burrell - D. March 11, 1892 - P. May 26, 1892
  Dau: Rebecca Ellen Gray
  Exec: Friend, R. J. Williams
  Wit: W. R. King, W. J. King

BLACKBURN, Hiram - D. Aug. 17, 1850 - P. May, 1858
  Wife: Nancy Blackburn
  Son: Allen M. Blackburn
  Daus: Jerusha Armstrong, Sarah Peterson
  Granddau: Mary Victor Herring
  Exec: Son, Allen M. Blackburn
  Wit: Lott Riche, L. A. Tatom, Wm. Johnson

BLACKBURN, William - D. Aug. 6, 1822 - P. Nov., 1822
  Sons: Burrell Blackman, Sion Blackburn, Hiram
                Blackburn
  Daus: Miriam Smith, Herodias Killet
  Grandson: Allen M. Blackburn
  Exec: Son, Hiram Blackburn
  Wit: Hiram Blackburn, Wm. Turns

BLACKMAN, Abigail - D. May 13, 1869 - P. Nov., 1876
  Son: William G. Blackman
  No identity: Kitsay West
  Exec: Son, William G. Blackman
  Wit: James C. Williams, James W. Lee
  Heirs: (As named in probate) Easter Godwin, Annie
                C. West, Nancy Langston, heirs of Mary Ellis
                and Calvin Blackman

BLACKMAN, Susannah - D. March 2, 1837 - P. May, 1839
  Daus: Ann Crawford, Olive McKinse, Mary Hooks
  Grandchildren: Sarah McKinse, Susy McKinse, Wm. McKinse,
                Betsey McKinse, Sarah Ann McKinse, John S.
                McKinse, Barnabas McKinse, Wm. Crawford,
                Eliza Stephens, Isaac Crawford, Betsey
                Crawford, Olive Crawford, Ashley R. Craw-
                ford, Nathan G. Crawford, Eveline Crawford,
                Alex. F. Crawford, William Hooks, Franklin
                Hooks, John Hooks

```
Exec:           Archibald Monk
Wit:            James Bennett, Joshua Craddoc
```

BLACKMAN, William - D. Nov. 20, 1840 - P. Feb., 1841
```
  Children:     Mentioned but names not given.
  Exec:         John Eason
  Wit:          Joel Joyner, Jr., Cader Blackman
```

BLAND, Isaac N. - D. Sept. 3, 1874 - P. (?)
```
  Sons:         Milton, James F., William, John G. Bland
  Daus:         Martha A. Rooks, Lavinia Vann, Sarah E. Pig-
                ford, Esther, Mary E. Bland
  Exec:         Son, William Bland
  Wit:          J. L. Pigford, J. G. Bland, Milton Bland
```

BLOUNT, John - D. Dec. 26, 1829 - P. May, 1830
```
  Wife:         Worthy Blount
  Son:          John W. Blount
  No identity:  Worthy Joiner
  Exec:         Wife, Worthy Blount
  Wit:          Hennant Byrd, Oliver Wooten
```

BLOUNT, John W. - D. July 17, 1884 - p. Oct. 29, 1884
```
  Dau.-inlaw:   Margaret
  Wit:          R. R. Bell, Wm. I. Thompson
```

BLOUNT, M. C. - D. May 25, 1866 - P. (?)
```
  Wife:         Louisa Blount
  Son:          Malcom Colan Blount
  Dau:          Arkansas Southerland
  Grandchildren:  Swenee, Emma, John, Wallace Southerland
  Exec:         J. B. Southerland
  Wit:          L. B. Millard, B. C. Bowden, John Blount
```

BLOUNT, Penelope - D. Feb. 11, 1835 - P. Nov., 1838
```
  Dau:          Cathran Bell
  Exec:         Louis F. Williams
  Wit:          L. F. Williams, William Rouse
```

BORDEAUX, William W. - D. Feb. 9, 1875 - P. March 13, 1875
```
  Wife:         Dicey A. Bordeaux
  Children:     L. H., J. C., Luther H., A. D., W. F.,
                Ira F., M. E. Bordeaux
  Exec:         Son, Loyd H. Bordeaux
  Wit:          A. N. Johnson, G. J. Rackley
```

BOYETTE, John - D. March 3, 1880 - P. April 27, 1882
Wife: Susan Boyette
Sons: C. T. Boyette, John E. Boyette
Daus: Mary J. Boyette, Sophia A. Anders
Exec: Son, J. E. Boyette
Wit: O. M. Matthis, Nathan Weeks

BOYETTE, Mary J. - D. May 16, 1888 - P. Aug. 15, 1888
Bros: C. T. Boyette, John E. Boyette
Exec: Bro., John E. Boyette
Wit: Jas. H. Stevens, Henry E. Faison

BOYKIN, Sarah - D. March 15, 1865 - P. Nov., 1865
Bro: Thomas W., Wm. H., John C. Boykin
Nephew: Tobias Underwood
Exec: Bro., Thomas W. Boykin
Wit: L. A. Powell, Everett Peterson

BRADSHAW, Jesse - D. Aug. 2, 1821 - P. --18--
Sons: Guilford, Thomas, Jno. Eliot, Sion, Alfred
Daus: Mary Ann Stanly, Edy Wiggins, Edney Daniel,
     Dicy Bradshaw
Exec: Son, Guilford Bradshaw
Wit: Jno. Bradshaw, Edmund Bradshaw

BRADSHAW, John - D. July 31, 1827 - P. Feb., 1829
Wife: Betsy Bradshaw
Exec: Wife, Betsy Bradshaw
Wit: William Thomas, Jesse Clifton

BRADSHAW, Thomas - D. Feb. 10, 1880 - P. April 5, 1880
Wife: P----- E. Bradshaw
Sons: Thomas, Jr., Jessy, Henry, John (dec'd),
     Charley
Daus: Susan Weeks, Catharine Britt, Mary Jane
     Martin, Elizabeth Overton, Eliza O'Quinn
Exec: Friend, W. A. Anders
Wit: W. A. Anders, Laura A. Weeks

BRANCH, Jesse - D. Oct. 14, 1852 - P. Aug., 1856
Wife: Nancy Branch
Sons: William, Kenan, Jonas Branch
Daus: Elizabeth, Rhoda Branch, Louisa Royal
Grandson: Albert Royal
Exec: Son, William Branch
Wit: R. C. Holmes, J. C. Owen

BREWER, Henry - D. Jan. 3, 1834 - P. Feb., 1840
  Sons: Edward, Henry, Herring Brewer
  Daus: Nancy Brewer, Catherine C. Brewer
  Exec: Ben Hargrove
  Wit: Ben Hargrove, I. Moore

BRITT, James - D. Feb., 1869 - P. June 11, 1891
  Wife: Tempy Britt
  Exec: Wife, Tempy Britt
  Wit: Wm. E. Barden, J. L. Stewart
  Heirs: (Named by Tempy Britt) Tempy Britt, Susan
              Stevens, Patience Lassiter, Mary West,
              Sallie Daughtery, Martha Smith, Julia
              McLamb's children, Mattie Sutton's children,
              Della McLamb

BRITT, Sarah A. - D. March 29, 1884 - P. Apr. 19, 1884
  Husband: Thomas Britt
  Exec: Husband, Thomas Britt
  Wit: James J. Huggins, L. M. Sanderson

BRITT, Sarah A. - D. Jan. 6, 1876 - P. Sept. 13, 1881
  Husband: Thomas Britt
  Wit: L. C. King, A. C. Standley

BROCK, Louisa - D. Aug. 1, 1885 - P. Oct. 16, 1885
  Husband: William L. Brock
  Exec: Husband, William L. Brock
  Wit: M. M. Hall, Fleet J. Cooper

BROWN, Arthur, Sr. - D. July 20, 1826 - P. Nov., 1830
  Wife: Lucy Brown
  Sons: Caleb, Arthur, Edward, Robert, John
  Daus: Mary Brewer, Dicy Odom, Sally Brewer, Nancy
              Newman, Peggy Brown
  Exec: Wife, Lucy Brown, Son, Arthur Brown
  Wit: G. Toole, James R. Toole, Willie M. Toole

BRYAN, John - D. Feb. 6, 1840 - P. Feb., 1840
  Wife: Eleanor Bryan
  Sons: Kedar, John A., Thomas K. Bryan
  Daus: Eleanor, Susan Mary, Eliza Jane Bryan
  Exec: David Murphy
  Wit: R. Parrish, Patrick Murphy, B. Stith

BRYAN, Susana - D. March 10, 1865 - P. Nov., 1865
 Sons: Josiah H., William H., John D. Bryan
 Daus: Sarah A. Bryan, Susan Cox
 Exec: Lewis C. King
 Wit: Alexander Benton, L. C. King

BULLARD, James - D. Jan. 30, 1883 - P. Oct. 25, 1886
 Wife: Elizabeth A. Bullard
 Sons: John, Thomas F., James L., Henry G.,
         Giles M. Bullard
 Daus: Elizabeth A. McLemore, Mary L. Bullard,
         Sallie M. Simmons, N. Matilda Bullard,
         Martha J. Averitt
 Exec: Son, James L. Bullard, David L. Bullard
 Wit: Amos Bullard, Carrie E. Bullard

BULLARD, William - D. June 13, 1882 - P. Jan. 4, 1887
 Wife: Elizabeth Ann Bullard
 Daus: Nancy Jane Maxwell, Charity Autry, Sabery
         Bullard, Lucy A. Autry, Frances Lee Williams
 Exec: Friends, Henry Bullard, William Maxwell

BUNCE, Charity - D. Feb. 27, 1863 - P. May, 1863
 Dau: Laura Ann Strickland
 Grandchildren: Anna Eliza Bunce, Henry Bradshaw
 Exec: Thomas Bradshaw
 Wit: Everett S. Bass, Hardy Fort

BUNTING, David - D. May 10, 1828 - P. Aug., 1828
 Sons: Richard C., Samuel, Owen, David, Thomas
 Daus: Penelope Morisey, Ann Morrisey

 Grandsons: David Morisey, David Bunting, Richard Mor-
         risey, Owen Morrisey
 Exec: Sons, David and Thomas Bunting
 Wit: James Blanks, Thomas Chesnutt

BUTLAR, Robert - D. March 26, 1802 - P. (?)
 Wife: Delilah Butlar
 Sons: John, Robert, Gabriel, Travis
 Wife's Son: Reddick Rhodes
 Daus: Sally, Patience, Betsy, Cherrywine, Lusia
         Brown, Suffer Ryals, Desia Culbrath
 Exec: Wife, Delilah Butlar
 Wit: Fleet Cooper, Wm. Butler, Robert Butler

BUTLER, Gabriel - D. June 6, 1823 - P. May, 1828
    Wife: Sophia Butler
    Sons: Jacob Butler, Redman Butler, John Butler,
                 Raiford Butler
    Daus: Jane Williams, Peggy, Susan, Mary Butler
    Exec: Brother, Travis Butler
    Wit: R. Royal, John Butler

BUTLER, Hartwell - D. March 4, 1838 - P. May, 1838
    Wife: Sarah Butler
    Sons: Jacob, John, Redden Butler
    Friends: Joseph D. Parker, Hardy Stevens
    Exec: Friends, Joseph D. Parker, Hardy Stevens
    Wit: Gabriel Holmes, Thomas Bunting

BUTLER, Mary - D. Aug. 11, 1875 - P. July 5, 1895
    Daus: Elizabeth A., Sabra Jane, Lucinda Butler
    Exec: Amos Crumpler, Sarah Bryant
    Wit: O. Holmes, A. Holmes

BUTLER, Robert - D. Nov. 3, 1857 - P. (?)
    Wife: Nancy Butler
    Sons: John, William, Adam Butler
    Daus: Ann Eliza, Sarah, Rebecca Eliza Butler,
                 Molsey Mariah Williams
    Exec: Joseph Herring, R. C. Holmes
    Wit: John R. Smith, David Smith

BUTLER, Stephen - D. Dec. 19, 1824 - P. Feb., 1830
    Wife: Jane Butler
    Son: Miles C. Butler
    Daus: Emma Jane, Betsey, Poley Butler
    Exec: Wife, Jane Butler
    Wit: Richard Parker, James Jorden

BUTLER, Travis - D. Oct. 23, 1857 - P. Nov., 1859
    Wife: Sally Butler
    Sons: Brazel, Ezekiel Butler
    Daus: Rebecca, Margaret Butler, Barbary Crumpler,
                 Nancy Porter
    Grandsons: Walter Dand, Zachariah Royal
    Exec: Son-in-law, Micajah Crumpler, Friend, R. C.
                 Holmes

BUTLER, Wiley - D. May 24, 1880 - P. May 17, 1885
  Wife: Romelia Butler
  Exec: Bro-in-law, Thomas M. Ferrell
  Wit: J. A. Ferrell, E. E. Howell

BYRD, Robert   D. Sept. 9, 1846 - P. (?)
  Wife: Nancy Byrd
  Exec: Daniel Bowden, Oates Lewis
  Wit: D. B. Newton, John C. Bowden

CAISON, Cannon - D. Oct. 1, 1842 - P. Nov., 1847
  Wife: Polly Caison
  Dau: Elizabeth Springs
  Granddaus: Lucinda, Matilda Caison
  Grandsons: William, Lewis Caison
  Exec: Jonathan Moseley, Nehemiah Chesnutt
  Wit: Thomas Bunting, Gabriel Holmes

CAISON, Jacob - D. Feb. 23, 1895 - P. April 23, 1895
  Niece: Fannie M. Caison
  Wit: J. O. Culbreth, Wm. H. Boykin

CARRAWAY, Bedreaden - D. May 9, 1844 - P. Aug., 1844
  Wife: Susannah Duprey Caraway
  Daus: Susannah Duprey, Gatsey Mage Caraway

  Nephews: John R. Beaman and son, Bedreaden Caraway
                   Beaman, Theophilus Caraway
  Exec: Wife, Susannah Duprey Caraway, Wyatt Magee,
                   John R. Beaman
  Wit: Duncan C. McPhail, Samuel J. Pope

CARROLL, Lewis - D. July 16, 1872 - P. Nov. 16, 1872
  Wife: Eliza Carroll
  Sons: George W., Wm. J., C. Tate, James L., Amma
                   B., Frank W. Carroll
  Daus: Rebecca P. Merriman, Mariah A. Southerland,
                   Mary E. Croom, Rachel C. Royal
  Exec: Sons, Franklin M. Carroll, James L. Carroll
  Wit: Archibald Matthis, Wm. S. Matthis

CARROLL, Sarah - D. Dec. 14, 1849 - P. May, 1855
  Children: Ann Matilda Herring, Winney Johnson, Dorcas
                   Bizzell, William Carroll

Grandchildren: Martha Jane Johnson, Sarah Catharine Her-
                ring, Sarah Elizabeth Bizzell, Edward Carroll
Exec: Friends, Sampson Bennett, Allen Williamson
Wit: Thomas Williamson, R. C. Holmes

CASHWELL, Herring - D. Oct. 12, 1878 - P. Nov. 2, 1878
Wife: Susan Cashwell
Sons: William H., Gaston B. Cashwell
Daus: Ann Pender, Lettie D. Cashwell, Susan C.
                Vann
Exec: Wife, Susan Cashwell
Wit: J. M. Hobbs, D. B. Watson, G. W. Hobbs

CHESNUTT, A. B. - D. July 19, 1881 - P. Oct. 25, 1887
Wife: Mentioned but not named.
Son: H. B. Chesnutt
Exec: James H. Stevens, James K. Morisey
Wit: J. L. Stewart, M. C. Richardson

CHESNUTT, Charles - D. March 21, 1832 - P. Aug., 1838
Wife: Elizabeth Chesnutt
Children: Dorcas Chesnutt, Paten C., Jonathan, Charles,
                Nicholas, Joseph, Anna
Exec: Alfred, Robert Chesnutt
Wit: Samuel I. Gavin, Jacob S. Chesnutt

CHESNUTT, David - D. Sept. 17, 1845 - P. Nov., 1846
Wife: Mary Chesnutt
Son: Joshua James Chesnutt
Daus: Sarah Herring, Dolly Jane Spearman, Polly
                Ann Chesnutt, Kitty Eliza Chesnutt
Exec: Son, Joshua James, Wife, Mary Chesnutt
Wit: Joshua R. Ezzell, H. Hollingsworth

CHESNUTT, Driver - D. Aug. 30, 1830 - P. Nov., 1830
Wife: Izzabell Chesnutt
Sons: Robert Driver, James Averet, Absolem Ches-
                nutt
Daus: Elizabeth, Julia, Avah, Unity, Becky Jane
                Chesnutt
Exec: Son, Robert Driver Chesnutt, Daniel Joyner
Wit: John Bryan, Dickson Sloan

CHESNUTT, Elizabeth - D. Feb. 15, 1855 - P. May, 1857
Sons: Alfred, Robert, William K., Jonathan,

                        Charles, Peyton, Nicholas Chesnutt
    Daus: Anna Merritt, Jemima Bryan, Dorcas Boon,
                        Kitty Register (dec'd)
    Exec: Sons, William K., Nicholas P. Chesnutt
    Wit: W. L. Robinson, Lewis Carroll

CHESNUTT, Joshua - D. Feb. 8, 1843 - P. Aug., 1850
    Wife: Nancy Chesnutt
    Sons: A. B. Chesnutt, A. M. Chesnutt
    Daus: Catharine Peterson, Frances Williamson
    Exec: Son, A. B. Chesnutt, Edward C. Gavin
    Wit: Dixon Killet, Elisha Peterson

CHESNUTT, Joshua J. - D. Feb. 21, 1851 - P. Aug., 1851
    Nephew: Lewis H. Herring
    Nieces: Martha I. Herring, Eliza Spearman, Mary P.
                        Alderman

    Exec: Friend, Joshua R. Ezzell
    Wit: Curtis C. Oates, Wm. H. Faison

CHESNUTT, Nicholas P. - D. Oct. 16, 1885 - P. Jan. 1, 1887
    Wife: Mary A. Chesnutt
    Sons: Albert P., Cornelius T., James A., Richard
                        C., Edward T. Chesnutt
    Daus: Josephine, Martha A. Chesnutt, Asia J. Hall,
                        Catharine Wilson
    Exec: Wife, Mary A. Chesnutt
    Wit: William S. Matthews, Archibald Matthis

CHESNUTT, Robert - D. March 29, 1863 - P. Nov. 28, 1868
    Wife: Rebecca Jane Chesnutt
    Exec: Wife, Rebecca Jane Chesnutt
    Wit: J. R. Beaman, W. K. Beaman

COLWELL, Elizabeth - D. Aug. 18, 1838 - P. Nov., 1838
    Son: John Colwell
    Daus: Caty, Peggy Colwell
    Exec: Son, John Colwell
    Wit: Edward C. Gavin, Henry E. Smith

COLWELL, John - D. Oct. 22, 1829 - P. Nov., 1829
    Wife: Elizabeth Colwell
    Sons: Richard Colwell, John Colwell

```
Daus:           Caty, Peggy Colwell, Elizabeth Hollings-
                worth, Nancy Barden, Polly Matthews
Exec:           Wife, Elizabeth Colwell, Son, Richard
                Colwell
Wit:            H. Hollingsworth, Edward C. Gavin
```

COLWELL, Richard - D. Jan. 1, 1860 - P. May, 1863
```
  Wife:         Jane Colwell
  Sons:         Henry Colwell, Edward J. Colwell
  Daus:         Susy Porter, Polly Rogers, Martha Chesnutt,
                Asha Williams
  Exec:         Sons, Henry, Edward J. Colwell
  Wit:          Isham Royal, Lewis Carroll
```

COOK, Perigreen - D. Nov. 23, 1846 - P. Nov., 1852
```
  Wife:         Charity Cook
  Sons:         Charles A., Perigreen, William R. Cook
  Daus:         Matilda, Hariet Cook, Polly Vann, Eliza
                Boon, Nancy Stevens, Sarah Ezzell
  Exec:         Son, Charles A. Cook
  Wit:          John K. Smith, John Colwell
```

COOPER, Fleet - D. Feb. 5, 1816 - P. Feb., 1828
```
  Wife:         Sarah Cooper
  Sons:         John, Jacob, Daniel, Wilson Cooper
  Daus:         Elizabeth Pope, Mary Butler, Nancy Cooper,
                Penelope Cooper, Dicy Cooper, Roda Cooper
  Exec:         Sons, Jacob, Daniel Cooper
  Wit:          Blackman Crumpler, Wilson Cooper
```

COOPER, John S. - D. July 26, 1863 - P. May, 1866
```
  County:       New Hanover
  Wife:         Elizabeth N. Cooper
  Sons:         Amos J. Cooper, Hiram J. Cooper, Daniel J.
                Cooper, Fleet Cooper
  Exec:         Wife, Elizabeth N., Daniel A. Cooper
  Wit:          Miles P. Owen, Sally Nance, Fleet Cooper,
                W. H. Harvard, Thomas B. Hall
```

COX, James Andrew - D. Jan. 10, 1885 - P. Sept. 23, 1881
```
  County:       Duplin
  Wife:         Flora J. Cox
  Exec:         Wife, Flora J. Cox
  Wit:          M. S. McCaleb, T. D. McCaleb
```

COX, Moses   - D. March 16, 1857 - P. May, 1857
  Children: Joab B. Cox, Uz W. Cox, Ann B. Craddock,
                 James P. N. Cox
  Exec: Sons, Joab B. Cox, Uz W. Cox
  Wit: A. Monk, James Britt

COX, Serena   - D. May 10, 1855 - P. Aug., 1856
  Son: Franklin Snead
  Grandsons: Walter Snead, George Snead, Thomas D. Snead,
                 Charles Snead, Edward Snead, Nathan Snead,
  Granddaus: Serena M. Cox, Laura Snead, Agnes Snead,
                 Catharine Snead, Ann F. Snead
  Exec: Nathan Williams
  Wit: Harry Bryan, Josiah H. Bryan
  Codicil: D. April 8, 1856
  Exec: Archibald Monk, Geo. H. Daughtry
  Wit: F. F. Allen, Uriah N. Westbrook

COX, William - D. May 20, 1831 - P. Feb., 1835
  Sons: Williams, Nixon, Blackman, Moses Cox
  Daus: Sarah Farrier, Mary Gray (dec'd), Ann,
                 Susanna Cox
  No identity - probably son: Daniel Cox
  Exec: Sons, Moses, Wm. Cox, Jr.
  Wit: A. Monk, Garry Draughon

CRADDOCK, Civil - D. April 17, 1867 - P. July 21, 1891
  Sons: William H., John T., Robert A., Walter J.
  Dau: Mary A. Barbrey
  Granddau: Annie F. Parker
  Exec: Son, Walter J. Craddock
  Wit: D. C. King, L. C. King

DARDEN, Joseph - D. Jan. 18, 1868 - P. Jan. 5, 1875
  Wife: Betsey Darden
  Sons: Simeon J., William H., Thomas B., James H.
  Daus: Elizabeth H., Sarah E., Nancy C. Darden
  Exec: Son, Simeon J. Darden
  Wit: P. B. Troublefield, W. A. Barbray

DAUGHTRY, Bryant - D. Dec. 30, 1846 - P. (?)
  Daus: Elizabeth Sutton, Nancy Turnage, Zilpha
                 Dawtry, Ann Turnage
  Grandson: Solomon Dawtry
  Exec: Isaac W. Lane
  Wit: A. Monk, W. H. Monk, James Oates

DAUGHTRY, Hardy - D. July 5, 1856 - P. Aug., 1856
  Sons: Adin, Jarrot, William Daughtry
  Daus: Patsey Daughtry, Elizabeth Westbrook
  Exec: G. H. Daughtry
  Wit: Josiah Jackson, Willie Keen

DAUGHTRY, S. R. - D. Aug. 19, 1893 - P. Oct. 7, 1893
  Sons: George L., Solomon Eugene, Ed Howard, James
                Bryan
  Daus: Mary F. Futrell, Nancy E. Parker, Della C.
                Weeks, Tempia A., Zilphia A., Lillie M.
                Daughtry
  Exec: Son, James Bryan Daughtry
  Wit: W. T. Sutton, J. D. Ezzell

DAWSON, David - D. June 4, 1844 - P. Aug., 1844
  Wife: Martha Dawson
  No identity: Ollen B. Mobley (son of Middleton Mobley),
                Lucinda (dau. of Middleton Mobley), Mary
                Elizabeth Dawson (dau. of Burrell Dawson)
  Bro: Joseph Dawson
  Exec: Kilbee Lassiter
  Wit: J. W. Mobley, Zilpha Branch

DAWSON, Joseph - D. July 13, 1837 - P. Nov., 1837
  Sons: David Dawson, Burrel Dawson, William Dawson,
                Henry M. Dawson
  Daus: Nancy Holley, Celia Gene, Zilpha Mobley
  Granddau: (Dau. of Burrell & Edith Dawson) Edithlizar
  Heirs of   Joel Dawson
  Dau. & Son: Elizabeth, Isaiah Warren
  Heirs of   Dau. Elizabeth
  No identity: Henry M., Sarah Jane Warren; Sally Jane,
                Lovet Warren; Joseph Isaiah Warren;
                Burrel Warren
  Trustee: (for Edithlizar Dawson) John G. King
  Exec: Son, David Dawson, Holley Gene Dawson
  Wit: Isaac Strickland, John Jones

DENNING, George W. - D. Dec. 24, 1887 - P. Jan. 27, 1888
  Bro: James W. Denning
  No identity: M---- Denning and wife Susan C.
  Exec: Friend, Jessy W. Denning
  Wit: R. S. Westbrook, J. W. Tart

DENNING, Jonas - D. July 6, 1860 - P. Aug., 1862
  Wife: Pearcey Denning
  Exec: Bro, James Denning
  Wit: David A. Bizzell, David Lee

DENNING, Nancy - D. March 12, 1857 - P. Oct. 9, 1871
  Sons: Robert, Jonas, Jas., Nathan, Thos. Denning

  Daus: Sarah Frazier, Elizabeth Hudson, Phebe
                  Murphy
  Son-in-law: Matthew Murphy
  Grandchildren: Nancy Ganey, Joanah Butler, Susannah
                  Sutton, Sarah Jane Murphy, Kesiah R.
                  Murphy, Thomas J. Murphy, Matthew Murphy,
                  Preston Murphy

  Exec: James Denning
  Wit: Joel Lee, H. G. Gainey

DENNING, Robert - D. Oct. 24, 1861 - P. Nov., 1861
  Wife: Mary Denning
  Children: Thomas J., Phebe, Mary Denning
  Exec: Bro-in-law, Uriah Westbrook
  Wit: Joel Tew, Wm. T. Westbrook

DEVANE, Eliza A. - D. Dec. 31, 1874 - P. Apr. 4, 1876
  Sons: Robert Harvey, William Thomas
  Exec: Sons, Robert Harvey, William Thos. Devane
  Wit: Thomas J. Herring, Preston R. Devane

DEVANE, Milton K. - D. March 22, 1883 - P. Jan. 30, 1889
  County: Duplin
  Wife: M. M. Devane
  Niece: Ollie C. Parrish
  Exec: Friend, A. Robinson
  Wit: G. W. Brinkley, W. C. Carroll

DODD, David   D. Aug. 7, 1813 - P. (?)
  Wife: Elizabeth Dodd
  Son: Willie
  Daus: Elizabeth Spell, Nancy Treadwell
  Grandchildren: Eliza Dodd, Abner Dodd, John Bolen Dodd
  Nephews: Benajah Dodd (son of John Dodd), David P.
                  Dodd (son of Daniel Dodd)
  Exec: Friend, John Herring, Son, Willie Dodd
  Wit: Lott Riche, Lewis Rich, John Paddison

DRAUGHON, Elizabeth R. - D. June 9, 1856 -P. (?)
Sons: Miles Sampson, James Walter, Robert Taylor
            Draughon
Daus: Martha Elizabeth, Augusta Jane, Rebecca
            Eliza, Mary Berrilla Draughon, Adelia Ann
            Pool
Exec: Bro., Hardy Bennett
Wit: Fleet Simpson, Richard Page

DRAUGHON, George - D. July 9, 1857 - P. May, 1866
Sons: Garry, James R., George W., Walter, Wm. C.
            Draughon
Daus: Mary Jane Williams, Rebecca E. Cox (dec'd)

Grandchildren: George T., Martha Jane, Wm. G., Frances
            A., Narcissa Bright, children of Garry
            Draughon, dec'd; Martha Jernigan, Delia
            A. Pool, Augusta J. Bell, Miles S., Rebec-
            ca Eliza, James Walter, Robert Taylor
            Draughon, children of James R. Draughon;
            Martha A. Walker, James D., William,
            Robert G., Susan J. Cox, children of R.
            E. Cox

Exec: Sons, Wm. C. Draughon, Geo. W. Draughon,
            Walter Draughon
Wit: J. R. Beaman, James Peterson

DREW, John - D. July 23, 1874 - P. Jan. 16, 1887
Wife: Julia A. Drew
Sons: Samuel James, Christopher H., Askew S.,
            David W., Dilliard L., Luther R., Marshal
            M., William M. Drew
Daus: Ann M., Margaret P., Catherine E. Rackley,
            Caroline Cook
Wit: J. B. Smith, J. M. Blanchard

DRIVER, William D. - D. Sept. 27, 1894 - P. Nov. 30, 1895
Wife: Eliza J. Driver
Son: George T. Driver
Daus: Ann E. Driver, Mary C. Driver
Exec: Son, George T. Driver
Wit: William S. Matthis, James M. Powell

DUDLEY, Laben - D. July 3, 1858 - P. Aug., 1861
Wife: Viney Dudley

```
Sons:          John, Laben, James Dudley
Daus:          Civil Lockaman, Sady West, Mary A. Dudley
Granddau:      Catharine
Exec:          Robert Wilson
Wit:           John Dudley, Jesse Wilson, John H. West
```

DUNCAN, Alfred - D. Oct. 31, 1883 - P. Nov. 23, 1883
```
   Wife:          Edith Duncan
   Son:           Henry J. Duncan
   Daus:          Mary Lewis, Jenette Murray, Elizabeth
                  Powell
   Exec:          Son, Henry J. Duncan
   Wit:           F. P. Jones, J. F. Duncan
```

ELLIS, Gorman - D. March 22, 1837 - P. Aug., 1837
```
   Wife:          Edith Ellis
   Sons:          Samuel, John Gorman, William N. Ellis
   Daus:          Martha Wiggs, Nancy Hudson, Mary Lee,
                  Jane Philips
   Exec:          Friend, Alexander Benton, Sr.
   Wit:           Asher Bizzell, Henry A. Bizzell
```

EVANS, Martha - D. April 5, 1847 - P. May, 1848
```
   Sons:          David Evans, Samuel Evans
   Dau:           Mary Rogers
   Exec:          Bizzell Johnson
   Wit:           W. M. Marley, Nathan W. Johnson, Catharine
                  Goff
```

EZZELL, John R. - D. Aug. 18, 1870 - P. Feb. 4, 1879
```
   Wife:          Catherine Ezzell
   Sons:          Charles W., John B., M. J., David
   Daus:          Mary A. Robinson, Sarah J. Robinson,
                  Catherine Peterson, Nancy Merritt, Luisa
                  Drew
   Exec:          Son, David Ezzell, Son-in-law, Josiah
                  Robinson
   Wit:           John C. Carroll, John E. Chesnutt
```

FAISON, Elias - D. Apr. 18, 1863 - P. (?)
```
   Wife:          Margaret Faison
   Sons:          Elias Kilbee (dec'd), Wm. Lucien  Faison
   Daus:          Margaret Ann Johnson, Narcissa E. Cromartie,
                  Eleanor I. Cromartie
   Granddau:      Margaret K. Faison
```

```
Exec:          Wife, Margaret Faison, Son, Wm. Lucien
               Faison
Wit:           N. C. Faison, John C. Carroll
Codicil:       D. Apr. 21, 1866
Wit:           James A. Bizzell, Allmand A. McKoy
```

FAISON, James - D. May 25, 1838 - P. Aug. 1838
```
Wife:          Elizabeth Faison
Dau:           Virginia Faison
Wit:           F. B. Millard, M. C. Blount
```

FAISON, Kilbee - D. Feb. 2, 1848 - P. May, 1848
```
Wife:          Mary Ann Faison
Sons:          John Haywood, Thomas Kilbee, William Elias
Daus:          Amelia Elizabeth, Ann Rebecca, Maria Louisa,
               Mary Virginia Faison
Exec:          Curtis C. Oates, William W. Faison
Wit:           Isham F. Hicks, Lewis C. Oates
```

FAISON, Mary A. - D. Dec. 14, 1866 - P. Sept. 13, 1882
```
Son:           William Elias Faison
Daus:          Ann Rebecca, Maria Louisa, Mary Virginia
Wit:           Thomas Wright, Thomas B. Wright
```

FAISON, Solomon J. - D. March 15, 1880 - P. May 18, 1880
```
Wife:          Helen J. Faison
Son:           John M. Faison
Exec:          Wife, Helen J. Faison, Son, John M. Faison
Wit:           W. A. Melvin, John M. Fennell
```

FAISON, Thomas I. - D. Feb. 8, 1860 - P. May, 1860
```
Nephews:       William, Preston K. Faison
Niece:         Mary Susan Faison
Exec:          Thomas I. Faison
Wit:           Elias F. Shaw, Wm. I. Thompson
```

FAISON, William - D. May 18, 1855 - P. Nov., 1857
```
Wife:          Susan Faison
Sons:          Matthew J., Edward L., Wm. A., Franklin J.,
               Abner M. Faison
Daus:          Eliza A. Murphy, Susan A. Shaw, Mary A.
               McDugald
Exec:          Sons, Matthew J. Faison, Wm. A. Faison,
               Patrick Murphy
Wit:           Nehemiah C. Faison, Julian P. Faison,
               Patrick Murphy
```

FAISON, William H. - D. July 2, 1889 - P. Aug. 1, 1890
  Wife: Sarah J. Faison
  Son: William S. Faison
  Daus: Elizabeth A. Pigford, Sarah S. Hufham
  Exec: Son, William S. Faison
  Wit: William I. Matthews, R. D. Matthews

FAISON, W. L. - D. April 3, 1891 - P. April 22, 1891
  Daus: Madge C., Mary E. Faison, Nannie H. Ander-
                 son, wife of Rev. N. L. Anderson
  Exec: Dau., Mary E. Faison
  Wit: A. F. Johnson, Henry E. Faison

FENNELL, Margaret - D. May 30, 1856 - P. Aug., 1854
  County: New Hanover
  Sons: Nicholas, Owen, John M. Fennell
  Daus: Margaret Ann Brown, Mary Jane Herring
  Grandchildren: Margaret Fennell, John Walis Fennell
  Wit: G. N. Robinson, John Robinson

FISHER, John - D. Dec. 27, 1819 - P. Aug., 1830
  Wife: Catharine Fisher
  Sons: Sandars, John, Ralph, Elijah Fisher
  Daus: Sally, Phebe, Penney Fisher
  Exec: Brother Worthy Fisher, Friend, Daniel
                 Parker
  Wit: James White, Solomon Faircloth, Leman
                 Sessoms

FISHER, Thomas - D. Jan. 4, 1861 - P. May, 1861
  Wife: Jane Fisher
  Son: Southy Fisher
  Daus: Cassa Fowler, Ann Hall
  Grandchildren: William T. Fisher, Marthy White, Percilla
                 Burten, Henry Howard
  Exec: Son-in-law, John Fowler
  Wit: Joseph Herring, R. C. Holmes

FLEMING, Alexander - D. Aug. 28, 1823 - P. Feb., 1824
  Wife: Jiney Fleming
  Son: William J. F. Fleming
  Wit: John Fellow, Jr., Joshua Craddock

FLEMING, John - D. July 28, 1840 - P. Aug., 1840
  Sons: Felix, David, James Fleming

Grandchildren: Kitsey Alen, Nancy (daus. of Susanah
Fleming), Elizabeth, James Allen, Hiram,
John Fleming
Exec: Friends, Gardner Parsons, John Benton
Wit: R. N. Herring, Sydney Parsons

FORT, Sarah - D. May 11, 1838 - P. Feb., 1842
Son: John Turner Fort
Exec: Son, John Turner Fort
Wit: Salmon Strong, John Sellers

FORT, John T. - D. Jan. 14, 1882 - P. May 23, 1882
Wife: Laura J. Fort
Son: John A. Fort
Daus: Frances A. McKinsie, Mary E., Emma J. Fort
Exec: Bro-in-law, Thomas L. Pugh
Wit: G. W. Highsmith, Blackman Hare

FORT, Milly - D. Aug. 24, 1859 - P. (?)
Nephew: Hardy Fort
Exec: Friend, Isaac M. Hobbs
Wit: Isaac M. Hobbs, Everett T. Bass

FORTNER, John E. - D. Feb. 7, 1851 - P. May, 1855
Wife: Sureany Fortner
Sons: William, John Everett Fortner
Dau: Nancy Fortner
Exec: J. R. Beaman
Wit: Langdon C. Hubbard, Alfred Johnson

FOWLER, Cassa - D. Oct. 19, 1875 - P. July 23, 1885
Sons: Leonard C., Miles B. Fowler
Daus: Sally A., Margaret R. Fowler, Susannah C.
Lewis, Matilda I. McLemore, Ellen C.,
Mary N. Fowler
Grandchildren: S. M., John R. Butler
Exec: Son, Leonard C. Fowler
Wit: R. C. Holmes, A. Holmes

FOWLER, Elizabeth - Sept. 5, 1884 - P. March 9, 1885
Sons: R. B., O. J., W. S. Fowler
Daus: Frances J. Sessums, Serena D. Lawhon
Exec: Son, R. B. Fowler
Wit: W. R. McKinzie, Jr., J. T. McKinzie

FRAZIER, Houston R. - D. Sept. 1, 1857 - P. Dec. 5, 1887
  Wife: Sarah Frazier
  No identity: Elsey Ann White (wife of James White, Jr.)
  Exec: Wife, Sarah Frazier
  Wit: G. H. Daughtry, Hardy Daughtry

FRAIZER, John - D. Feb. 24, 1837 - P. Feb., 1848
  Wife: Elizabeth Fraizer
  Son: Houston Fraizer
  Daus: Nancy, Elsey Fraizer
  Exec: Wife, Elizabeth Fraizer, Alexander Benton,
               Jr.
  Wit: James Wilson, Noel Williams, Alexander
               Benton, Sr.

FREDERICK, James - D. Jan. 12, 1819 - P. --Term 18--
  Bro: William K. Frederick
  Father: William Frederick
  Grandfather: Watson Barton
  Sisters: Catharine Houston, Jane Lester, Polly Wilkin-
               son, Nancy, Betsey Frederick
  Nephews: Henry F. Frederick, James Houston
  Exec: Bro., William K. Frederick
  Wit: J. K. Hill, Stephen Slocumb

FRYAR, John - D. Sept. 25, 1882 - P. May 28, 1884
  Sons: James, George, Daniel Fryar
  Daus: Elizabeth Johnson, Sarah, Rachel, Margaret
  Exec: Friend, George W. Ward
  Wit: A. M. Johnson, J. J. Ward

FRYAR, Jonathan - D. Feb. 22, 1819 - P. Nov., 1821
  Son: William Fryar
  Daus: Charity Fryar, Polly Moore, Edith Blanks,
               Fanny Bloodworth
  Sons-in-law: Joseph Moore, James Blanks
  Exec: Son, William Blanks, son-in-law, Joseph
               Moore
  Wit: J. Moseley, Lemuel Chesnutt

FRYAR, William - D. Aug. 10, 1881 - P. Jan. 3, 1883
  Wife: Mary Ann Fryar
  Sons: A------ Blackman, Martin Luther, William
               Jefferson

```
Daus:            Celestia Ann, Emily Idella, Malisa Electa,
                 Mary Cornelia, Louisa Bailey
Exec:            Sons, Azariah Blackman, Martin Luther Fryar
Wit:             C. C. Johnson, S. W. Johnson
```

GAINEY, Bartholomew - D. June 28, 1818 - P. --Term 18--
```
  Sons:          William, Redick, Elias, Abram, Noel (dec'd)
  Daus:          Kiziah Carathers, Dicey Lee, Edney West-
                 brook
  Sons-in-law:   Westbrook Lee, Moses Westbrook
  Dau-in-law:    Polly Thornton
  Grandchildren: Noel West, Willis West, Sally Peters,
                 Edney Lee, Nancy West, Handy West, Lawed
                 West, Allen West, Bartholomew Westbrook,
                 Blackman, Reals Gainey, Redick Carathers
  Exec:          George Lassiter
  Wit:           L. Lee, King Vann
  Addition:      Blackman Gainey (grandson) changed to Josiah
                 Gainey
```

GAINEY, Martha - D. June 6, 1894 - P. Aug. 16, 1894
```
  Children:      L. G., Bodie, Vina B. Gainey
  Exec:          C. J. Hudson
  Wit:           Otis Ward, Pennington West
```

GAINEY, Thaddeus G. - D. March 17, 1894 - P. Sept. 12, 1895
```
  Wife:          Nancy J. Gainey
  Children:      Cenora, Thaddeus G., Claudius, Roy Gainey
  Exec:          Daniel P. Dameron
  Wit:           Daniel P. Dameron, Charlie Lassiter
```

GAINEY, Wm. G. - D. June 19, 1883 - P. Nov. 20, 1883
```
  Wife:          Sena A. Gainey
  Sons:          Hiram M., Wilton F., Blackman L., Wm. H.,
                 Thadeus G., Hinton M. Gainey
  Daus:          Franklin D., Mary A. Lee
  Exec:          Sons, Hinton M. Gainey, Wilton F. Gainey
  Wit:           Robinson Ward, Ransom West
  Codicil:       D. Oct. 20, 1883
  Dau:           Amanda A. Lee
```

GAVIN, Edward C. - D. April 30, 1850 - P. Nov., 1850
```
  Wife:          Charity Gavin
  Son:           Samuel James Gavin
```

Daus: Mary Belenda Smith, Margaret Ann Hines, Susan Matilda Pigford, Sally Jane Torrence

Exec: Sons-in-law, James B. Pigford, William H. Smith

Wit: Joshua R. Ezzell, John West

GODWIN, Elizabeth - D. Aug. 9, 1866 - P. Sept. 30, 1869
Son: William David Godwin
Daus: M. -. -. Elizabeth, Silvania Godwin, Rachel Lockaman, Eley E. Phillips
Exec: M. K. Tew
Wit: J. H. Elmore, Louise A. Stone

GODWIN, John - D. June 7, 1864 - P. Dec. 2, 1873
Wife: Elizabeth Godwin
Children: Henry, Nathan, Jonathan, John, Elizabeth, Jr., one infant not named
Exec: Wife, Elizabeth Godwin
Wit: Kilbee Lassiter, John H. West
Named in Probate: Penny, Polly, Bud, David Godwin

GODWIN, Nathan - D. Nov. 3, 1882 - P. Nov. 18, 1882
Children: Lucinda E., Artie M., William A., Sophoronia J. Godwin
Exec: Bro., Jonathan Godwin
Wit: Robinson Ward, Ransom West

GODWIN, Nathan - D. Jan. 12, 1821 - P. Aug., 1823
Sons: Jonathan, John, Joel, David Godwin
Daus: Jerusha, Rachel, Anna Starling, Edna Laton
Grandsons: Handy, Royal Godwin
Exec: Son, John Godwin
Wit: Demey Laton, Handy Godwin

GRANTHAM, Needham - D. Dec. 24, 1873 - P. May 5, 1879
Sons: Hiram, Barfield, Needham J. Grantham
Exec: C. Monk
Wit: John E. West, James Crusenbury

GREGORY, Asa - D. Feb. 4, 1857 - P. May, 1861
Son: Owen Gregory
Daus: Nancey Rackley, Louisa Dollar, Polley Ann Peterson, Sally Shepherd Smith

```
Friend:      John R. Beaman
Exec:        Friend, John R. Beaman
Wit:         G. W. Atkins, James A. Bizzell
```

GREGORY, Elijah - D. Sept. 22, 1843 - P. Feb., 1844
```
Sons:        William, Lewis, Marshal, Hubert Francis,
             James, Thomas, Henry, Lewis Gregory
Daus:        Meriah Williamson, Anny, Laney, Sally
             Jane, Nancy, Elizabeth C. Gregory
Wit:         H. Hollingsworth, Wright Gregory
```

GREGORY, Elisha - D. Nov. 17, 1870 - P. April 17, 1878
```
Son:         Wright Gregory
Dau:         Anna Jane Bowden
Grandchildren: Sydney Forest Gregory, Hettan Broadhurst
Exec:        Son, Wright Gregory
Wit:         Wm. S. Matthis, L. R. Carroll
```

GREGORY, Jane - D. June 12, 1871 - P. Sept. 27, 1871
```
Children:    James William, Lewis, Monk, Mary A. Denning,
             Beck, Eliza Gregory
Exec:        John T. Gregory, H. C. Monk
Wit:         J. C. Monk, Jno. T. Hudson
```

GREGORY, Wright - D. Aug. 12, 1891 - P. July 23, 1892
```
Dau:         Mary E. Thomson
Friend:      William S. Matthews
Exec:        Walter O. Thomson
Wit:         Wm. S. Matthews, Wellington L. Matthews
```

GREGORY, Lott - D. Jan. 9, 1811 - P. --Term 18--
```
Wife:        Nancy Gregory
Sons:        Asa, Elijah, Elisha, Owen Gregory
Daus:        Sarenia, Lena Simpler, Lelah Dinkins
Granddaus:   Molsey, Louiza
Exec:        Hardy Holmes, Son, Elijah Gregory
Wit:         Louis F. Peck, J. Moore, F. Holmes
```

GREGORY, Lott - D. Jan. 24, 1823 - P. Feb., 1824
```
Wife:        Nancy Gregory
Sons:        Elijah, Elisha, Asa
Daus:        Alia Vann, Lena Simpler, Serena Fortner
Granddau:    Molsey Fryer
Exec:        William Robinson, Son, Asa Gregory
Wit:         Benjamin Watters, W. Robinson
```

GUY, William - D. July 30, 1846 - P. May, 1847
  Wife: Mary Ann Guy
  Wit: J. W. Moseley, Rufus I. Herring

HALL, Elizabeth - D. June 29, 1863 - P. May, 1864
  Children: Wm. S., Charles H., Ferebe Hall
  Exec: William Bullard
  Wit: James Autry, William H. Autry

HARGROVE, Ann W. - D. March 27, 1871 - P. April 6, 1871
  Bro: Benjamin F. Hargrove
  Exec: Bro., Benjamin F. Hargrove
  Wit: James H. McCullen, Solomon McCullen

HARGROVE, Sallie - D. July, 1886 - P. Aug. 1, 1887
  Husband: Alvin Hargrove
  Niece: Dicey Ann Thomson
  Exec: Friend, Reddin T. Carr
  Wit: L. C. King, John T. Gregory

HERRING, G. W. - D. Aug. 25, 1892 - P. June 12, 1893
  Sons: Edger C., Solomon, Poidres Herring
  Daus: Mary V. Fowler, Ira Ann Packer, Mittie G.
                 Corbett, Elvira C. Herring
  Exec: Sons, Poidres, Edger C. Herring
  Wit: Columbus G. Robinson, James M. Corbett
  Codicil: D. Sept. 15, 1892
  Wit: Columbus G. Robinson, James M. Corbett

HERRING, Gabriel - D. March 12, 1845 - P. Feb., 1846
  Wife: Janet Herring
  Sons: Nathan, William James Herring
  Daus: Elizabeth Herring, Mary Jane Butler
  Wit: Allen M. Blackburn, G. S. Bronson, A. N.
                 Treadwell

HERRING, Joel - D. April 9, 1828 - P. Nov. , 1832
  Sons: Lewis Herring, Joel Herring
  Dau: Ann Wetherington
  Grandchildren: Eliza, Mary, Murdock, Benajah
  Exec: Son, Joel Herring, Moses Cox
  Wit: R. R. Lee, William House

HERRING, Nathan - D. Oct. 5, 1883 - P. Nov. 20, 1883
  Wife: Sara Herring

```
Sons:          Lucian, John Otice, Dallas, Adolphus Herring
Exec:          Sons, Lucian, John Otice, Dallas Herring
Wit:           W. K. Anders, W. E. Herring
```

HERRING, Nehemiah - D. March 7, 1876 - P. Nov. 22, 1890
```
  Wife:          Sarah A. Herring
  Son:           Amos M. Herring
  Daus:          Julia Kelly, Nancy C. Tatom, Dicey C.
                 Williams, Emily Herring, Sarah E. Herring
  Exec:          Son, Amos M. Herring
  Wit:           J. E. Barden, W. E. Barden
```

HERRING, Stephen - D. May 12, 1834 - P. Feb., 1839
```
  Wife:          Dicey Herring
  Sons:          John, Hardy, Amos, Stephen, Nehemiah,
                 Richard, George Washington Herring
  Daus:          Elizabeth, Sally, Dicey Herring
  Exec:          Sons, John, Hardy Herring
  Wit:           Gabriel Herring, Mary I. Herring, William
                 Herring
```

HERRING, Thomas W. - D. Sept. 16, 1852 - P. Nov., 1852
```
  Wife:          Sarah Herring
  Sons:          Thomas I., Isaac W., Luther W. Herring
  Daus:          Sarah E., Nancy I. Herring
  Exec:          Wife, Sarah Herring, David F. Rivenbark
  Wit:           John Colwell, John West
```

HIGHSMITH, Jacob - D. July 22, 1869 - P. Sept. 28, 1869
```
  Wife:          Miriam Highsmith
  Sons:          Robert, George Highsmith
  Dau:           Susan Highsmith
  Exec:          Sons, Robert, George Highsmith
  Wit:           A. F. Lawhon, W. R. Highsmith
```

HIGHSMITH, Lewis - D. April 26, 1884 - P. June 14, 1884
```
  Wife:          Elizabeth Highsmith
  Sons:          Lewis D., Luther R. Highsmith
  Dau:           Phebe Eleanor Herring
  Exec:          Son, Luther R. Highsmith
  Wit:           N. F. Highsmith, L. F. Bland
```

HIGHSMITH, Noah - D. Nov. 8, 1872 - P. March 20, 1877
```
  Sons:          George Washington, Owen E., Isaac M., Noah
                 F., Richard A., James H., Joseph Sydney High-
                 smith
```

Daus: Ann Julia Colwell, Rebecca Susan Bland,
                    Mary E. Highsmith
Exec: Son, Noah Franklin, Owen Alderman
Wit: A. E. Colwell, Jacob Wells

HIGHSMITH, William L. - D. Jan. 5, 1885 - P. Feb. 21, 1890
  Wife: M. E. Highsmith
  Daus: C. C. Highsmith, M. E. Waters, A. S. High-
                    smith
  Exec: In probate, W. R. Highsmith, D. F. Johnson
  Wit: In court, J. R. Beaman, A. J. Johnson, D.
                    F. Johnson

HILL, Edward - D. May 1, 1862 - P. Feb., 1864
  Wife: May C. Hill
  Dau: Mary E. Hill
  Wife's bro. as her trustee: James C. Williams
  Exec: Bro-in-law, James C. Williams
  Wit: E. W. Sanders, C. C. Bell, Elijah Taylor

HINES, James - D. Sept. 2, 1844 - P. Feb., 1845
  Wife: Margaret Ann Hines
  Sons: Albert, William Hines
  Exec: Son, Wm. Hines, Edward C. Gavin
  Wit: John W. Grice, Thomas Byrd

HOBBS, Abram, Sr. - D. Oct. 23, 1858 - P. (?)
  Wife: Mary Ann Rebecca Hobbs
  Sons: William P., Hosea J., Isaac, Abram, Gaston
                    Mears Hobbs
  Daus: Cynthia Ann Boykin, Mary Hobbs, Elizabeth
                    C. Boykin
  Grandsons: Judson, William
  Exec: J. R. Beaman
  Wit: J. H. Robinson, J. S. Hines
  Addition: D. Dec. 7, 1858
  Wit: J. H. Robinson, H. A. Bizzell
  Addition: D. Jan. 28, 1859
  Wit: J. A. J-----, J. H. Robinson
  Addition: D. July 27, 1859
  Wit: J. W. Atkins, H. H. Register

HOBBS, Gabriel - D. March 20, 1848 - P. Feb., 1858
  Sons: Simon P., George W. Hobbs
  Daus: Sarah Eliza Moseley, Elizabeth M. Darden

```
Exec:          James Moseley, Simon P. Hobbs, Son
Wit:           A. Monk, B. G. Carr
Addition:      D. July 4, 1849
Wit:           Laura Ann Strickland, A. Monk
```

HOBBS, Mary A. R. - D. Apr. 28, 1870 - P. Dec. 10, 1875
```
Son:           Gaston M. Hobbs
Exec:          Son, Gaston M. Hobbs
Wit:           Abram Hobbs, Jonathan L. Stewart
```

HOBBS, Simon P. - D. June 18, 1883 - P. Oct. 9, 1884
```
Wife:          Mary E. Stevens
Sons:          Mortimer E., Charles M., David W., Henry
               A., Edwin H. Hobbs
Exec:          Son, Mortimer E. Hobbs
Wit:           O. F. Herring, G. H. Daughtry
```

HOBBS, William - D. (?) - P. Aug., 1866
```
Wife:          Rebecca Eliza Hobbs
Exec:          Wife, Rebecca Eliza Hobbs
Wit:           Isaac M. Hobbs, Lewis Hobbs
Original was destroyed.
```

HOBBS, William - D. Jan. 6, 1836 - P. Aug., 1836
```
Children:      Nanney, Phanna, Pleasant, Susanna, Reddin
Exec:          Henry Lee
Wit:           Hardy House, Aden Daughtry
```

HOLDER, Jesse - D. Sept. 25, 1845 - P. Aug., 1848
```
Sons:          Abel, Nathan, Ezrael, Jesse, John Holder
Daus:          Dorcas West, Clarkey Peters, Elizabeth
               Holder
Grandsons:     Zachariah Holder, Joel Nicholas Holder
Exec:          Son, Abel Holder
Wit:           Isaac Strickland, Samson Strickland
```

HOLLEY, James - D. April 17, 1824 - P. Nov., 1831
Wife, Sons, Daughter mentioned but not named.
```
Exec:          Friend, Edmon Godwin, William Williford
Wit:           Alexander Benton, Sr., John Fleming
```

HOLLINGSWORTH, Henry - D. Feb. 23, 1836 - P. Nov., 1840
```
Sons:          Zebulon, Guilford
Daus:          Fanny Bass, Nancy Ballard, Elizabeth
               Hollingsworth
```

Exec: Edward C. Gavin
Wit: James D. Brown, Elijah Gregory

HOLLINGSWORTH, Jacob - D. Jan. 22, 1844 - P. Feb., 1844
  Wife: Elizabeth Hollingsworth
  Sons: Henry, James Hollingsworth
  Daus: Fanny M. Heath, Nancy I. Sheffield, Eliza-
                 beth Wilson, Catherine E. Hollingsworth,
                 Peggy Ann Hollingsworth
  Exec: Wife, Elizabeth, Son, James Hollingsworth
  Wit: Edward C. Gavin, John West

HOLMES, Ann - D. May 5, 1852 - P. May, 1852
  Son: Richard C. Holmes
  Daus: Ann Brown, Penelope Whitfield, Mary Holmes
  Exec: Son, Richard C. Holmes
  Wit: Langdon C. Hubbard, Malcom C. Conoly

HOLMES, Hardy - D. May 27, 1825 - P. Feb., 1852
  Son: Hardy Lucian Holmes
  No identity: Michael J. Kenan
  Exec: Son, Hardy L. Holmes
  Wit: William Webb, Robert Ship

HOLMES, James C. - D. April 22, 1861 - P. Nov., 1865
  Wife: Eliza J. Holmes
  Exec: Father, Richard C. Holmes, Wife, Eliza J.
                 Holmes
  Wit: Thomas Bunting, Lewis Carroll

HOLMES, Owen - D. Sept. 13, 1835 - Aug., 1840
  County: New Hanover
  Wife and 3 children not named.
  Exec: Gabriel Holmes
  Wit: R. C. Holmes, Mary Holmes
  Col. Samuel Ashe gave slaves to O. Holmes

HONEYCUTT, W. B. - D. Sept. 11, 1891 - P. Nov. 19, 1891
  Wife: Sarah J. Honeycutt
  Children: Not named
  Exec: B. A. Honeycutt
  Wit: M. O. Jackson, M. C. Honeycutt

HONEYCUTT, William - D. July, 1876 - P. Sept. 16, 1876
  Wife: Malsis Honeycutt

Sons:	John, William A., Blackman Honeycutt
Dau:	Mary M. Knowles
Wit:	Miles C. Simmons, J. F. Jones
Exec:	Son, William B., Son-in-law, Isham McLamb
Heirs:	Named in probate, Malsis, M. C., Civil McLamb, Chillin, Charles, John G., Redin A., Blackman, B. A. Honeycutt

HOUSE, Dollie S. - D. Nov. 18, 1884 - P. April 14, 1885

Bros:	Franklin P., Luther J., David E., Ira D. Alderman
Sis:	Nancy Carroll, Duella Powell, Estella, Sarah C. Alderman
Exec:	Bros, Franklin P., Luther J. Alderman
Wit:	Wm. S. Matthews, James M. Powell

HOUSE, John - D. Oct. 4, 1849 - P. Nov., 1849

Son:	William House
Dau:	Nancy Hobbs
Grandchildren:	(Children of Hardy House, dec'd) Susan Ann, Polley Jane, Caroline, Francis Elizabeth House; Wm. House, Franklin House
Exec:	Son, William House
Wit:	Matt Murphy, B. M. Herring

HOUSE, John C. - D. June 5, 1880 - P. June 25, 1880

Wife:	Dolly S. House
Exec:	Wife, Dolly S. House
Wit:	E. F. Royal, F. P. Alderman

HOWARD, Mary - D. Feb. 3, 1870 - P. Dec. 10, 1883

Friends:	Priscilla Faircloth, Wm. Thomas Cooper, John R. Cooper & wife, Spicey Cooper
Exec:	Friend, John R. Cooper
Wit:	John C. Carroll, Allmand A. McKoy

HOWARD, Minson - D. Oct. 22, 1864 - P. Aug. 21, 1869

Wife:	Mary Howard
Niece:	Spicy Cooper
Exec:	Wife, Mary Howard
Wit:	Allmand McKoy, John H. Crumpler
Codicil:	D. July 3, 1869
Nephew:	William T. Cooper
Wit:	A. M. Lee, Allmand A. McKoy

HUDSON, Holley - D. April 23, 1849 - P. May, 1849
    Wife: Jane Hudson
    Exec: Joel Hudson
    Wit: Crawford Wooten, D----- Hudson

HUDSON, Sarah M. - D. Feb. 6, 1892 - P. July 21, 1893
    Sons: William W., J. H. Hudson
    Exec: Son, J. H. Hudson
    Wit: L. C. King, R. T. Carr

HUDSON, Thomas I. - D. Oct. 14, 1884 - P. Dec. 5, 1884
    Bros: Benajah, William H., Joel, Hawley Hudson
    Sis: Lucinda Wooten, Eady A. Hargrove
    Half-Sis: Rebecca E. Bass
    Exec: Ransom West
    Wit: C. C. Jackson, B. B. Jackson

HUDSON, William - D. April 9, 1829 - P. May, 1829
    Wife: Anna Hudson
    Son: Samuel Hudson
    Daus: Nanna Hudson, Dicy Hudson
    Exec: Joel Hudson, R. Benjamin Hudson
    Wit: Lewis McClam, John Wilson

INGRAM, Abner - D. June 1, 1844 - P. Aug., 1844
    Wife: Pherebe Ingram
    Son: Abner Ingram, Jr.
    Daus: Phebe Jackson, Elizabeth Ann Ingram
    No identity: William R. Ingram
    Exec: Son-in-law, Willie B. Jackson
    Wit: Cader Blackman, Powel Blackman

IRELAND, Samuel R. - D. Jan. 16, 1873 - P. Aug. 7, 1888
    Wife: Eliza Ireland
    Sons: James Daniel, Henry Bizzell Ireland
    Daus: Octavie Josephine Ireland, Mary Elenor
                 Pass, Margaret Louize Giddens
    Exec: (Codicil) Son, Jas. D. Ireland
    Wit: Isham R. Faison, Jno. A. Oates

IVEY, Thomas - D. Sept. 19, 1896 - P. --Term 18--
    Sons: Thomas, Claburn Ivey
    Daus: Charlotte, Elizabeth, Rebecca, Lucy Thompson
    Grandson: Thomas Routledge Ivey
    Exec: Sons, Thomas, Claburn Ivey
    Wit: Thomas Sewell, William Tatom

JACKSON, Eden - D. Dec. 21, 1871 - P. April 9, 1872
```
  Wife:         Leanna Jackson
  Son:          Eden, James, Lewis Jackson
  Daus:         Charity Jane Jackson, Nancy Green Barefoot
  Son of John Wily Jackson:  Julius E. Jackson
  Exec:         John Robert Barefoot
  Wit:          Kinon Barefoot, J. J. Hudson
```

JACKSON, Henry - D. Feb. 17, 1876 - P. Oct. 16, 1877
```
  Wife:         Anna Jackson
  Children:     Malinda Strickland, Hezekiah, Raiford,
                Susan Jerusha Jackson
  No identity:  Adaline Burnett
  Exec:         H. W. Jernigan
  Wit:          James Turnage, Kinon Barefoot
```

JACKSON, Irvin - D. Sept. 4, 1844 - P. May 18, 1852
```
  Wife:         Nancy Jackson
  Sons:         Irvin, Nathan, Needham, James T.
  Daus:         Four not named.
  Exec:         Son, Irvin Jackson
  Wit:          Silas Baggat, Josiah Baggat,  John Baggat
```

JACKSON, John - D. Oct. 22, 1831 - P. Nov., 1831
```
  Wife:         Elizabeth Jackson
  Son:          James
  Daus:         Rachel, Mary, Martha
  No identity:  John H. Hays
  Exec:         Children, Rachel, Mary, Martha, James
  Wit:          Isaac Strickland, Alexander Strickland
```

JACKSON, Lemmon - D. March 9, 1857 - P. Aug., 1857
```
  Wife:         Jennet Jackson
  Exec:         Brother, John N. Jackson
  Wit:          Thomas N. Jackson, Willie B. Jackson
```

JACKSON, Richard - D. June 16, 1822 - P. Nov., 1822
```
  Wife:         Mary Jackson
  No identity:  Clarkey Dorman (dau. of Benjamin Dorman),
                Nanney Hall, John Jackson, Lewis Jackson,
                Fredrick Jackson, Sally Hays, James Dorman,
                John Allen Dorman
  Wit:          B. Dorman, James Holly, William Cruse
```

JACKSON, William - D. May 25, 1870 - P. Sept. 5, 1870
```
  Daus:         Elizabeth Ingram, Penny Norris
```

```
Grandson:      Jesse Martin Ingram
Exec:          Robert Norris
Wit:           John Dudly, O. M. Jackson
```

JACKSON, Willie B. - D. June 21, 1860 - P. Aug., 1860
```
  Wife:        Phebe Jackson
  Sons:        Ollen Jackson, Matthew E. Jackson
  Daus:        Nancy E. Tew, Aquilla Warren, Kizziah,
               Mary Adline Jackson
  Exec:        Sampson D. Jackson, Samson B. Jackson
  Wit:         Bright Bass, Samson Hawley, Willie B.
               Jackson
```

JAMES, Thomas - D. June 30, 1828 - P. Nov., 1835
```
  Wife:        Sabry
  Children:    Not named
  Exec:        John Bryan, George W. Robinson
  Wit:         Peyton R. Parker, W. Robinson
```

JERNIGAN, Ferney - D. Jan. 26, 1864 - P. Aug., 1867
```
  Wife:        Martha Jernigan
  Niece:       Harriet Elizabeth Rainer
  Exec:        Kilbee Lassiter
  Wit:         Batt Lee, L. H. Lee
```

JOHNSON, Amos - D. Feb. 9, 1871 - P. (?)
```
  Wife:        Elizabeth Johnson
  Son:         Amos J. Johnson
  Daus:        Margaret M. Carter, Zilpha J. Rackley, Mary
               E. Highsmith, Elizabeth Bordeaux, Charlotte
               M. Johnson, Kitty Ann Peterson, Susan R.
               Powell, Martha Caroline Chesnutt, Helen P.,
               Alice R. Johnson
  Exec:        Son, Amos J. Johnson, Josiah Robinson
  Wit:         Columbus G. Robinson, Joseph J. Harvell
```

JOHNSON, Bright, - D. (?) - P. May, 1866
```
  Wife:        Elizabeth Johnson
  Brother's Children: (Samuel Johnson) Owen H., Eliza,
               Rebecca Killett, Tabitha Lewis Carr, Ann
               M., Elizabeth N. Cooper, Caroline Owen
  Brother's Children:  (Stephen Johnson) Elizabeth, Sarah
               Jane, Samuel K., Stephen W., Thomas Johnson
  Nieces:      Mary J. Ward, Catherine Carter
  No identity: R. C. Burton, James Reid, Wm. Carter, L. S.
               Campbell, Ira T. Wade, Wm. Barringer
```

Nephews:	Amos N. Johnson, Jno. B. Robinson
Exec:	J. B. Robinson
Wit:	Kilbee Merritt, Richard Parish, D. B. Nicholson

JOHNSON, Joab - D. Feb. 26, 1842 - P. May, 1842

No identity:	Robert Charles Goff, Milton Henry Goff, Luther Franklin Goff
Exec:	Friend, Allen Johnson
Wit:	George Johnson, John Fryer

JOHNSON, John - D. Aug. 13, 1859 - P. Aug., 1860

Wife:	Mary Johnson
Nephews:	Everrett Johnson, J. M. Goff
Nieces:	Ann N. Johnson, Margarett M. Johnson
Exec:	John Balkcum
Wit:	G. M. Johnson, John Balkcum

JOHNSON, Jno. - D. Nov. 17, 1875 - P. Dec. 13, 1875

No identity:	Fanny A. Sessums
Niece:	Margaret M. Johnson
Daus:	Electy Johnson, Martha A. Peterson
Wit:	W. E. Herring, Lucian Herring

JOHNSON, Nancy - D. Jan. 28, 1888 - P. Dec. 3, 1888

Friend:	Stephen Pearce
Exec:	Friend, Stephen Pearce
Wit:	E. C. Smith, J. C. Wells

JOHNSON, Matthew - D. Aug. 13, 1851 - P. Aug., 1852

Wife:	Charity Johnson
Son:	Aaron Johnson
Sis-in-law:	Anna Peterson
Niece:	Keziah Katharine Johnson
Exec:	Allen M. Blackburn
Wit:	William H. Vann, Valentine Vann

JOHNSON, Nathan - D. March 15, 1851 - P. Aug., 1854

Wife:	Kezziah Johnson
Sons:	Bizzell, Nathan Washington, Robert Calvin, Allen Chatham
Daus:	Dorcas Lee, Mary Ann Fryer, Trecy Newton, Kezziah Jane Ward
Exec:	Son, Bizzell Johnson, Son-in-law, William Fryer

```
Wit:            Hardy Herring, O. M. Lewis
```
One acre of land given to school committee of Evergreen
  Academy.

JOHNSON, Soasbe - D. Aug. 28, 1822 - P. Nov., 1822
```
    Wife:           Sarah Johnson
    Son:            Solomon Johnson
    Exec:           Son, Solomon Johnson, E. Herring
    Wit:            E. Herring, Wm. Miller, John Robinson, Sr.
```

JOHNSON, Solomon - D. Aug. 14, 1830 - P. Feb., 1832
```
    Sons:           King, Samuel, Stephen, Bright, Amos, Enoch
                    (dec'd)
    Daus:           Sarah Carty, Rebecca Robinson
    Dau.-in-law:    Mariah Johnson
    Exec:           Friend, George W. Robinson
    Wit:            Benjamin Robinson, Cornelius Devane
```

JOHNSON, Warren - D. April 18, 1895 - P. July 13, 1895
```
    Wife:           Mary E. Johnson
    Exec:           Wife, Mary E. Johnson
    Wit:            Jno. D. Kerr, A. M. Lee
```

JOHNSON, Wm. C. - D. (?) - P. Nov. 17, 1875
```
    Sons:           Alpheus Marshal, Wm. Samuel, David Clark
    Daus:           Mary E., Frances Marion Johnson, Sophiah
                    Helen Jones, Hariet Harvel
    Exec:           Friend, Josiah Robinson
    Wit:            Allen Johnson, Stephen Pierce
```

JONES, Lancelot - D. July 24, 1854 - P. Nov., 1862
```
    Wife:           Ann Jones
    Exec:           Wife, Anna Jones, Noel Jones
    Wit:            R. N. Herring, William McLane
```

JORDEN, Richard - D. Oct. 13, 1863 - P. May, 1864
```
    Wife:           Mary Ann Jorden
    Nieces:         Hariet M. Williams, Caroline Stith, Jane
                    Smith, Elizabeth Jorden
    Dau:            Mary Jane Jorden
    Granddau:       Mary Susan Jorden
    Nephew:         Richard Jorden
    Exec:           Henry Faison
    Wit:            W. B. Darden, O. H. Darden
```

KEEN, James R. - D. May 22, 1889 - P. July 23, 1890
Wife: Sally J. Keen
Children: John, Marion, Franklin, Mary J., Ema
             Hattie, Jim, George, Henry
Exec: Son, George Keen
Wit: R. K. Herring, J. C. McLamb

KELLY, Felix - D. May 24, 1860 - P. Aug., 1864
Sons: Sylvester R., Thomas O., Isaiah I., Mar-
             shal M. Kelly
Daus: Minney Ellen, Edith M. Kelly
Granddau: Amelia Chesnutt
Exec: Friend, Dr. Thomas Bunting, Son, Thomas
             O. Kelly
Wit: Alfred¹ Johnson, James A. Bizzell

CANNADY, Patrick - D. Sept. 9, 1811 - P. (?)
Sons: Hardy Cannady, Samuel Cannady, Patrick
             Cannady, John, George, James Cannady
Daus: Susannah, Kisiah Cannady, Nancy Cannady,
             Mary Holland
Exec: Son, Patrick Cannady, Jr., George Hobbs
Wit: Jacob Godwin, Kizziah Cannady

KERR, Jacob - D. June 20, 1895 - P. Nov. 8, 1895
Sons: Andrew D., Hayes B., Henry R., Noah T.,
             Jacob D., Robert Gales, Hatter L., Daniel
Grandson: John T. Kerr
Wit: James T. Hayes, William H. Hayes
Exec: Exhibited in court by J. T. Hayes

KERR, James - D. July 2, 1872 - P. Dec. 12, 1872
Wife: Jane Ellen Kerr
Son: Charles S. Kerr
Sis: Catherine Kerr
Exec: Wife, Jane Ellen, Son, Charles S. Kerr
Wit: William Robinson, P. L. Cromartie, John Kerr

KILLET, Alexander - D. March 7, 1848 - P. Feb., 1849
Wife: Herodias Killet
Son: Sion Killet
Daus: Susannah Peterson, Miriam Highsmith, Charity
             Highsmith
Granddau: Miriam Elizabeth Highsmith
Exec: Son, Sion Killet
Wit: W. McKoy, Wm. H. McKoy

KILLETT, Julian A. - D. Jan. 17, 1890 - P. April 4, 1891
  Mother: Mrs. Rebecca Killett
  Exec: M. M. Killett
  Wit: J. R. Williams, E. W. Kerr

KING, Bryan - D. March 22, 1835 - P. May, 1835
  Wife: Polly King
  Sons: Barney, Henry King
  Daus: Clarisey, Sally King
  Exec: J. L. Clifton
  Wit: Edmond King, Mitchel Giddens

KING, David C. - D. Oct. 21, 1864 - P. Nov. 26, 1872
  Wife: Rosa A. A. King
  Children: Sallie King, Laura C. King, Julius S.,
                  Marion D., Walter M. King
  Exec: Bro., Lewis C. King
  Wit: F. Westbrook, Wm. Gregory

KING, Edmund - D. Feb. 14, 1860 - P. Feb., 1863
  wife: Harriett King
  Sons: William B., Richard J., Robert T., John B.,
                  Nathan J. King
  Dau: Sarah C. King
  Exec: Sons, Robert T., John B. King
  wit: R. R. Bell, Jethro Oates

KING, Henry - D. March 24, 1875 - P. March 4, 1880
  Wife: Eliza R. King
  Sons: J. W., Steven S., George W. King
  Daus: Mary Jane, Sarah Ann, Serena Catharine,
                  Rhoda E., Virginia, Julia, Dolly, Arkansas
                  King, Eliza Wilkins, Caroline Bass
  Exec: Wife, Eliza R. King
  Wit: R. R. Bell, Wm. Russell

KING, Jenny - D. Feb. 28, 1856 - P. Aug., 1856
  Son: Alvin Houstin King (Others not named)
  Exec: David Oates
  Wit: Benjamin Hargrove, J. K. Darden

KING, Jethro - D. Jan. 5, 1823 - P. Feb., 1823
  Wife: Michel King
  Bros: Michael, John, Charles, Allen, Benajah,
                  Alvin, Irvin King

```
Sis:            Elizabeth Lowell, Anny Cogdell
Exec:           Bros., Michael, Charles King
Wit:            Benjamin Hargrove, C. H. Monk
```

KING, Richard J. - D. Dec. 31, 1861 - P. Aug., 1868
```
  Mother:       Harrett King
  Bro:          John B. King
  Sis:          Sarah C. King
  Exec:         Friend, James Bell
  Wit:          Jno. A. Oates, Joth. Oates
```

KING, Seney - D. Nov. 15, 1836 - P. May, 1844
```
  Sons:         Alworth, Stephen, James, Henry, Michael,
                Nathan, Jethro, John, Allen, Thomas King
  Daus:         Caroline Bass, Patsey Bizzell, Ann Darden,
                Polly, Amy, Sally King
  Exec:         Son, Alworth King
  Wit:          Ben Hargrove, Henry King
```

KIRBY, William - D. Oct. 4, 1838 - P. Nov., 1843
```
  Wife:         Elizabeth Kirby
  Son:          William Turner
  Daus:         Mary Ann Pugh, Elizabeth McDaniel
  Grandsons:    William Kirby, John C. Kirby, George L.
                Kirby, Joseph M. Stephens
  Exec:         Wife, Elizabeth, Son, William Kirby
  Wit:          Wm. B. Meares, W. McKoy, Owen Holmes
                $50 each to Baptist and Methodist Missionary
```

KORNEGAY, David - D. March 7, 1821 - P. (?)
```
  Wife:         Zilpha Kornegay
  Children:     Sarah, Margaret, George O., James F.
                Kornegay
  Mother-in-law: Sarah Oliver
  Exec:         Wife, Zilpha Kornegay, Son, George O.
                Kornegay, Jonathan Thomas
  Wit:          Henry Faison, Allen Morris
```

LAMB, J. H. - D. Aug. 30, 1888 - P. Dec. 5, 1889
```
  Wife:         Nancy C. Lamb
  Sons:         Allen W., John D., James C., William B.,
                Colin T. Lamb
  Daus:         Anna E. Lamb, Betty H. Draughon
  Exec:         Son, James C., Wife, Nancy C. Lamb
  Wit:          Daniel Robinson, J. W. L. Robinson
```

LAMB, Rebecca - D. Dec. 6, 1859 - P. Feb., 1861
   Sons: Thomas C., George W. Lamb
   Daus: Cathrine E. Carroll, Mariah A. Chesnutt,
                 Rebecca P. Bordeaux
   Exec: Son, George W. Lamb
   Wit: Archibald Matthews, William S. Matthews

LASSITER, Kilby - D. Sept. 19, 1874 - P. Jan. 2, 1882
   Wife: Louisa Lassiter
   No identity: Giden M. Cooley, James F. Cooley
   Exec: Giden M. Cooley
   Wit: Nathan Barefoot, George Jones

LEE, Batt - D. Nov. 1, 1870 - P. Sept. 26, 1871
   Wife: Wife or children not named
   Exec: Erasmus Lee, John H. Elmore
   Wit: John C. Williford, S. W. Williford
   Heirs: (In probate) Wife, Susan C. Lee, H. N.,
                 Samuel B., Catharine, Troy, Susan S., Robert
                 E., Ulissis, Nancy Lee

LEE, Batt - D. March 3, 1834 - P. May, 1834
   Wife: Kezia Lee
   Sons: James B., Major D., Erasmus B., Lemuel H. Lee
   Daus: Susan, Keziah Lee, Harriet Jernigan
   Exec: Wife, Kezia Lee, Son, Lemuel H. Lee
   Wit: Kilba Lassiter, Powel Blackman

LEE, Bethany - D. June 1, 1886 - P. April 19, 1890
   Sons: Jesse, David Lee
   Dau: Martha Lee
   Exec: Sons, Jesse, David Lee
   Wit: D. H. Cox, Marshall Lee

LEE, Blackman - D. June 9, 1877 - P. Sept. 3, 1877
   Niece: Mrs. Polly Bizzell
   Granddau: Muriel H. Evritt
   Exec: John E. West, Isaac Williams, Friends
   Wit: David Lee, R. F. Rose
   Wife: (Named in dissent of will) Laura A. Lee

LEE, Burchet - D. Feb. 1, 1818 - P. Feb., 1824
   County: Orange
   Wife: Delilah Lee
   Bro.-in-law: Altha Lindsay

```
Exec:           Bro-in-law, Altha Lindsay
Wit:            John Lindsey, Nathan Edwards
```

LEE, Curtis - D. May 27, 1859 - P. Nov., 1859
```
Sis:            Polly Bizzell
Bro-in-law:     David A. Bizzell
Exec:           Named in court:  D. A. Bizzell
Wit:            In court:  Henry A. Bizzell, Sinon B. Killet,
                Wm. Lee
```

LEE, Gardner - D. Feb. 16, 1894 - P. May 10, 1894
```
Sons:           Joseph Gardner, Samuel Lee
Dau:            Elcy Ann Bryan
Wit:            David Lee, L. Bizzell
```

LEE, Jesse, Sr. - D. Oct. 28, 1831 - P. Nov., 1831
```
Wife:           Susannah Lee
Sons:           Jesse, Jas. W., John, Jonathan Lee
Grandson:       Powell Blackman
No identity:    Joab Lee; Elizabeth Ingram; Joseph Blackman;
                Susah Jernigan, wife of Wm. Jernigan; Eliza-
                beth Blackman; Susannah Smith, wife of Samuel
                Smith; Edy Lee, dau of Josiah Lee; Joel Lee;
                Nancy Johnson; Pharaba Lee
Exec:           Wife, Susannah Lee, Joel Lee, Powel Blackman
Wit:            Cader Blackman, John Tart, Westbrook Lee
```

LEE, Joab - D. March 20, 1858 - P. Feb., 1860
```
Wife:           Bethany Lee
Sons:           Josiah, Blackman, David, Jesse, Westbrook,
                Joseph, Joab Lee
Daus:           Nancy, Martha, Polly, Bethany, Jr., Appy
                Lee, Betsey Johnson, Susan Tart
Exec:           Wife, Bethany Lee, Sons, Westbrook, Joseph
                Lee
Wit:            Joel Lee, Nathan Denning
```

LEE, Peter - D. Oct. 1, 1846 - P. Nov., 1846
```
Son:            Peter R. Lee
Daus:           Jane Saur, Mary Noles, Pherabe Lee, Kitsey
                Tart, Vianna Lee
Granddaus:      Spicey J., Pherabe A. Hudson -- Simon H. Lee
                guardian of same
Exec:           Gary Draughon
Wit:            John Holley, Erasmus B. Lee
```

LEE, Pharoah - D. Aug. 3, 1868 - P. May 22, 1875
  Servants: Guard, Boyet, Calvin, George, John, Fox,
                   Henry Lee
  Attorney: M. C. Richardson
  Wit: Clifton Ward, Joseph Wilson
                   All legatees were former servants.

LEE, Thomas M. - D. Jan. 29, 1879 - P. April 21, 1881
  Sons: A. M., R. H., Matthew L., Thomas J. Lee
  Daus: S. Addelaid McKinnon, Sarah Rowena Micks,
                   M. Elizabeth F----
  Exec: Algernon M. Lee, Richard Henry Lee, Sons
  Wit: D. A. Culbreth, Allmand A. McKoy

LEE, William - D. Aug. 12, 1882 - P. March 3, 1883
  Wife: Nancy Jane Lee
  Daus: Tilley Catherine, Susan Ann, Milly Jane Lee
  Sons: Lovett James, Wm. Henry, John Thomas Lee
  Step-son: George Allman Daughtry
  Exec: Wife, Nancy Jane Lee
  Wit: G. W. Highsmith, James Anders

LEWIS, Ollen M. - D. April 22, 1887 - P. Nov. 1, 1890
  Wife: Susan Lewis
  Sons: Charles Tate, Julian Franklin Lewis
  Daus: Mariam Elizabeth Ward, Ann Julia Highsmith
  Exec: Sons, Julian Franklin, Charles Tate Lewis
  Wit: Josiah Robinson, L. K. Taylor

LEWIS, Tabitha - D. Nov. 12, 1884 - P. Sept. 27, 1891
  Husband: J. C. Lewis
  Wit: W. R. Carter, M. C. Cashwell

LANIER, John - D. Jan. 15, 1820 - P. --Term 18--
  Wife: Esther Lanier
  Children: Killy Jane, Killery, Nancy, Betsey
  Exec: Bro., Thomas Lanier, John Carlton
  Wit: Wm. Sillars, Robert Merritt, Felix Merritt

LUCAS, George A. - D. July 1, 1887 - P. Nov. 12, 1887
  Mother: Sophia A. Lucas
  Bro-in-law: Alexander Johnson
  Exec: Fleet R. Cooper
  Wit: Frank Boyette, A. H. Herring

MAINOR, F. D. - D. Sept. 19, 1890 - P. Nov. 3, 1890
  Son: William Ottis Mainor
  Dau: Mary A. Gainey
  Wit: Otis Ward, C. C. Jackson

MANUEL, Ishmael - D. June 2, 1851 - P. Feb., 1853
  Wife: Martha Manuel
  Children: C------, Rebecca Eliza, Alpha Jane
  Exec: Wife, Martha Manuel, Sampson D. Jackson
  Wit: John Tew, John I. Spell

MARLEY, Robert - D. Aug. 26, 1835 - P. May, 1837
  Sis: Eliza Marley
  No identity: William Henry Merritt (Dickson Sloan,
                guardian)
  Exec: Dickson Sloan
  Wit: Patrick Murphy, David Murphy

MATTHEWS, Joel - D. June 9, 1821 - P. --Term 18--
  Wife: Katharine Matthews
  Wit: John Johnston, Robert Williams, Alen Porter

MATTHIS, A. N. - D. Dec. 13, 1873 - P. Sept. 1, 1876
  Wife: Eliza Jane Matthis
  Sons: J. B., J. Tate, T. J. Matthis
  Daus: Susan C. Matthis, Mary A. N. Chesnutt,
                Rachel C. Lamb
  Exec: W. A. Matthis
  Wit: Josiah Robinson, O. P. James

MATHIS, Frederick - D. May 6, 1889 - P. Aug. 21, 1890
  Daus: Matilday Williams, Cherry Lewis, Mary J.
                Boone
  Grandchildren: Anderson Lewis, Alford Lewis, A. Lewis
  Exec: Friend, Daniel Williams
  Wit: J. R. Maxwell, A. E. Royall

MATHIS, James - D. Oct. 28, 1844 - P. Feb., 1851
  Wife: Mary Ann Matthis
  Sons: Thomas B., Fleet C., Abram N., David S.,
                Edmond Matthis
  Daus: Penney, Lavina Jane, Nancy Matthis, Sarah
                Caroline Henry
  Grandchildren: Elizabeth Matthis, Sloan Matthis, Luther
                Rice Matthis, Sabra Matthis, Margaret Jane
                Matthis

Exec: Son, Abram N. Matthis, John Vann
Wit: Lazarus Matthis, E. Vail

MATTHIS, Marshal H. - D. June 23, 1882 - P. Feb. 10, 1887
  Wife: Elizabeth A. Matthis
  Sons: John O., George E., Marshal M., Willie L.,
                Perry C. Matthis
  Daus: Asa V., Ellen E., Elizabeth C., Mary T.
                Matthis, Emmer Lee
  Exec: Josiah Robinson
  Wit: John W. Moore, Burriess W. Robinson

MATHIS, Mary - D. Jan. 11, 1859 - P. Aug., 1864
  Sons: Henry, Marshal Mathis
  Dau: Janetta Roberson
  Grandchildren: Silvester R. Mathis, Albert Mathis, Thomas
                Vail, Lorenza D. Vail, Elizabeth Vail, Sarah
                Vail
  Exec: Son, Marshal Mathis
  Wit: John Colwell, E. J. Colwell

MATHIS, Mary - D. July 14, 1853 - P. Aug., 1864
  Son: Thomas B. Mathis
  Wit: Edward Vail, Fleet C. Mathis

MELVIN, Daniel - D. Sept. 14, 1874 - P. Jan. 17, 1876
  Wife: Elizabeth L. Melvin
  Son: Stephen H. Melvin
  Daus: Sarah A. Highsmith (dec'd), Celia N. Carter,
                Anna C. Smith, Mary B. Lucas, Catherine
                Carter
  Great-granddau: Lavony Crosby Fowler
  Grandchildren: Daniel H., Robert G., John F., James H.,
                William C., & Stephen B. Melvin, Mary E.
                Waters, Caroline, Anna Highsmith
  No identity: William B. Owen, Lucinda Melvin, wife of
                Stephen Melvin
  Exec: Jno. R. Beaman, A. B. Chesnutt
  Wit: Miles P. Owen, Langdon C. Hubbard

MERRITT, Benajah C. - D. June 28, 1861 - P. May, 1863
  Bros: Lewis L., Alexander H. Merritt
  Sis: Rachel A. Merritt, Susan J. Johnson
  Exec: Friend, Bryant Merritt
  Wit: W. J. Watson, Killbee Merritt

MERRITT, Elizabeth - D. Feb. 18, 1854 - P. May, 1864
  Son of Haywood Merritt: William Nicholas Merritt
  Exec: Friend, Robert Merrett
  Wit: Patrick Merritt, Patrick Murphy

MERRITT, Gabriel - D. June 3, 1820 - P. --Term 18--
  Wife: Sally Merritt
  Son: Wright Merritt
  Dau: Tempy Jane Merritt
  Exec: Bro., Patrick Merritt
  Wit: John Bryan, David Merritt

MICKS, Eliza J. - D. Dec. 28, 1891 - P. Nov. 9, 1895
  No identity: Mildred H. Bunting
  Sis: Mary P. Brown
  Exec: Sis., Mary P. Brown
  Wit: Marion Butler, H. B. Chesnutt

MICKS, Dr. Wm. G. - D. Sept. 2, 1875 - P. Dec. 14, 1875
  Wife: Eliza J. Micks
  Exec: Wife, Eliza J. Micks
  Wit: J. M. Chesnutt, Allmand A. McKoy

MILLARD, Bithana - D. Oct. 30, 1823 - P. Feb., 1830
  Son: Felix B. Millard
  Daus: Charity Jones, Betsey Ann Millard, Hepsey
               Jane Millard, Eleanor Millard
  Grandson: Thomas Isaac Jones
  Exec: John Ingram
  Wit: John Hines, William S. Hicks

MILLARD, Felix B. - D. June 12, 1872 - P. June 3, 1873
  Wife: Sallie Millard
  Son: Richard W., David S., Junius M. (dec'd),
               Luther R. Millard
  Exec: Sons, Richard W., David S. Millard
  Wit: W. J. Thomson, J. B. Southerland

MOBLEY, Ollen - D. Oct. 19, 1840 - P. Feb., 1841
  Wife: Susan Mobley
  Children: Betsey Ann House, Wiley O. Mobley, Fanny A.
               Mobley
  Exec: Dr. Thomas Bunting, Whitney Royal, Hardy
               House
  Wit: Salmon Strong, G. Parsons

MOLTON, John T. - D. March 14, 1827 - P. Jan. 7, 1882
  Wife: Ann Molton
  Exec: Wife, Ann Molton, William Faison
  Wit: Nehemiah Chesnutt, Jacob Hollingsworth

MONK, Archibald - D. May 29, 1856 - P. Aug. 14, 1869
  Sons: Julius Alexander, John C., James M.,
                Claudius B., Henry C. Monk
  Exec: Sons, John C., James M. Monk
  Wit: In probate, James Oates, Kilbee Lassiter, Wm.
                H. Herring.

MONK, B. R. - D. Dec. 26, 1878 - P. Feb. 26, 1879
  Wife: Lizzie N. Monk
  Daus: Mary, Waneta E. Monk
  Bro: As guardian, H. C. Monk
  No identity: Ethan Allen
  Exec: A. B. Barbrey, H. C. Monk
  Wit: Alvin H. King, Ethan Allen

MONK, John C. - D. May 8, 1877 - P. Sept. 17, 1877
  Bro: Rufus, Henry Monk
  Daus: Anna, Flora Monk
  Wit: J. H. Benton, R. J. Bell

MOORE, James - D. Oct. 16, 1845 - P. Feb., 1846
  Wife: Jane Moore
  Sons: Walter O. (dec'd), James, Henry W. Moore
  Daus: Jane Thompson, Sarah W. Brothers, Ann
                (dec'd), Harriet O. Moore, Mariah O.
                Moore
  Son-in-law: Rufus Herring
  Exec: Son, James Moore
  Wit: Salmon Strong, Alworth King

MOORE, Mary - D. (?) - P. April 20, 1874
  Sons: William, John, Thomas Moore
  Granddau: Mary Moore
  Exec: Son, Thomas Moore
  Wit: Allmand A. McKoy, Wright Gregory

MOORE, W. H. - D. Sept. 23, 1889 - P. Nov. 15, 1889
  Daus: Mary E. Rackley, Eliza J. Johnson, Sarah A.
                Culbreth
  Granddau: Mabel Culbreth

```
Exec:          D. A. Culbreth, Dr. A. M. Lee
Wit:           Henry E. Faison, E. E. Johnson
```

MORISEY, J. K. - D. Feb. 24, 1882 - P. June 10, 1882
```
  Bro:           William H. Morisey
  Exec:          Bro., Wm. H. Morisey
  Wit:           George W. Hargrove, Milton Pope
```

MORISEY, Richard B. - D. Sept. 21, 1853 - P. Nov., 1853
```
  Mother:        Ann E. Morisey
  Sis:           Elizabeth C. Morisey, Ann B. Morisey
  Bro:           William G. Morisey
  Exec:          Wm. H. Morisey
  Wit:           A. B. Chesnutt, Robt. A. Mosely
```

MORISEY, William H. - D. Jan. 25, 1879 - P. Oct. 29, 1885
```
  Nephews:       Robert G., James K. Morisey
  Nieces:        Fanny Chesnutt, Carrie Morisey, Mary Lou
                 Brown, Eliza J. Morisey, Mary P. Morisey
  Exec:          Bro., James K. Morisey
  Wit:           W. L. Faison, A. F. Johnson
```

MOSELY, Robert A. - D. July 28, 1863 - P. (?)
```
  Wife:          Mary A. Moseley
  Exec:          Wife, Mary A. Moseley
  wit:           J. C. Carroll, Allmand A. McKoy
```

McARTHUR, John A. - D. April 8, 1848 - P. May, 1848
```
  Wife:          Margaret A. McArthur
  Children:      James O., John Thomas, Mary E., William A.
                 McArthur
  Exec:          Rice P. Matthis, James T. Matthis
  Wit:           John Vann, Harmon Matthis
```

McDONALD, Sarah - D. Jan. 1, 1848 - P. Aug., 1848
```
  Cousins:       Daniel McDonald, Mary Ann McDonald,
                 Catharine McDonald

  Exec:          Cousin, Daniel McDonald
  Wit:           John MacKay, Middleton Mobley
```

McDUFFIE, Catharine J. - D. Apr. 22, 1876 - P. Nov. 5, 1877
```
  Son:           William Archibald McDuffie
  Daus:          Susan Alice, Laura Electa, Anna Cornelia
                 McDuffie, Elizabeth Jane Black
```

```
Exec:          Son-in-law, Archibald R. Black, Bro. Robert
               Henry Murphy
Wit:           Archibald Sellers, Edwin Sellers
```

McDUFFIE, Wm. A. - D. March 28, 1891 - P. June 19, 1893
```
  Sis:         Susan A., Anna C. McDuffie, Laura E.
               McDonald, Elizabeth J. Black (dec'd)
  Exec:        Rev. Kenneth McDonald
  Wit:         H. W. Moore, J. M. Corbett
```

McKOY, A. A. - D. Feb. 14, 1860 - P. Nov. 13, 1885
```
  Wife:        Lydia A. McKoy
  Exec:        Wife, Lydia A. McKoy
  Wit:         Josiah Robinson, B. Hill, E. E. Johnson
```

McLAMB, Percy - D. May 10, 1874 - P. Aug. 29, 1874
```
  Husband:     John McLamb
  No identity: Joseph B. Westbrook

  Exec:        Uriah N. Westbrook
  Wit:         Wm. H. Bryan, J. H. House
```

McPHAIL, Duncan - D. Oct. 12, 1838 - P. Feb., 1841
```
  Wife:        Thereby McPhail
  Sons:        Duncan C. McPhail, Isaiah McPhail
  Daus:        Mary Herring, Elizabeth Herring, Ann Eliza
               McPhail, Catharine McPhail
  Exec:        Joseph Herring, Son, Duncan C. McPhail
  Wit:         Daniel Maxwell, Thomas I. Bulla
```

NEWMAN, Jacob - D. April 17, 1858 - P. (?)
```
  Wife:        Mary Ann Newman
  Son:         Archibald Newman
  Daus:        Anna Maria Reynolds, Mary Ann Honeycutt,
               Susan Honeycutt, Elizabeth A. Newman
  Exec:        Ollen Royal, Isham Royal
  Wit:         W. Royal, Sr., Whitney Royal, Jr.
```

OATES, David - D. Nov. 6, 1873 - P. Aug. 18, 1875
```
  Wife:        Malinda J. Oates
  Sons:        Jethro W., David Oates
  Daus:        Susan, Serena F. Stevens
  Exec:        Wife, Malinda J. Oates, Friend, Calvin J.
               McCullen
  Wit:         Milton C. Richardson, Abner G. Cooper
```

OATES, Elizabeth - D. Aug. 17, 1836 - P. Feb., 1839

  Sons: John, Jethro, Thomas I., Curtis C., Claiburn

                I. Oates

  Dau: Mary Ann Faison

  Exec: Son, Curtis C. Oates

  Wit: S. R. Ireland, Jas. P. Beck, A. B. Wright

OATES, James - D. Apr. 22, 1876 - P. Nov. 24, 1877

  Wife: Mildred J. Oates

  Daus: Susan Ann Grice, Martha J. Roberson, Vir-

                ginia A. Benton, Ann E., Mary B., Louetta

                W. Oates

  Exec: Wife, Mildred J. Oates

  Wit: A. B. Chesnutt, James K. Morisey

OATES, Jethro - D. March 12, 1821 - P. May, 1823

  Wife: Eliza Oates

  Sons: John, Thomas, Curtis Caraway, Claborn Ivey,

                Jesse O., Stephen Oates

  Dau: Mary Ann Oates

  Grandson: John Olen Oates

  Exec: Son & Dau., John, Eliza Oates, Thomas Wright

  Wit: John Oates, Gibson Merrett, Salmon Strong

OATES, Mary Ann - D. Aug. 25, 1821 - P. --Term 18--

  Children: Fanny Brown, M---- Brown, Anny Williams,

                Lenny King, Calvin Oates, Michael, Stephen,

                James Oates

  Exec: James Oates, Son

  Wit: John Brown, Rhody Cam---

OATES, Stephen - D. Feb. 17,1822 - P. Aug., 1835

  Wife: Elizabeth Oates

  Wit: Samuel J. Pope, Robert Shipp

ODUM, Dicey - D. Dec. 3, 1889 - Jan. 18, 1890

  Kinfolks: Polly Brown, & son, James L. Brown

  Exec: T. W. King

  Wit: A. Holmes, J. W. King

OWEN, John - D. July 29, 1858 - P. Aug., 1859

  Wife: Sarah Owen

  Sons: Miles P., William T., Thomas I., Benson S.,

                John W., Edmund B. Owen

Daus: Mary E. Williams, Martha Jane Owen, Sarah
                 A. Smith
Wife's Assistant: Asha Faircloth
Grandchildren: Millard F. Owen, Junius P. Owen, Martha A.
                 Owen, Mary Allia Owen
Exec: Sons, Miles P. Owen, Benson S. Owen

Codicil: D. Feb. 22, 1829
Wit: In court, Hosea J. Hobbs, Isaac C. Wright

OWEN, Miles P. - D. Aug. 25, 1876 - P. July 26, 1880
   Wife: Caroline Owen
   Sons: John W., Leonidas C., Henry L., Edward J.,
                 Samuel W., George P. Owen
   Daus: Sarah E. Parker, Margaret J. Brock, Mary A.
                 Hobbs, Martha A., Ann E. Owen
   Exec: Wife, Caroline Owen
   Wit: In probate, James M. Mosely, Thomas J. Lee,
                 Charles P. Johnson, Daniel L. Brock

OWEN, Owen - D. July 2, 1829 - P. Aug., 1838
   Wife: Patsey Owen
   Sons: Bernice B., Irvin, Reden
   Daus: Mary, Elizabeth, Letetia, Jennetta, Patsey
                 Owen, Sabra Parker
   No identity: Gabriel Owen (son of Wm. Owen, dec'd),
                 Jemima Grozier (wife of Wm. Grozier)
   Exec: Son, Irvin Owen, John Owen, Sr.
   Wit: Neal Campbell, William Fowler

   Codicil: May 20, 1831
   Codicil: D. Sept. 18, 1837
   Granddau: Martha Owen

OWEN, Reddin - D. Oct. 13, 1865 - P. (?)
   Wife: Rody Owen
   Son: David C. Owen
   Exec: George W. Autrey
   Wit: John W. Matthews, J. C. Howard

PARKER, Ann - D. Aug. 11, 1835 - P. May, 1837
   Son: Denis Parker
   Dau: Sophia Parker
   Exec: Son, Denis Parker
   Wit: John Owen, Daniel Horn, William J. Owen

PARKER, Charity M. - D. --187- - P. March 21, 1887
  Sons: Samuel J., David F., John W. Parker
  Dau: Mary E. Carroll
  Exec: Friend, Isaac W. Herring
  Wit: C. C. Smith, W. A. Gavin

PARKER, Harriet - D. Jan. 15, 1857 - P. Feb., 1866
  Friends: Abraham N. Matthis, J. R. Beaman
  Dau. of A. N. Matthis: Rachel Caroline Matthis
  Exec: Abraham N. Matthis
  Wit: Lewis Carroll, Jonathan Pearson

PARKER, Jemima - D. Sept. 26, 1836 - P. Nov., 1843
  Sis: Bathsheba Parker
  Exec: Sis., Bathsheba Parker
  Wit: Dickson Sloan, W. L. Robinson

PARKER, John - D. Oct. 7, 1856 - P. Aug., 1859
  Sons: William W., Charles K., Robert A., John B.,
              Joseph L., Timothy S., James W. Parker
  Daus: Elizabeth Ann Owen, Mary J. Underwood,
              Molsey Parker, Rachel C. Parker, Sarah I.
              Parker
  Grandchildren: David B., Susan A., James C. Parker
  Exec: Sons, William W., Robert A. Parker
  Wit: R. C. Holmes, John J. Highsmith

PARKER, Joseph D. - D. (?) - P. Dec. 23, 1890
  Wife: Mary J. Parker
  Sons: Joseph D., Jr., James M., Lucien E. Parker
  Daus: Martha J. Lockaman, Ellen S. McPhail,
              Zilpha A. Royal, Mary K. Smith, Margaret E.
              Newman, Sarah E. Cobb, Laura Howard
  Exec: Son, Joseph D. Parker, Jr.
  Wit: Thomas L. Owen, John D. Ezzell

PARKER, Thomas - D. Sept. 28, 1852 - P. Feb., 1861
  Wife: Cathrine Parker
  Son: Gabriel Parker, Joseph Parker
  Dau: Edney Parker
  Exec: John Owen
  Wit: Benson S. Owen, Silas Herring
  Codicil: L. M. White as executor
  Dated: Dec. 21, 1859
  Wit: B. S. Owen, W. F. Culbreth

PEARSON, Thomas E. R. - D. Aug. 12, 1863 - P. Aug., 1864
  Bro: William D. Driver
  Sis: Sallie Eliza Bell
  Exec: Friend, Jonathan Pearson
  Wit: C. Tole Murphy, John G. Powell

PETERS, Samuel - D. Aug. 31, 1847 - P. Feb., 1851
  Wife: Lucretia Peters
  Sons: Samuel, Jr., Josiah, Jesse Peters
  Daus: Edney Bass, Barbary Peters
  Grandchildren: Jennett Holder, Mary Jane Holder,
                Sampson Holder
  Exec: Son, Jesse Peters, Sampson Holder
  Wit: Isaac Strickland, Shepard Bass

PETERSON, Aaron - D. Sept. 8, 1823 - P. Nov., 1823
  Wife: Sarah Peterson
  Son: Charles Peterson

  Grandchildren: Laban, Gabriel, Patrick, Enock, Allen,
                Anna Peterson, Charity Johnston
  No identity: Adonisam Peterson
  Exec: Angus Johnston, Son, Charles Peterson
  Wit: Angus Johnston, Harmon Matthis

PETERSON, Charles - D. March 25, 1869 - P. Aug., 14, 1869
  Sons: Aaron, Raiford, Laban, Nixon, Fleet
  Grandson: Larkin Peterson
  Daus: Dicy, Rebecca Hudson
  Exec: Son, Aaron Peterson
  Wit: W. L. Robinson, Josiah Robinson

PETERSON, Elisha - D. Aug. 16, 1849 - P. Nov., 1849
  Wife: Not named
  Daus: Polly Robinson, Hariet Peterson, Sophia
                Purvis
  Exec: William D. Robinson, Stephen Purvis
  Wit: A. B. Chesnutt, J. C. Carroll

PETERSON, Elizabeth - D. Sept. 16, 1850 - P. May, 1863
  Nephew: Milton Powel
  Exec: Nephew, Milton Powel
  Wit: W. L. Robinson, Wm. L. Peterson

PETERSON, Hiram - D. Feb. 7, 1881 - P. Nov. 14, 1881
  Wife: Dilcy Peterson

```
Sons:           Milton, George, Winslow, Richard, Robinson
Daus:           Francis, Rachel Peterson
Exec:           B. W. Robinson
Wit:            Josiah Robinson, Ira Robinson
```

PETERSON, Ross - D. Jan. 23, 1876 - P. Feb. 21, 1876
```
Wife:           Lucy Peterson
Son:            Lewis, Bryant (other children not named)
Exec:           Wife, Lucy Peterson
Wit:            Josiah Robinson, Burress W. Robinson
```

PETERSON, Stephen - D. Apr. 10, 1889 - P. Aug. 26, 1895
```
Wife:           Sabrah A. Peterson
Sons:           David T., Henry B. Peterson
Daus:           Ann G. Gregory, Helan C. Owen, Lena A.
                Barden, Rebecca E. Martin, Sarah R. Rackley,
                Mary S. Lewis
Exec:           Wife, Son, Sabrah, David T. Peterson
Wit:            William S. Matthis, A. C. Peterson
```

PETERSON, Thomas - D. March 22, 1838 - P. May, 1838
```
Daus:           Nancy Powel, Miriam Peterson, Elizabeth
                Peterson
Son-in-law:     Sion Bracher
Grandson:       Moses Bracher
Exec:           Elisha Parker, Zachariah Parker
Wit:            Asa Gregory, Zachariah Parker
```

PETERSON, William D. - Feb. 17, 1881 - P. Dec. 28, 1881
```
Wife:           Sarah Jane Peterson
Son:            William F. Peterson
Exec:           Robert Highsmith, Wife, Sarah Jane Peterson
Wit:            George Highsmith, R. Highsmith
```

PHILLIPS, Samuel - D. March 23, 1832 - P. Nov., 1832
```
Wife:           Hannah Phillips
Son:            James J., David Phillips
Grandson:       Samuel J. Philips
Exec:           John Godwin
Wit:            Joseph Dawson, John Rainor
```

POWELL, Luke - D. March 8, 1838 - P. Feb., 1842
```
Wife:           Rebeckah Powel
Wife's Nephew:  Thomas Edward Randolf Pearson
Exec:           Jonathan Pearson
Wit:            John Bryan, Dickson Sloan, Peyton R. Parker,
                J. T. Treadwell
```

POWELL, Mark - D. June 5, 1836 - P. Aug., 1836
```
  Wife:          Zilpha Powell
  Children:      Peyton M., Patience, Cora N., Anne, Benj. J.,
                 Mary, Luke A., John G., Amos S. C., Sherod
                 C., Anom L., Arcada Powell
  Exec:          Son, Peyton M. Powell
  Wit:           John Bryan, Luke Powell
```

PRIDGEN, William E. - D. May 11, 1864 - P. Feb. 13, 1882
```
  Wife:          Emily J. Pridgen
  Exec:          Wife, Emily J. Pridgen
  Wit:           Thomas H. Holmes, R. A. Moseley, Samuel C.
                 S. Shelly, T. H. Best
```

PRIDGEON, Mathew - D. Oct. 19, 1820 - P. --Term 18--
```
  Sons:          Luke, Matthew Pridgeon
  Daus:          Peggy, Ann Jane, Jemima, Rebecca, Deborah
  Exec:          Alfred Wood, Robert Ward
  Wit:           John Carlton, Nathan Jones
```

RACKLEY, Nancy - D. Feb. 19, 1835 - P. May, 1835
```
  Grandsons:     Elisha Tew, Pleasant A. Tew
  Granddau:      Nancy Elizabeth Tew
  Exec:          Joab Tew
  Wit:           Isaac Strickland
```

RAINOR, Amey - D. Aug. 1, 1833 - P. Feb., 1834
```
  Sons:          William, Samuel, Joab, Matthew, Richard
                 Rainor
  Daus:          Ann Hudson, Elizabeth Eldridge, Phereba
                 Thornton
  No identity:   John Rainer, Jarris J. Rainer, Pearcy
                 Draughon
  Exec:          Archibald Monk
  Wit:           James Oates, Susy McLamb
```

REGISTER, Gibson - D. Apr. 12, 1866 - P. Feb., 1868
```
  Wife:          Sally Register
  Sons:          Edward S., Henry H., Newton Francis Register
  Daus:          Adline A. Waters, Mary J. Bland, Nancy L.,
                 Sarah E. Register
  Exec:          Son, Newton F. Register
  Wit:           J. Dickson Pearsall, Geo. W. Moseley
```

REGISTER, Harmon H. - D. Jan. 28, 1878 - P. May 17, 1878
  Wife: Mellissa A. Register
  Sons: John W., James H., Henry M., William E.
                  Register
  Exec: William S. Matthis, James M. Powell
  Wit: William S. Matthis, A. C. Garris

REGISTER, John - D. Aug. 17, 1820 - P. Nov., 1832
  Wife: Edith Register
  Sons: Gibson, Edmond
  Exec: Son, Gibson Register
  Wit: W. Robinson, Wm. L. Robinson

REGISTER, Joseph - D. 1822 - P. Aug., 1823
  Wife: Mary Register
  Exec: M. Register
  Wit: John Register, Aaron Vann, Burrell Register

REGISTER, William - D. July 26, 1851 - P. Aug.,1851
  Wife: Susan Register
  Daus: Margaret Ezzell, Sarah Walker, Susan
                  McLemore, Dorcas Bradshaw
  Exec: R. C. Holmes
  Wit: Joseph Herring, James M. Robinson

REID, David - D. Aug. 14, 1858 - P. Oct. 4, 1858
  County: Madison Co., Tennessee
  Wife: Sophia Reid
  Son: Alexander
  Exec: Bros., James W. Reid, Ambrose R. Reid
  Wit: John R. Alston, John A. Tyson, Jr.
    (Estate settled in Sampson County, May, 1859. Patrick
  Murphy, Administrator.)

RICH, Lott - D. Jan. 15, 1879 - Oct. 20, 1879
  Sons: James O., Lott Jasper Rich
  Daus: Margaret M. Rich, Sarah A. Rich, Dicey L.
                  Bird, Harriett D. Lawhon
  Exec: Sons, James O., Lott J. Rich
  Wit: In court, John C. Wright, Amma B. Chesnutt,
                  William R. Highsmith, Kedar Vann

RICH, Lott, Sr., - D. July 9, 1838 - P. Nov., 1840
  Sons: Lott Rich, Owen Rich
  Daus: Harriet, Dicey, Becky Peterson, Jinny Fisher,

Susannah Spell, Polly
Granddau: Mary Jane Rich, Harriet Chesnutt
Exec: Sons, Owen, Lott Rich
Wit: Gabriel Holmes, Love A. Tatom

RIVENBARK, David F. - D. Sept. 18, 1857 - P. Nov., 1857
  Children: Owen J., William J., Daniel J., Matthew J.,
  Exec: Son, William J. Rivenbark
  Wit: J. R. Ezzell, Willis Wilson

ROBINSON, George - D. June 30, 1865 - P. Nov., 1865
  wife: Eleanor Robinson
  Son: L. W. Robinson,
  Daus: Missouri F?, Julia B., Annabella, Elizabeth
               H., Susan M. Robinson
  wit: W. R. Tatom, James C. Robinson, L. W.
               Robinson

  Heirs: In probate: Neill McDugald and wife,
               Margaret J., William K. Chesnutt and wife,
               Charlotte, A. Herring Hall and wife, Eliza
               E., James C. Robinson, Lucien W. Robinson,
               five daus. as named above.
will written after death by witnesses named above.

ROBINSON, George R. - D. Feb., 1869 - P. Nov. 16, 1874
  Wife: Margaret Robinson
  Sons: J. Monroe, Oliver P. Robinson
  Daus: Tabitha Robinson, Elizabeth A. Matthis,
               Arabella Rackley, Sarah Highsmith
  Exec: Friend, W. L. Robinson
  Wit: J. J. Harvel, William L. Johnson

ROBINSON, George W. - D. July 9, 1872 - P. Oct. 30, 1882
  No identity: Helen Highsmith, Louisa Vann, Isabella Ward,
               Nancy Robinson, Sarah Tatum, Mary Vann,
               (dec'd)

  Exec: Sons, Abner Robinson, Josiah Robinson
  Wit: In probate, John R. Beaman, A. B. Chesnutt,
               A. J. Johnson, Joseph Robinson

ROBINSON, James - D. Aug. 4, 1846 - P. Spring Term, 1854
  Wife: Rebecca Robinson
  Sons: John Bright, George R.
  Daus: Elizabeth McLeod, Tabitha Robinson, Mary

Jane, Sophia Ann, Katharine Robinson,
Nancy Devane, Eley Sessoms, Margaret Her-
ring, Charlotte Treadwell
No identity: E. G. Ward
Exec: Son, George R. Robinson, Friend, George W.
Robinson
Wit: Hardy Herring, Abner Robinson
Codicil: D. July 22, 1852

Wit: David D. Sloan, Bright Johnson, Bizzell
Johnson

ROBINSON, J. W. - D. Sept. 18, 1895 - Oct. 9, 1895
Bros: Wm. Henry, Duncan Thomas Robinson
Sis: Sarah Bertha Ross, Mary Catherine Robinson
Exec: Bro., Duncan Thomas Robinson
Wit: J. W. S. Robinson, D. I. Robinson

ROBINSON, John - D. Feb. 13, 1866 - P. Oct. 10, 1868
Sons: John F., William D. Robinson
Dau: Molcy Jane Robinson
Granddau: Caroline Mathis
Exec: Bro., W. L. Robinson, Son, John F. Robinson
Wit: G. W. Robinson, Josiah Robinson

ROBINSON, Oliver P. - D. Oct. 8, 1877 - P. Feb. 4, 1878
Wife: Dicey A. Robinson
Dau: Harritta C. Robinson
Exec: Wife, Dicey A. Robinson
Wit: Jas. B. Highsmith, Daniel T. Johnson

ROBINSON, William - D. May 15, 1841 - P. May, 1843
Sons: John, George W., William L. Robinson
Daus: Elizabeth Ward, Marget Robinson, Mary Ward,
Arabella Marly, Nancy Herring
Exec: Sons, George, Wm. L. Robinson
Wit: (In court) Thomas K. Morisey, Dr. John Owen,
Dr. William McKay

ROBINSON, Wm. D. - D. Aug. 19, 1879 - P. March 17, 1883
Son: Abner
Granddau: Sarah C. Pipkin
Exec: Son, Abner Robinson, Stephen Pipkin
Wit: Jas. H. Stevens, A. B. Chesnutt

ROBINSON, William L. - D. March 7, 1870 - P. Apr. 30, 1870
  Wife: Jenetta Robinson
  Sons: Thaddeus, Otavey, Ferdinand, Burress W.
  Daus: Victoria E. Robinson, Jenetta Tate, Mary
               K. Mosley, Lenora Vann, Virginia J. Rackley
  Exec: Friend, Josiah Robinson
  Wit: D. J. Knowles, Kilbee Chesnutt

ROYAL, A. - D. July 15, 1879 - Jan. 15, 1880
  Wife: Sarah J. Royal
  Sons: Albert B., Timothy L., Ivey A. Royal
  Dau: Miney N. Royal
  Exec: Wife, Sarah J. Royal, Hardy L. Spell
  Wit: In probate, Adolphus Williamson, R. L. Lewis,
               Sylvester Carter

ROYAL, Catharine - D. Aug. 26, 1882 - P. Oct. 19, 1882
  Bro: Stephen Williamson, Wm. C. Williamson
  Sis: Jane Morgan
  Exec: A. F. Johnson
  Wit: Edwin W. Kerr, Wm. A. Johnson

ROYAL, Hardy E. - D. Nov. 8, 1845 - P. Nov., 1849
  Sis: Athanasia Hicks, Mary A. Royal
  Exec: Wife, not named
  In court: Albert R. Hicks, Mariah Royal
  Wit: Joel Parker

ROYAL, Hardy, Sr. - D. March 1, 1832 - P. May, 1832
  Wife: C--- Royal
  Sons: William Rufus, Hardy Elverton Royal
  Daus: Althenisa Royal, Mary Adeline Royal, Mary
               Jane Faison
  No identity: Lucy Carroll
  Exec: Elias Faison, Whitney Royal, Hardy Stevens
  Wit: Thomas Brown, Daniel Johnson

ROYAL, Isham - D. May 8, 1832 - P. Aug., 1833
  Wife: Elizabeth Royal
  Sons: Whitney Royal, John Royal, Hardy Royal
  Exec: Son, Whitney Royal
  Wit: W. D. Stephens, Eliza J. Stephens

ROYAL, John - D. March 20, 1862 - P. Aug., 1862
  Sons: Hardy S., Alexander, Amos Royal

```
Daus:           Susanna A. Royal, Betsey Carr
Grandchildren:  Mary C., Susanna E., Amos E. Carr
Wit:            Jas. C. Williams, Elias T. Royal
```

ROYAL, Rezin - D. Aug. 1849 - P. Nov., 1854
```
Wife:           Catharine Royal
Sons:           Young, Josiah, John Royal
Dau:            Edith Carver
Grandsons:      John D. Carver, Alexander, Josiah Carver
Exec:           Wife, Catharine Royal, John Royal, Son
Wit:            Thomas J. Morisey, Frank N. Robert
```

ROYAL, Noah - D. Sept. 17, 1853 - P. Feb., 1855
```
Wife:           Polly Royal
Sons:           Ollen, Moulton Royal
Exec:           John T. Moulton, Amma B. Chesnutt
Wit:            Alfred Johnson, Robert A. Mosely
```

ROYAL, Ollen - D. Dec. 10, 1874 - P. March 1, 1875
```
Wife:           Nellie
Sons:           John Allen, Gabriel H., Ollen J. M. Royal
Exec:           Son, John Allen Royal, John Thomas Warren
Wit:            A. J. Johnson, D. A. Culbreth
```

ROYAL, Owen - D. May 7, 1820 - P. --Term 18--
```
Wife:           Lucy Royal
Children:       Dicy Jackson, Willis, William, Labon, John,
                Biggers Royal, Zilpha Butler
Dau-in-law:     Nancy Royal
Exec:           Ollen Mobley
Wit:            Ollen Mobley, Horatio J. Mosley
```

ROYAL, Sarah J. - D. Feb. 14, 1882 - P. March 18, 1882
```
Sons:           Owen R. Rich, Timothy L. Royal, Ivey Adlas
                Royal, Albert Bernard Royal
Dau:            Minnie Novelle Royal
Exec:           James W. Wright
Wit:            Enoch W. Alderman, Adolphus Williamson
```

ROYAL, Whitney - D. March 30, 1864 - P. Sept. 1, 1869
```
Wife:           Sarah Royal
Sons:           Wm. R., Alvin, Isham, Elias F., Whitney
Daus:           Mary Ann Underwood, Hepsey M..Holmes,
                Elizabeth Maria Royal
Exec:           Sons, Alvin, Isham Royal
Wit:            W. B. Draughon, Alexander Royal
```

ROYAL, William - D. 1831 - P. Feb., 1832
  Wife: Tabitha Royal
  Children: William, Alfred, Thomas, Vinson, Jona-
                than, Elizabeth
  Wit: D. Dawson, David Phillips

ROYAL, Young - D. July 12, 1818 - Feb. 15, 1894
  Wife: Edith Royal
  Sons: Rezin, William, Wilson, Raiford
  Daus: Sallie Butler, Sabra Brown, Betsy Westbrook,
                Polly Royal, Nancy Butler
  Exec: Son, Rezin Royal, son-in-law, Travis Butler
  Wit: H. Royal, Robert Butler

ROYAL, Zacheriah - D. June 28, 1869 - P. March 12, 1870
  Wife: Louisa Royal
  Sons: Oliver, Allen, Rice, Albert
  Daus: Emily, Nancy Royal
  Exec: Son, Oliver Royal
  Wit: R. C. Holmes, Lofton H. McLemore

SEAVEY, J. B. - D. May 18, 1881 - P. Oct. 28, 1881
  Wife: Ann J. Seavey
  Son: Jeremiah B. Seavey
  Daus: Hannah W. Seavey, Mary B., Eugenia F. Moore
  Exec: Wife, Ann J. Seavey
  Wit: A. West, O. P. Rogers, H. S. Devane

SESSUMS, Blake - D. Oct. 17, 1833 - Nov., 1841
  Wife: Rachel Sessums
  Sons: Irvin, John Nelson, Solomon, Miles
  Daus: Polly Hanah, Elizabeth Ann
  Exec: Nicholas Sessums, Guy Sessums, John Sessums
  Wit: Enoch Hall, Sophia Sessums

SESSUMS, Solomon, Sr. - D. Aug. 25, 1831 - P. Aug., 1832
  Children: Blake, John, Solomon, Nicholas, Owen, Lemmon,
                Gray, L-------- Hailes, Elizabeth Holland,
                Sophiniah, Mary Ann Sessums
  Grandson: Colan
  Exec: Sons, Nicholas, Gray Sessums
  Wit: William Hall, Gray Sessums

SIKES, Murdock M. - D. Sept. 27, 1862 - Nov. 10, 1873
  Sis: Elva J. Sikes

```
County:        New Hanover
Heirs:         Named in probate:  Daniel M. Sikes, Charles
               M. Sikes, Dorcas Melvin, Elva J. Sikes
Will was written in a letter at Richmond, Virginia.
```

SIKES, John - D. March 17, 1849 - P. May, 1849
```
Son:           James H. Sikes
Daus:          Elizabeth Underwood, Margaret Ann McArthur,
               Rhoda Catharine Mathis
Friend:        John T. Molton
Exec:          Friend, John T. Molton, Son-in-law, Rice P.
               Matthis
Wit:           R. C. Holmes, B. Stith
```

SHINE, Francis - D. Apr. 23, 1831 - P. May, 1831
```
Sons:          Thomas T., James K., William R., Alexander,
               John Shine
Daus:          Ellen Jane, Sarah Green, Margaret Ann Shine
Exec:          Sons, Thomas T., James K. Shine
Wit:           H. J. Marley
```

SHIP, Ann - D. July 11, 1839 - P. Aug., 1840
```
Sons:          Robert Ship, Michael Ship
Daus:          Elizabeth Oates, Susannah McQueen, Ann
               Robertson, Jane Ship
Exec:          James Moore, Benj. Hargrove
Wit:           Alworth King, Harry Brewer
```

SLOCUMB, Martha A. - D. Oct. 20, 1887 - P. Nov. 20, 1894
```
Sons:          John C., William, R. K. Slocumb
Exec:          Sons, John C., William, R. K. Slocumb
Wit:           A. F. Johnson, H. B. Giddens, Howard J.
               Peterson
```

SLOCUMB, Stephen - D. Aug. 8, 1827 - P. Nov., 1828
```
Sons:          John C., William, Stephen
Daus:          Elizabeth, Sivel, Isabella, Dolly Slocumb
Exec:          John Ingram, Son, John C. Slocumb
Wit:           Alexander Chesnutt, Redin Williams
```

SLOCUMB, William K. - D. May 1, 1854 - May, 1854
```
Sis:           Mary B. Eliot
No identity:   John C. Slocumb, Thomas B. Ashford, George
               Thomas King, Flora I. King, Margaret E. King
Exec:          Jesse G. Shepherd
Wit:           J. W. Lane, John B. Lane
```

SMITH, David - D. Nov. 9, 1854 - P. Aug., 1857
  Wife: Catharine Smith
  Sons: John, David, James, George, Franklin
  Daus: Matilda, Margaret, Ann, Elizabeth, Caledonia,
                 Jane

  Exec: Wife, Catharine, Children, John, David,
                 James, George, Franklin

  Wit: A. A. McKoy, Thomas M. Clarkson

SMITH, Henry E. - D. July 29, 1873 - P. Sept. 3, 1877
  Wife: Anna Smith
  Sons: Jefferson D., Thomas, Christopher C.,
                 Edward C., Jesse T., Yancy B., Amos J.
  Daus: Margaret A. Royal, Mary P. Howard
  Exec: Son, Edward C. Smith
  Wit: Wm. S. Matthis, Wm. F. Hines

SMITH, James M. - D. May 18, 1889 - P. June 5, 1891
  Wife: M------- F. Smith
  Sons: George E., Robert L., David, James M.
  Daus: Elizabeth C., Clara Smith
  Exec: Sons, George E., Robert L. Smith
  Wit: A. M. Lee, J. L. Stewart

SMITH, John - D. April 16, 1880 - P. April 5, 1881
  Wife: Rhody Smith
  Son: P. B. Smith
  Exec: Son, P. B. Smith
  Wit: W. D. Hawley, Autry Baggett

SMITH, John - D. July 2, 1880 - P. Sept. 6, 1883
  Wife: Della Smith
  Servants: Rufus, Alexander, Marcellus Smith
  No identity: Joseph B. Elwell, Isaac Rich, Betsy Norris,
                 Hannon Smith, Richard Smith, Andrew Smith,
                 Bennett Smith, M. Cashwell
  Exec: Fleet H. Armstrong
  Wit: C. E. Beard, F. H. Armstrong

SMITH, John - D. March 23, 1830 - P. Aug., 1834
  Grandsons: Henry E. Smith, William H. Smith
  Great-Grandson: John K. Smith
  Exec: Grandsons, Henry E. Smith, Wm. H. Smith
  Wit: Nehemiah Chesnutt, James D. Brown

SMITH, John W. - D. May 2, 1885 - P. Jan. 21, 1891
  Sons: John D. Smith, George W. Smith
  Daus: Sarah C. Smith
  Exec: H .W. Jernigan
  Wit: L---- Lee, H. F. Warren

SMITH, William H. - D. May 19, 1871 - P. Sept. 1, 1873
  Wife: Mary P. Smith
  Sons: Julius R., Edward E., Charles H., James K.
  Daus: Sally J. Carlton, Susan S. Smith, Charity
               P. Rodgers
  Exec: Sons, Charles H., James K., Julius R.,
               Edward E. Smith
  Wit: Wm. S. Matthis, L. R. Carroll
  Heirs: (In probate) Elizabeth A. Middleton, Mary
               C. Stokes, and above named.

SOUTHERLAND, Arkansas - D. Apr. 5, 1887 - P. Sept. 10, 1887
  Sons: Robert B., Charley, Mack Southerland
  Daus: Mary T. Bowden, Kittie Southerland
  Exec: Bro., M. C. Blount
  Wit: R. R. Bell, W. Southerland

SPEARMAN, Dolly J. - D. Apr. 14, 1885 - P. June 13, 1885
  Son: James E. Spearman
  Daus: Eliza Sanderlin, Ella Jane Smith, Mary Ann,
               Agnes Eldora Spearman
  Exec: Son-in-law, Amos J. Smith
  Wit: E. C. Smith, F. P. Alderman

SPELL, John, Sr. - D. Dec. 11, 1853 - P. Feb., 1854
  Wife: Sarah Spell
  Sons: Jacob H., John J., Lewis Spell
  Daus: Hariet, Margaret Matilda
  Granddau: Elizabeth Katherine
  Exec: Sons, Lewis, John J. Spell
  Wit: Sampson D. Jackson, Morning D. Tew

SPELL, Margaret J. - D. Nov. 4, 1885 - Apr. 23, 1886
  Children: Betty, Archie, Minnie, Cora Spell
  Wit: M. M. Hall, W. W. Herring, Sarah E.
               Crumpler

SPELL, W. D. - D. Feb. 27, 1892 - P. Apr. 22, 1893
  Wife: Mary M. Spell

```
Sons:           Olive, David D., Burnice B., Hardy A.
Daus:           Elizabeth Holland, Lilly J. Strickland,
                Mary F. Autry, Letty N. Crumpler, Virginia
                D. Spell, Polly E. Spell
Exec:           J. M. Spell, B---- Spell
Wit:            J. M. Spell, C. G. Autry, B---- Spell
Wife dissented will of W. D. Spell.
```

STEVENS, Jemima - D. Sept. 23, 1831 - P. Nov., 1831
```
Bro:            John Stevens
Sis:            Druzilla Cooper
Exec:           Bro., Hardy Stevens
Wit:            G. Toole, W. Royal
```

STEVENS, John - D. Jan. 1, 1824 - P. Aug., 1829
```
Wife:           Mary Stevens
Sons:           Hardy, Wilber D., William, John, Barnaby
Daus:           Zilpah Cooper, Drusilla Cooper, Susannah
                Morgan, Sabrah Stevens, Jemima Stevens,
                Sally T. Stevens, Mary Ann Stevens, Eliza
                Jane Stevens

Exec:           Son, Hardy Stevens
Wit:            G. Toole, Fanny Toole
```

STEVENS, Mary J. - D. Oct. 2, 1879 - P. March 18, 1891
```
Husband:        W. D. Stevens
Exec:           R. R. Bell
Wit:            B. H. Hatche, Lewis Jackson
```

STEVENS, William J. - D. Nov. 24, 1836 - P. Nov., 1841
```
Wife:           Sarah Jane Stevens
Son:            Charles Thomas Stevens
Daus:           Elizabeth, Mary Jane, Angelina Stevens
Exec:           Father, Charles Stevens
Wit:            Thomas I. Faison, John Royal
```

STEWART, Daniel - D. Jan. 22, 1875 - P. May 7, 1875
```
Wife:           Nancy
Sons:           Daniel, John
Grandchildren:  Mary Eliza, Nancy Evaline Stewart
Exec:           Son, Daniel Stewart
Wit:            H. L. Hall, J. T. Mathews
```

STEWART, John - D. May 8, 1841 - P. Aug., 1846
```
Sons:           James, Will, Daniel, Dougal (dec'd)
```

```
Daus:            Katharine Shaw
Granddau:        Christian
Exec:            Daniel Bain, Daniel McMillan
Wit:             Isaac Strickland, Blackman Jackson
```

STRICKLAND, Holly - D. Oct. 21, 1822 - P. Nov., 1822
```
  Wife:          Betsey Strickland
  Sons:          John, Martin Strickland
  Daus:          Nancy Queen Jackson, Sopheah Odum
  Grandchildren: Wm. Haywood Smith, Betsey Van Smith
  Exec:          Wife, Betsey, Son, Martin Strickland
  Wit:           Abraham Naylor, Sr., Willis Daniel, Abraham
                 Naylor
```

STRONG, Salmon - D. Oct. 8, 1848 - P. Nov., 1848
```
  Children:      William A., George V., Catharine M., Henry
                 R., Robert C., Michael I. Strong
  Exec:          Son, George V. Strong
  Wit:           Warren Johnson, Jas. A. Moore
```

SUTTON, Barnabas - D. Nov. 29, 1878 - P. Jan. 25, 1879
```
  Wife:          ' Susan Sutton
  Grandson:      Josiah Sutton, Jr.
  Granddau:      Sarah Ann Sutton, Virginia S. Sutton
  Exec:          William T. Sutton
  Wit:           James J. Huggins, Luther S. Bell
```

SUTTON, Edmond - D. May 22, 1863 - P. May, 1864
```
  Wife:          Nancy Sutton
  Exec:          Son, Oswin Sutton
  Wit:           L. C. King, Daniel C. King
```

SUTTON, Elizabeth - D. Jan. 23, 1882 - P. Jan. 2, 1885
```
  Sons:          Bryant, Stephen W., Barnabas, William R.
  Daus:          Ann Mariah Sutton, Sarah Lindsey, Penny
                 Stanly, Susan T. Sanderson, Nancy Anders,
                 Martha E. King
  Grandsons:     William Alfred Smith, Bryant McKoy Sutton
  Exec:          Son, William R. Sutton
  Wit:           W. R. Sutton, Jr., A. M. Sutton, W. A.
                 Anders
```

SUTTON, James - D. Aug. 18, 1884 - P. March 22, 1889
```
  Wife:          Nancy J. Sutton
  Sons:          Joseph R., George W., Thomas H., William,
```

```
Daus:           Sena C., Elizabeth C., Hepsy A. Sutton
Grandchildren:  Lela Bryant, Georgianna Bryant, Granger
                Bryant, John Bryant, Nancy Bryant
Exec:           Sons, Joseph R., Wm. T. Sutton
Wit:            D. C. King, Julius S. King
```

SUTTON, John B.- D. March 26, 1886 - P. Nov. 2, 1891
```
Wife:           Hepsy Sutton
Dau:            C. E. Britt
Grandson:       Percy Darden
Exec:           Son-in-law, Edwin T. Britt
Wit:            L. C. King, John T. Gregory
```

SUTTON, Joseph - D. Jan. 27, 1835 - P. Feb., 1835
```
Wife:           Elizabeth Sutton
Sons:           James, Lewis, Benjamin, Josiah, Stephen,
                Thomas J. Sutton, Barnabas Sutton
Daus:           Artesha, Ann Mariah Sutton, Nancy Byrd,
                Penny Byrd, L------- Glessen, Betsey Ann
                Cole
Exec:           Bryan Daughterry, Barnabas Sutton, Son
Wit:            Edmund Sutton, A. Monk
```

SUTTON, Luke W. - D. June 29, 1837 - P. Aug., 1837
```
Wife:           Sylvia Sutton
Sons:           Theophilus, John Brown, William Rufus Sutton
Daus:           Mary Jane, Sally Ann, Clarissa Sutton
Exec:           Wife, Sylvia Sutton
Wit:            Bryan McCullin, Benjamin Sutton, Stephen
                Sutton
```

SUTTON, Matilda - D. Feb. 20, 1877 - P. July 19, 1877
```
Sons:           John H., Benjamin, Joseph, Lewis Sutton
Daus:           Ann Williams, Penelope Sutton, Treacy Jones,
                Nancy Precythe
Grandau:        Mary F. Sutton
Exec:           Son, Lewis Sutton
Wit:            Jesse S. Sanderson, Barney Creel
```

SUTTON, Theophilus - D. Feb. 3, 1892 - P. Apr. 6, 1893
```
Sons:           Julius, Theophilus, Thomas W.
Daus:           Julia Hollingsworth, Sylva Odom, Sarah Best,
                Clarisa Best
Son of Ezekiel Sutton:  J. H. Sutton (No identity)
Exec:           Son, Thomas W. Sutton
```

Wit: L. C. King, H. G. Williamson

TART, Thomas - D. Dec. 26, 1848 - P. May, 1850
  Sons: John, Thomas, Jr., Nathan, James Tart
  Daus: Sarrah Hanes, Patsey Ward, Nancy Denning,
             Pharebee McLamb, Elizabeth McLamb
  Grandchildren: John Westbrook, Sarah Byrd, Mary Miles,
             Wm. Westbrook
  Exec: Son, James Tart, Archibald Monk
  Wit: Sarah Tart, T. G. Bennett, William Gregory

TATOM, Joshua - D. (?) - P. Feb., 1834
  Wife: Sarah Tatom
  Sons: Dickson, Richard Tatom

  Grandchildren: Molsey Jane Tatom, Mary Johnson, Nancy
             Peterson, Betsy Crumpler & dau., Treacy
             Crumpler, James Armstrong
  Exec: Archibald Murphy
  Wit: E. Herring, Arch. Murphy, Hanson W. Herring

TATOM, Laban - D. Aug. 6, 1830 - P. Aug., 1835
  Wife: Sooky Tatom
  Sons: Wm. R., Love A. Tatom
  Daus: Dicey, Zilpah, Mary, Elizabeth, Sally, Sooky,
             Marget, Beckky
  Exec: Son, Love A. Tatom, Wm. Robinson
  Wit: G. W. Robinson, W. Robinson

TAYLOR, Ransom - D. Dec. 11, 1885 - P. June 7, 1886
  Widow of Henry Massengill: . Nelly Massengill
  No identity: Festus F. Raynor, Sarah Mariah Raynor
  Exec: James M. Crusenberry
  Wit: J. E. West, James Crusenberry

TEW, Daniel - D. Nov. 5, 1853 - P. Nov., 1860
  Sons: John, Daniel, Wiley Tew
  Daus: Sarah Tew, Patience Tew, Jennet Tew, Jane
             Strickland, Jinny Wilson, Janetty Butler
  Exec: Nephew, Daniel Wooten
  Wit: Alexander McRae, Samuel S. Pope

TEW, Emily Jane - D. Aug. 28, 1886 - Jan. 9, 1893
  Husband: Lewis Tew
  Exec: Husband, Lewis Tew
  Wit: A. F. Johnson, D. A. Culbreth

TEW, Holley - D. Feb. 15, 1853 - P. Aug., 1853
  Wife: Aley Tew
  Sons: Huston Hobbs, John Holley, Alston, Morning
                 Dawson, Bedford Tew
  Dau: Mariah Tew
  Exec: D. M. Jackson
  Wit: E. L. Perkins, Jesse H. Hawley

TEW, Lewis - D. Jan. 16, 1853 - P. Aug., 1857
  Wife: Elizabeth Tew
  Sons: John, M. Tew
  Daus: Apsilla Royal, Elizabeth Godwin, Rachel Tew,
                 Elcey Tew, Luiza Tew
  No identity: Elizabeth Mobley, Jessie Martin Mobley
  Exec: M. Tew, Son
  Wit: Isaac Strickland, Allen Strickland

TEW, Philip - D. May 8, 1830 - P. Feb., 1831
  Wife: Mary Tew
  Son: Robert, Osburn, Logan, Alexander Tew
  Exec: Holley Tew, Robert Tew
  Wit: Isaac Strickland, Redding Strickland,
                 Jeremiah Strickland

THORNTON, Benjamin - D. March 25, 1815 - P. May, 1823
  Wife: Elizabeth Thornton
  Sons: Wright, Whitfield, Averitt
  Daus: Polly Robinson, Sally Thornton
  Exec: Nathaniel Thornton, Alexander Flemming,
                 Right Thornton
  Wit: Thomas Thornton, Sr., Eldridge Thornton,
                 Handy Thornton

THORNTON, Benjamin S. - D. Nov. 14, 1848 - P. Nov., 1848
  Wife: Elizabeth Thornton
  Step-dau: Sally Ward
  Son: Samuel Thornton
  Exec: Thomas Ward
  Wit: A. Monk, Alexander Benton

THORNTON, Nathaniel - D. Dec. 8, 1821 - P. --Term 18--
  Wife: Millie Thornton

```
Children:        Benjamin Sims, Uriah, Samuel Sugs, Millie,
                 Joseph, Susanna, Sarah Lee, Pherebee Lee,
                 David, Thomas, Nathaniel, Elizabeth,
                 Christian, Eldridge, Bershaby Thornton
Exec:            Son, Eldridge Thornton, Samuel Lee
Wit:             Thomas Thornton, Sr., Jonathan Lee
```

THORNTON, Susannah - D. March 15, 1830 - P. May, 1830
```
Bros:            Benjamin Sims, Uriah Thornton
Wit:             Sarah Thornton, A. Monk
```

TINDAL, Jannetta - D. Sept. 3, 1883
Widow of Joshua Tindal dissented will of said J. Tindal.

TINDAL, Joshua - D. May 19, 1877 - P. June 20, 1883
```
Daus:            Sarah, Rebecca Eliza, Nancy
Sons:            Joshua Lawrence, Young Tindal
Granddau:        Selesia Jewel Tew
Exec:            Son, Joshua Lawrence Tindal
Wit:             R. D. Moseley, L. C. Hubbard
```

TORRANS, Martha - D. Sept., 1829 - P. Nov., 1839
```
Niece:           Eleanor E. Stanford, Eleanor Bryan, Susan
                 Mary Bryan
Nephew:          John A. Bryan, Kedar Bryan, Thomas Kenan
Bro-in-law:      John Bryan
Exec:            Bro-in-law, John Bryan
Wit:             Needham Bryan, Thomas James, Red. Crumpler
```

TORRANS, Thomas K. - D. March 25, 1820 - P. --Term 18--
```
Wife:            Elizabeth Torrans
Children:        Samuel, Thomas, Martha, Margaret Torrans
Exec:            William Faison, Stephen Hines
Wit:             (in court) William Morisey, David Kornegay,
                 Daniel Love
```

TREADWELL, James P. - D. Feb., 1867 - P. Nov., 1867
```
No identity:     Nancy Brewington
Exec:            Robert J. Murphy
Wit:             J. C. Carroll, A. A. McKoy
```

TREADWELL, John - D. Nov. 24, 1819 - P. Feb., 1822
```
Son:             John Treadwell
Daus:            Miriam Devane, Elizabeth Portevint, Zilpah
                 Moulton, Lucretia Rogers, Charlotte Robinson
```

```
Son-in-law:    Abraham Moulton (married Zilpah)
Exec:          Son, John Treadwell, Enoch Herring
Wit:           W. Robinson, John Molton
```

TROUBLEFIELD, Peter B. - D. Dec. 24, 1872 - P. Jan. 15, 1873
```
Wife:          Nancy E. Troublefield (named in probate)
Children:      Named in probate:  Sallie E., S-- William,
                Mary, Marshall, Lizzie, Barbrey, Alexander
Exec:          Wife, Nancy E. Troublefield, Benjamin Monk
Wit:           A. B. Barbary, Elizabeth Barbary
```

TURNER, Elizabeth - D. (?) - P. May, 1837
```
Nieces:        Sally Fort, Mason Fort, Milly Fort
No identification:  John Jack Turner Fort; Hardy Fort, Son
                of Mason Fort
Exec:          Owen Holmes
Wit:           Richard C. Holmes, Gabriel Holmes
```

TURNER, Lyttleton - D. May 10, 1853 - P. (?)
```
Nephew:        William Turner
Bros:          William, Sprattiff, David, Henry Turner
No identity:   Page Williamson, John Burks
Exec:          Amma B. Chesnutt, Thomas I. Faison
Wit:           Warren Winslow, Thomas Bunting
```

UNDERWOOD, John - D. Jan. 27, 1860 - P. May, 1860
```
Sons:          Thomas R., Joseph B., David D., John P.
Daus:          Sarah J., Louisa A.
Exec:          Sons, David D., Joseph B. Underwood
Wit:           Murdock White, Jas. H. Turlington
```

UNDERWOOD, Josiah - D. March 24, 1854 - P. Aug., 1854
```
Sons:          Thomas, Theophilus (dec'd), Jacob, Uriah,
                Eli Underwood
Daus:          Marthy Cooper, Penelope J. Howard, Anna-
                mariah Butler, Rebecca A. Butler, Sarah
                J. Crumpler, Alpha Branch (dec'd)
Exec:          Sons, Thomas, Uriah Underwood
Wit:           Owen Butler, Haywood Butler
```

UNDERWOOD, Sarah - D. July 30, 1847 - P. May, 1849
```
Son:           David, and wife Sabra Underwood
Grandchildren: Sarah Ann, Margaret Ann, Eliza Ann, Mary
                Ann, Sabrey Swan Underwood
Exec:          Son, David Underwood
```

Wit: Jacob Underwood, Micajer Crumpler

UNDERWOOD, Wright L. - D. Dec. 27, 1858 - P. Aug., 1859
    Wife: Elizabeth B. Underwood
    Son: John Walter
    Daus: Julia Frances, Emma Catharine
    Exec: Wife, Elizabeth B. Underwood
    Wit: John M. Matthews, L. M. White

VANN, Enoch - D. Sept. 5, 1847 - P. Nov., 1847
    Wife: Rebecca Vann
    Sons: Wm. H., Kedar, James, Valentine Vann
    Daus: Margaret Boon, Catherine Peterson, Elizabeth
                   Boney
    Exec: Sons, Kedar Vann, Valentine Vann
    Wit: G. W. Robinson, Benajah V. Carroll

VANN, Henry - D. Dec. 20, 1886 - P. Oct. 31, 1887
    Sons: Dennis J., W. R., Franklin, Andrew C.,
                   Arthur Vann
    Daus: Lou Holland, Phareby Elizabeth, Mary Frances,
                   Margaret Ann, Dolsey Ida, Dicey Ellen Vann
    Exec: Friend, J. R. Beaman
    Wit: Nathan McLamb, Isham T. McLamb

VANN, John - D. Dec. 16, 1841 - P. May, 1842
    Wife: Sally Vann
    Sons: James, Valentine, Enoch, Aaron Vann, Thomas
    Daus: Macy Carroll (dec'd), Katherine Parker,
                   Miriam Mathis, Sally Carroll, Civil, Mary
                   Vann
    Grandchildren: Nancy, Louisa, Sarah, Polly Ann Gregory;
                   Charlotte, Sally Ann, Catherine Carroll;
                   Mary Jane Vann; (John's sons) John, Robert,
                   William
    Exec: Sons, James, John Vann
    Wit: G. W. Robinson, Sihon Killet

VANN, James - D. Aug. 16, 1865 - P. (?)
    Wife: Mary Vann
    Daus: Miriam Peterson, Susan Anders, Nancy Jane
                   Barden, Polly Ann Powell, Sally Jane Butler
    Exec: John R. Beaman, Allmand A. McKoy
    Wit: Thomas B. Matthis, H. H. Register
    Codicil: D. Nov. 19, 1866

```
Wit:              John Vann, Robinson James
Codicil:          D. Nov. 14, 1866
Dau:              Charlotte C. Stevens
Granddaus:        (In will) Martha Jane Lockamay, Molsey
                  Powell
Wit:              G. W. Moseley, Jonathan Pearson
```

```
VANN, Needham - D. June 10, 1833 - Nov., 1833
  Wife:           Elizabeth Vann
  Son:            William Vann
  Dau:            Nancy Owens
  Granddau:       Nancy Vann, Zilpha Owen
  Exec:           Son, William Vann
  Wit:            Harmon Owen, John Underwood
```

```
VANN, Owen - D. (?) - P. (?)
  Sis:            Charity Vann
  Bro:            Daniel Vann
  Nephew:         George D. Moore
  Exec:           Bro., Daniel Vann
  Wit:            W. L. Robinson, J. H. Spearman
```

```
VANN, Susan A. - D. Oct. 28, 1874 - P. Feb. 8, 1875
  Sons:           Isham D. Godwin, Joel N. Godwin, James H.
                  Vann, Robert D. Vann
  Exec:           John T. Wilson
  Wit:            Wiley Brewer, J. D. Linsey
```

```
VANN, Thomas - D. Sept. 16, 1838 - P. Nov., 1838
  Wife:           Judith Vann
  Sons:           Henry, Daniel, Thomas, Owen Vann
  Daus:           Charity, Nancy, Elizabeth, Margaret Vann,
                  Priscilla Peterson, Susan Peterson, Lucrecia
                  More
  Exec:           Son, Daniel Vann
  Wit:            G. W. Robinson, A. D. Vann
```

```
VANN, Valentine - D. Oct. 27, 1887 - P. Feb. 29, 1888
  Sons:           Lewis F., Lott, J. E. Vann
  No identity:    H. L. Vann, M. T. Cain, L. Francis Howell
  Exec:           H. B. Fryar
  Wit:            A. L. Ezzell, J. M. Fryar
```

```
VANN, William H. - D. July 31, 1863 - P. May, 1864
  Wife:           Marion M. Vann
```

```
Exec:        Bros., Kadar, James Vann
Wit:         Valentine Vann, Thomas B. Mathis
```

WARD, Mary - D. Oct. 16, 1867 - P. Sept. 10, 1885
```
  Children:    Adeline Bland (dec'd, wife of Timothy Bland),
               Robinson Ward, Elizabeth Ann Wilson, Clifton
               Ward, Mary Dameron
  Exec:        Son, Robinson Ward
  Wit:         G. W. Robinson, John Robinson
```

WARD, Nancy - D. Oct. 27, 1883 - P. July 9, 1888
```
  Niece:       Nancy E. West & husband W. J. West, and dau.
               Mary M. W. West, Elizabeth Blackburn
  Husband:     Edbridge G. Ward
  Nephew:      John D. Fussell
  Exec:        Cousin, James C. Williams
  Wit:         Nancy J. Johnson, Ira J. Johnson
```

WARD, Thomas - D. July 31, 1844 - P. Aug., 1856
```
  Wife:        Clarissa Ward
  Sis:         Elizabeth Thornton, Sarah Ward (Dautrey)
  Bro:         Jesse, John Ward
  Niece & nephew:  Isaac Ward, Susan Thornton
  Exec:        Wife, Clarissa Ward
  Wit:         John C. Monk, A. Monk
```

WARD, William - D. July 26, 1835 - P. Nov., 1836
```
  Sons:        Alfred, Robert, William, Samuel
  Daus:        Sophia White, Nancy Carlton, Nancy Jane
               Evan, Eliza Matilda Merritt
  Exec:        Sons, Alfred, Robert Ward
  Wit:         Robert Marley, A. Johnson
```

WARREN, Bennett - D. April 9, 1889 - P. Aug. 5, 1889
```
  Wife:        Annie Warren
  Sons:        Archy, Samson, Camel, Blake, Ashley, Lovitt,
               John Warren
  Daus:        Jennett, wife of George Keen; Katie, wife of
               Gaston Jones
  Bro:         J. C. Warren (dec'd)
  Exec:        Son, John Warren
  Wit:         J. A. Beaman, R. H. Beaman
```

WARREN, Isaiah - D. Sept. 4, 1846 - P. Aug., 1847
```
  Wife:        Nancy Warren
```

```
Sons:           Isaiah, Jr., Needham (dec'd)
Grandchildren:  Richard, Blake, Right Warren, Handy
                Warren, Phereba McPhail, Nancy Jackson,
                Mary Williford, I. Warren, Jr.
Exec:           Son, Isaiah Warren, Jr.
Wit:            Willis B. Jackson, Isaac Strickland
```

WARREN, Richard - D. Nov. 29, 1850 - P. (?)
```
Son:            William Hawley Warren
Daus:           Nancy Watkins, Hester Weeks
Grandchildren:  Nancy Jane Watkins, Miny Cindy, Rachel Ann,
                Richard Townly, Lavina, Hester
Exec:           Bro., Isaiah Warren
Wit:            B.  Stith, Isaiah McPhail, Samuel S. Pope
```

WEEKS, Benajah - D. March 29, 1888 - P. May 23, 1888
```
Wife:           Eliza Weeks
Sons:           Joshua, Jasper, John, Willie
Dau:            Margaret
Exec:           Chosen by court, James H. McCullen
Wit:            J. L. Stewart, W. H. Darden
```

WEEKS, John - D. Aug. 1, 1843 - P. May, 1851
```
Wife:           Nancy Weeks
Sons:           Arthur Moore Weeks, Benjamin, John Wright,
                James Weeks
Wife's son:     William Rufus
Daus:           Harriet Weeks, Mary Warren
Exec:           Son, Arthur Moore Weeks
Grandson:       William Rufus Weeks
Wit:            Isaac W. Lane, Henry Weeks, James Andrews
Codicil:        D. Sept. 20, 1844
Wit:            Redn. Hobbs, Young Wilson
```

WEEKS, Kenon - D. Feb. 22, 1888 - P. July 21, 1893
```
Wife:           Mary Weeks
Son:            James H. Weeks
Granddau:       Ula May Weeks
Exec:           Son, James H. Weeks
Wit:            L. C. King, J. B. Sutton
```

WEST, Hardy - D. July 21, 1884 - P. May 4, 1885
```
Daus:           Meritta Ann, Matilda Ann (others unnamed)
Exec:           Friend, Ransom West
Wit:            Wm. H. West, Westbrook Lee
```

WEST, Loyed, Sr. - D. March 14, 1881 - P. April 11, 1881
   Sons: Uriah, Gainey, Ransom, Noel
   No identity: Mrs. Abigail Wilson
   Exec: Sons, Noel, Ransom West
   Wit: Robinson Ward, Loyd West, Jr.

WILKINS, Sally Ann - D. Dec. 2, 1887 - P. Dec. 19, 1887
   Bro: George King
   Children: William Isaac, James, Eliza Jane Wilkins,
              Francis Russell, Virginia Carr
   Exec: Bro., George King, also as guardian
   Wit: Nathan Weeks, Oates S. King

WILLIAMS, Barnaby - D. Nov. 17, 1820 - P. --Term 18--
   Grandson: Louis F. Williams
   Exec: Grandson, Louis F. Williams
   Wit: John Bell, Thomas Byrd

WILLIAMS, Blaney - D. March 5, 1833 - P. May, 1852
   County: Duplin
   Wife: Mary Jane Williams
   Exec: Wife, Mary Jane Williams
   Wit: J. H. Everts, Isaac Ship

WILLIAMS, Elizabeth - D. Jan. 8, 1873 - P. Aug. 7, 1876
   Bro: Sam R. Williams and wife Margret Jane
              Williams
   Exec: Friend, Robert Williams
   Wit: J. R. Maxwell, John Culbreth

WILLIAMS, Joel - D. Sept. 30, 1840 - P. May, 1841
   Wife: Effy Williams
   Children: Not named
   Exec: John C. Williams
   Wit: Lewis F. Carr, Daniel M. Culbreth

WILLIAMS, Robert - D. May 11, 1830 - P. May, 1831
   Wife: Margret Williams
   Son: John Williams
   Exec: Wife, Margret Williams
   Wit: David Spell, Rebeccah Butler

WILLIAMS, Robert - D. Oct. 30, 1827 - P. Nov., 1827
   Sis: Rosey Williams

Heirs: Elizabeth Catharine, James Sessom, Mary
                Clarrilly
Exec: Harper Williams, James Williams
Wit: Bedn. Caraway, Alfred Turner, John Eliot, Jr.

WILLIAMSON, Allen - D. Apr. 19, 1877 - P. Dec. 27, 1877
  Sons: Benjamin, David, Allen, Henry, Julian, James,
                Adolphus
  Daus: Sophiah McKenzie, Elizabeth (wife of Raiford
                Butler)
  Exec: Son, James Williamson
  Wit: R. C. Holmes

WILLIAMSON, Burrell - D. Dec. 28, 1874 - P. March 13, 1875
  Wife: Ritta Williamson
  Sons: Alley D., John A., Erskin Williamson
  Sis: Polly
  Daus: Virginia, Jerusha J., Euphenia
  Exec: Son, John A. Williamson, A. B. Chesnutt
  wit: A. M. Lee, Abner Robinson
                Named in probate: Charity Ann, and above
                named.

WILLIAMSON, H. G. - D. Aug. 9, 1878 - P. Feb. 15, 1879
  Wife: Charity Ann Williamson
  Sons: David Ashly, Henry Lee
  Daus: Francis Jane, Stella, Minnie
  Exec: John A. Williams
  Wit: M. M. Killett, J. A. Killett

WILLIAMSON, Mary - D. July 30, 1831 - P. Nov., 1831
  No identity: William M. Williamson, Giney Morgan, Katha-
                rine, Elizabeth Williamson
  Exec: Son, William M. Williamson
  wit: John Boykin, Katharine Williamson

WILLIAMSON, Ollen - D. Aug. 4, 1860 - P. May, 1861
  Wife: Ann J. Williamson
  Sons: Henry G., Wm. Wright Williamson
  Daus: Lucinda, Hepsey, Sarah Williamson
  Exec: Son, Henry G. Williamson
  Wit: J. C. Carroll, A. Johnson

WILLIAMSON, Stephen H. - D. Feb. 8, 1884 - P. Jan. 2, 1885
  Wife: Lucy Ann Williamson

```
Sons:          Edward W., John W., Albert M. Williamson
Daus:          Mary S., Amanda Williamson
Exec:          Friend, A. F. Johnson
Wit:           A. B. Chesnutt, W. G. Hubbard
```

WILLIAMSON, Wright - D. Sept. 6, 1820 - P. --Term 18--
```
Wife:          Charity Williamson
Sons:          Ollen, William, Burrel, Owen Williamson
Dau:           Mary
Exec:          James Williamson, Thomas Boykin, Blen Gow
Wit:           Willis Wiggins, John Peterson
```

WILLIFORD, Jason - D. Aug. 4, 1868 - P. Aug. 5, 1878
```
Wife:          Susanna Williford
Sons:          Martin Andrew, S. W. Williford
Daus:          Mary E., Martha J. Williford, Susan C. wife
               of S. L. Hawley
Exec:          Warren Williford, Sydnia T. Smith
Wit:           J. H. Elmore, M. K. Tew
```

WILLIFORD, Mary E. - D. Feb. 14, 1880 - P. Aug. 31, 1881
```
Bro:           Warren, William, Marshal A. Williford
Sis:           Martha Jane, wife of Sidney T. Smith, Susan
               C. Hawley
Nephew:        Jason C. Williford (5 years old)
Niece:         Margaret Ann Williford
Exec:          Friend, John H. Elmore
Wit:           J. C. West, M. K. Tew
```

WILLIFORD, Micajah - D. Sept. 22, 1832 - P. May, 1833
```
Wife:          Rebecca Williford
Sons:          Thomas, Benton, William Williford
Dau:           Rachael Warren
Grandson:      James M. Williford
Granddau:      Rebecca Williford
Exec:          Son, William Williford, John Godwin
Wit:           Andrew Odam, Ransom Godwin
```

WILSON, Isham - D. July 3, 1851 - P. Nov., 1851
```
Wife:          Elinor Wilson
Sons:          Willie Elisha M., John T. Wilson
Daus:          Sarah Jane, Susan C. Wilson, Mary Ann King
Granddau:      Susan Ann Wilson
No identity:   Needham, Nancy Warren
Exec:          Sons, Elisha M., John T. Wilson
```

Wit: G. W. Stith, Kenan Weeks

WILSON, Joseph - D. June 22, 1880 - P. Aug. 27, 1881
 Wife: Elizabeth A. Wilson
 Sons: Joseph J. F., Adolphus R., Robert B.,
                Calvin D. Wilson
 Daus: Elvira Wilson, Mary F. Wilson, Eugenia A.
                Harper, Margaret E. Highsmith, Elizabeth
                C. Mathews
 Exec: Friend, Robeson Ward, Son, A. R. Wilson
 Wit: Jas. C. Williams, Wm. R. Lee

WILSON, Robert - D. Sept. 22, 1882 - P. Jan. 14, 1884
 Friend: Bronson Baggett
 Exec: Friend, Bronson Baggett
 Wit: John Dudley, N. B. Barefoot

WOLF, Richard - D. Feb. 14, 1844 - P. Nov., 1848
 Son: Seaborn I. Wolf
 Daus: Icey, Sally Wolf Elizabeth Bennett, Susey
                Bell (dec'd), Peggy Bell
 Exec: Son, Seaborn I. Wolf
 Wit: T. B. Millard, Wm. S. Hines

WOODARD, Any Ann - D. April 23, 1859 - P. Aug., 1864
 Daus: Amey Ann Harper, Martha Jane
 Exec: Friends, E. A. Bizzell, J. C. Eason
 Wit: Averitte Thornton, Eleazar Rich

WOODARD, James - D. Dec. 10, 1831 - P. Feb. 10, 1840
 Sons: Isaac, William C. Woodard
 Daus: Martha Jean, Amey Ann, Katherine, Rachel
 Exec: Bedreden Caraway, Dau., Amey Woodard
 Wit: Robert N. Herring, Lancelot Jones

WRENCH, James - D. March 24, 1864 - P. May, 1864
 Sons: Thomas E., Hugh L., Joseph, John
 Daus: Mary Lockamy, Elizabeth Haise
 Exec: Son, Joseph Wrench
 Wit: Joel Jackson, John A. Strickland

WRIGHT, Eliza J. - D. March 24, 1875 - P. Aug. 25, 1880
 Sons: John C., James W. Wright
 Daus: Kate E. Murphy, Margaret C. Wright, Ann E.
                Boykin (dec'd)

```
Exec:           Son, John C. Wright
Wit:            Miles P. Owen, Henry L. Owen

WRIGHT, Isaac C. - D. Jan. 10, 1864 - P. Feb., 1864
  Wife:         Eliza J. Wright
  Sons:         James W., John C. Wright
  Daus:         Catherine E., Margaret C. Wright, Ann E.
                Boykin
  Exec:         Sons, John C., James W. Wright
  Wit:          Arthur Brown, John H. Campbell, Almond A.
                McKoy

WRIGHT, John, Sr. - D. Nov. 20, 1835 - P. Nov., 1848
  Wife:         Penelope Wright
  Children:     Isaac, John, Nancy (dec'd) Wright
  Granddau:     Penny Prown, Rebecca, Polly, Betsy
  Exec:         Sons, John, Isaac Wright
  Wit:          W. Robinson, David Smith, Raiford Carroll
```

Deed Record Book No. 2

Wills, Births and Marriage Records
This Book is in Register of Deeds Office

BEVERET, Benjamin - D. Oct. 25, 1749 - P. July 11, 1750
   County: New Hanover (Registered in Duplin)
   Sons: Benjamin (3 others and wife unnamed)
   Wit: William Savage, Hugh McCanne
   Exec: Henry Calter, Thomas Kenan
   Clerk: John Dickson for John Sampson, Register

BARFIELD, Richard - D. May 1, 1754
   County: Duplin
   Sons: Henry, Isaac, Solomon Barfield
   Daus: Mary, Tebeth Barfield, Ann Grady, Catrrun
               Taler
   Granddau: Tebeth Taler
   Exec: Son, Solomon Barfield, Jesse Barfield
   Wit: James Barfield, John Morris, Solomon
               Barfield

CARR, William - D. Dec. 5, 1753
   County: Duplin
   Wife: Hannah Carr
   Son: Archibald Carr
   Dau: Jane Carr, Unborn child
   Exec: Wife, Hannah
   Wit: John Dickson, William McRee, Susannah
               McAlexander

HAWKINS, John - D. March 29, 1756
   County: Duplin
   Daus: Mary, Ann, Lettess Hawkins
   Exec: Daus., Mary, Ann, Lettess Hawkins
   Overseer   Friends, Benjamin Fussall, Jacob Fussall
   Wit: Benjamin Fussall, Jacob Fussall, Thomas
               Davis, Richard Perry, Edward Spearmon

ISHAM, James - D. Nov. 2, 1753
  Wife: Jane Isham
  Dau: Margaret Isham
  Sons: James, Charles Isham
  Exec: Wife, Jane Isham, brother-in-law, Evan Ellis,
                Edward Harrison, Jr.
  Wit: William Houston, William McRee, John Dunn

JONES, John - D. March 15, 1759 - P. June 2, 1759
  County: Duplin
  Wife: Ann Jones
  Son: William Jones
  Daus: Patte, Catherine, Elizabeth, Mary Ann, Sarah
                Jones
  Exec: Wife: Ann Jones, John Jones
  Wit: William Whitfield, Ann Jones, Ann Williams
  Clerk: John Dickson

LOVE, Daniel - D. Nov. 6, 1752
  County: Duplin
  Wife: Cathrin Love
  Children: Sarah, James Love
  To pay debts: James McKeen, James Paxton
  Exec: William McKee, John Smith, Wife, Cathrin Love
  Wit: Geo. Bruce, Richard Cockburn, James Paxton

MERADITH, Joseph - D. June 15, 1750 - P. June 19, 1751
  County: Duplin
  Wife: Elizabeth Meradith
  Son: Nathan Meradith
  Daus: Ann, Hannah, Sarah Meradith
  Exec: Wife, Elizabeth Meradith, John Anderson, Jr.
  Wit: Richard James, John Williams, James Wright
  Clerk: John Dickson for John Sampson, Register

McREE, William - D. March 30, 1751
  County: Duplin
  Sons: John, James, William, Robert, Samuel McRee
  Daus: Sarah McRee Smith, Alace McRee Williams,
                Susanna McRee
  Grandson: William Williams
  Exec: Son, William McRee, Son-in-law, John Smith
  Wit: Sarah McAlexander, Wm. Kenan, Elizabeth
                Chambers

SNELL, Roger - D. Oct. 27, 1758 - P. June 2, 1759
    County: Duplin
    Wife: Ann Snell
    Sons: James, Roger Snell
    Daus: Partheny Snell, Mary King, Rebecca Herring,
                Ann King
    Son-in-law: Abram Herring, Michael King
    Exec: Michael King, George Bell
    wit: John King, John Canady, Jesse Bell
    Clerk: John Dickson

WILLIAMS, Anthony - D. July 3, 1751 - P. May 4, 1752
    County: Duplin
    Wife: Mary Williams
    Sons: Stephen, Benjamin Williams
    No identity: Edward Carter
    Brother: John Williams
    Daus: Mary, wife of Moses Powell, Penelope Will-
                iams, Pherabe Williams, Easter Williams
    Grandson: Cader Powell
    Cousin: Anthony Bevely
    Exec: Friends, Job Brooks, William Meares
    Wit: Samuel Jones, George Smith, John Williams
    Clerk: John Dickson, Deputy Register

WILLIAMS, Joyce - D. Nov. 22, 1749 - P. April 8, 1752
    County: New Hanover
    Brother: Evan Thomas
    Wit: John Thomas, Edward S. Williams, Morgan
                Humphrey
    Clerk: John Dickson, Deputy Register

                 ANN COCK'S Birthday
              Duplin County, North Carolina

    Ann Cock, daughter to Charles Cock and Francis Sena Cock,
his wife of Duplin County, was born the ninth day of February
in the year of our Lord one thousand seven hundred and forty
eight, 1748. Certified according to her said father and
mother. Return this thirtieth (30th) day of August, anno
domini, one thousand seven hundred and fifty-four, 1754.
    Duplin County - John Dickson, Register

JOSEPH and MARY WILLIAMS
Births, etc.

The following marriages, births, and burials is registered
in this Book, Register Book B, which is the names thereof:
Joseph Williams, Esquire, was joyned in the holly state of
marriage to Mary Hicks, the eighth day of August in the year
of our Lord, one thousand and seven hundred and forty-six
1746. (John Howard, Justice of the Peace - Onslow County.)

Hester Williams, daughter of Joseph Williams and Mary Hicks
was born the ninth 9th day of September, one thousand seven
hundred and forty seven, 1747. Declared by the parents was
born in Onslow County.
Mary Williams, daughter of Joseph Williams and Mary Hicks,
was born in Onslow County the 22nd day of February in the
year of our Lord one thousand seven hundred and forty eight,
1748. Declared by her parents.
Daniel Williams, son of Joseph Williams and Mary Hicks, was
born in Duplin County the fourth day of January in the year
of our Lord one thousand, seven hundred and fifty one, 1751.
Benjamin Williams, son of Joseph Williams and Mary Hicks,
was born in Duplin County on the thirtieth day of December,
one thousand seven hundred fifty two, 1752. Declared by his
parents.
(Unnamed) son of Joseph Williams and Mary Hicks was born
in Duplin County the nineteenth (19th) day of January in the
year of our Lord, one thousand seven hundred and fifty five,
1755. Declared by his parents.
(Register Book "B" is now Deed Record 2).

Unrecorded Wills

JOHN SAMPSON

I, John Sampson of Duplin County,Esquire, being of sound mind and memory, do make and ordain this my last will and testament in manner and form following, that is to say:

I commend my soul into the hands of Almighty God, the Creator and Preserver of all Mankind, and my body to the earth to be buried in a christian and decent manner near my dear deceased wife, trusting to the merits of my Blessed Redeemer, Jesus Christ, for a happy ressurection to eternal life; and I also desire and request that my executors hereafter named, do as soon as conveniently can be, procure one neat tombstone sufficient to cover the graves of me and my said dear deceased wife, and that one-half acre of ground around these graves be laid off and reserved as a burial place for my heirs and family, who at all times shall have free ingress and regress thereto, and the same shall not at any time or on any pretense whatever be alienated, sold or conveyed.

ITEM: I will and require that all my debts and funeral charges be paid as soon as possible,and for the more speedy discharge thereof, I desire that my slaves be employed in such labor as my executors shall judge most effectual for the purpose.

ITEM: I give and bequeath to.Mrs. Mary Blunt, wife of William Blunt, and daughter of Caleb Grainger, deceased, one young Negro wench. (Blunt - Blount).

ITEM: I give and bequeath all my wearing apparell to be divided amongst my household Negroes.

ITEM: I give and bequeath to my Negro woman, Moll, her

liberty and freedom immediately on my death as a reward of
her long and faithful services.

ITEM: I give and bequeath unto my Mulatto woman, Hannah,
daughter of the aforesaid Moll, her liberty and freedom immediately on my death, as a reward for her constant and dil-
igent attention to her deceased mistress in her illness, and
her great care and attendance on myself when sick, and her
faithfullness in all cases.

ITEM: I give and bequeath unto my grand-nephew, James
Sampson, son of my nephew James Sampson, the plantation
whereon I now live, called Sampson Hall, (preserving the
burying ground before mentioned for the use and purposes before specified) containing about one thousand acres be the
same more or less bounded by lands of Richard Clinton, Gabriel Holmes, James Sampson and vacant lands, and also the
slaves hereafter mentioned, namely: Chloe, Joe, Darcy, Molly,
Arthur, Peggy, Johnny, Ben, Tommy, (Hatira) Billy, Candice,
Ivey, Becky, Aaron, Old Toney, Polly, Roland, Charlie and
Harriot; and all the plantation tools which shall be deliv-
ered and put into the possession of him, the said James Sampson whenever he may attain the age of twenty one years and not
before. But in case he should die before he attain that age,
then I give and bequeath the same unto the next surviving
eldest son lawfully begotten of my said nephew James Sampson, and on default of any such, then I give and bequeath
the same unto any daughter or daughters the same James Sampson may have lawfully begotten. But in case my said nephew,
James Sampson, should die without any child lawfully begotten, then I give and bequeath the said plantation, slaves
and plantation tools unto Richard Clinton and his heirs forever, but it is my express will and meaning that my executors
do as soon as possible after my death, put into the possession of my aforementioned nephew, James Sampson, the
plantation, slaves and tools, that he may enjoy the profits
and revenues thereof during the minority of his child or
children, after deducting the charges for a liberal education which I desire May be given, and in case he should sur-
vive all his children, then he shall enjoy the same all his
life, and it is my express request that he keep the buryings
on the said plantation in good repair, and on the death of
him, the said James Sampson, without lawful issue, then
Richard Clinton or his heirs shall enter into the property
of the said plantation and slaves, and not before.

ITEM: I give and bequeath unto the children of Richard Clinton the residue of all the slaves I may die possessed of exclusive of those before devised or set free to be divided in manner following, that is to say, six young Negroes (one-half to be males, the other half females) to his daughter Ann, and the remainder of the slaves to be equally divided amongst the other children of the said Richard Clinton and his present wife Penelope, now has or may have, and in the case of the death of the said Ann, or any of the other children during their minority, the survivors shall succeed in equal porportions to their rights, and my will is that my executors shall as soon as possible after my death put into possession of the said Richard Clinton all the said slaves for the uses and purposes aforesaid, and that he shall apply the profits of the labour of the six young slaves given to his daughter Ann, towards her maintenance and education, and the labour of the other slaves during the minority of the children aforesaid, he may apply to his own proper use and behalf, giving them a proper education.

ITEM: I give and bequeath unto Richard Clinton, my grist mill, and the lands thereunto belonging.

ITEM: I give and bequeath unto Richard Clinton, his heirs or assigns forever, all the lots and lands I may die possessed of in this State and not before devised.

ITEM: I give and bequeath unto Richard Clinton all my 'smiths tools and everything thereunto belonging.

ITEM: I give and bequeath unto Richard Clinton my silver headed sword and watch.

ITEM: I give and bequeath my still worm and tubs, barrells and all other utensils thereunto belonging equally between my nephew James Sampson and Richard Clinton.

ITEM: I do require that my executors hereafter mentioned if they think it necessary, sell and dispose of all my household and kitchen furniture, riding carriages, horses, cattle, hogs and sheep to the most advantage for the more speedy payment of my debts. But in case they shall not think it necessary, then I give and bequeath the same unto my nephew James Sampson and Richard Clinton to be equally divided between.

ITEM: I give and bequeath unto John Hay, Esquire, five Guineas to purchase a mourning ring.

ITEM: I give and bequeath unto Richard Clinton all the rest of residue of my estate, real and personal, and I do request that my nephew James Sampson and Richard Clinton should live in peace and harmony.

LASTLY, I do nominate, constitute and appoint my friend, John Hay, James Sampson and Richard Clinton executors of this, my last will and testament, hereby revoking, disanulling and making void all former wills by me heretofore made.

IN TESTIMONY WHEREOF I have hereunto set my hand and seal this twenty-seventh day of October, One Thousand seven hundred and eighty-three.

JOHN SAMPSON.

SIGNED, Sealed, pronounced and declared by the testator as his last will and testament in presence of us,
James M... , Richard Brocas, Lewis Moore.

State of North Carolina
Sampson County

December Term, 1784.
Then was the within will proved in open court by the oath of Richard Brocas and Lewis Moore, subscribing witnesses, and ordered to be recorded.

C. Ivey, Clerk.

SAMPSON, Jane - D. August 22, 1817
Son: James Sampson
Daus: Lucy Sampson, Eliza Sampson, Sally Swann,
            Mary Ann Jocelyn

No identity: Michael Dunn
Exec: Son, James Sampson, Kinsmen, Frederick J.
             Hill, Wm. B. Meares
Wit: Wm. B. Meares, Wm. H. Williams

KING, William, Sr. - D. August 28, 1816
  Wife: Margaret King
  Sons: Devane King, Thomas D. King, William R. King
  Daus: Margaret Beck, Tabitha Kornegay, Helen King,
                 Ann King
  Granddau: Catherine M. Parrish
  Exec: Sons, Thomas D., Wm. R. King, Son-in-law,
                 John Beck
  Wit: Isham Wilson, Shadrack Wilson

ALDERMAN, David B. - D. November 18, 1884
  Wife: Sarah Alderman
  Sons: David E. Alderman, Ira D. Alderman, John E.
                 Alderman, Franklin P. Alderman, Luther J.
                 Alderman
  Exec: Sons, Franklin P. and Luther J. Alderman
  Wit: William S. Matthews, James M. Powell
  Codicil: Dated - November 17, 1886
  Wit: Abner T. Cooper

BELL, Mary - D. Feb. 6, 1804
  County: Robeson
  Sons: Joseph Atkinson, William Atkinson, John
                 Atkinson
  Dau: Lucy, wife of James Barnes
  Exec: James Barnes, Jos. Lee
  Wit: Robert Inman, Josiah Inman, William Lusso
    Copy from original will filed in office of Clerk on June
            13, 1840

BLACKMAN, Joab - D. April 9, 1819
  Wife: Susanna Blackman
  Granddaus: Betsey Ann Cox, Ann Cox, Susanna Cox
  Grandsons: Joseph John Cole, Blackman Cox
  Exec: Alexander Fleming, Alexander Benton
  Heirs: (Orphans) Fleming Vail, Elizabeth Vail,
                 (Friend) William Cox
  Wit: King Vann, Jos. Eldridge

BOYETTE, William H. - D. August 10, 1900
  Wife: Francis A. Boyette
  Sons: John K. Boyette, Steven J. Boyette
  Daus: Susah J. McCullen, Zilphia A. Britt, Mary E.
                 Sutton, Tempie Estella Boyette
  Grandson: William A. Britt

```
Exec:        C. T. Boyette
Wit:         F. R. Cooper, W. A. Britt
```

CARTER, John - Undated
```
Wife·        Sarah Carter
Sons:        A. J. Carter, H. J. Carter, Joseph D. Carter,
             King S. Carter, John M. Carter
Exec:        Son, Joseph D. Carter, friend, William L.
             Robinson
Wit:         J. P. Treadwell, J. C. Robinson
```

DAUGHTRY, Alley - D. Feb. 15, 1881
```
Friends:     James M------, son of T. D. Jones; Jeromey,
             son of T. D. Jones; Charley D., son of T. D.
             Jones; Elizabeth A. Jones
Exec:        Arthur Lee
Wit:         John V. Eason, E. Barefoot
```

HALL, Henry - D. Feb. 9, 1871 - P. October 4, 1872
```
Wife:        Nancy Hall
Exec:        Haywood Peterson
Wit:         Miles P. Owen, Haywood Peterson
```

LASSITER, Patience - D. June 23, 1898
```
Sons:        Charley, Joseph W., John T. Lassiter
Daus:        Euphemia Lassiter, Susanna Lassiter
Exec:        Son, Charley Lassiter
Wit:         W. J. Craddock, N. C. Giddens, P. W. McPhail
```

LASSITER, Robert - D. October 15, 1813
```
Bro:         George Lassiter
Sis:         Delaney (wife of Samuel Eldridge), Polly
             (wife of Elias Peters), Media (wife of Joel
             Lee), Linda (wife of William Wood)
Exec:        Brother, George Lassiter, Friend, Joab Black-
             man
Wit:         Peter Lee, ----- Adams
```

LEE, Joseph - D. July 4, 1819
```
Wife:        Eliza Lee
Son:         George R. Lee
Brother:     John Lee
Exec:        (Friend) Nathaniel Thornton, Sr.
Wit:         L. Eldridge, Eldridge Thornton
```

LOCKERMAN, Jacob - D. June 3, 1845
  Wife: Sarah Lockerman
  Sons: Odam, Aaron, Dennis Lockerman
  Dau: Betsey Ann Lockerman
  Wife's Sons: Raiford and Thomas Hair
  Exec: John Hair (Friend)
  Wit: James Calhoun, Thomas Hair

LOCKERMAN, James - Undated
  Wife: Mary Lockerman
  Son: James Lockerman, Jr.
  Grandchildren: Suviah, Catharine (children of Ruth
                 Lockerman
  Exec: John Simmons, Sr.
  Wit: John Simmons, Archibald Colbraith, Ruth
                 Lockerman

LUCAS, Lewis - D. November 15, 1806
  Wife: Elizabeth Lucas
  Sons: Charles Lucas, Raiford Lucas, Sherod Lucas,
                 Lewis Lucas
  Daus: Therebee Davis, Elizabeth Lucas, Priscilla
                 Lucas
  Exec: Wife, Elizabeth Lucas, Charles Lucas
  Wit: Daniel Coor, Charles Bullerd, John Lucas

MERRITT, Daniel - D. Feb. 22, 1841
  Wife: Mary Merritt
  Daus: Margaret Bowen, Ann Sellars, Jane Sellars,
                 Elizabeth Rackley
  Grandchildren: Mary Jane, Martha, Nancy Sellars, Catherine
                 Merrett, Molsey Swan and Elizabeth Emeline
                 Rackley
  Sons-in-law: Bradly Merret, Lewis Bowen
  Exec: Friend, David Murphy
  Wit: Haywood Merrett, Wiley Stallings

MERRITT, Mary - D. July 11, 1861
  Dau: Elizabeth, wife of James S. Rackley
  Grandchildren: Amariah Sellars, Jane Sellars (widow of
                 Everitt Sellars)
  Heirs: Margaret Bowen, Ann Sellars, Jenny Sellars,
                 Molsey Merritt
  Exec: Lewis L. Merritt, William L. Robinson
  Wit: Alexander H. Merritt, John L. Register

McGEE, Betsey Ann - D. August 22, 1864
   Son: Hardy W. McGee
   Niece: Arabella Butler
   Heirs: William Martin Butler, Reddin Egbert Butler
                 (sons of Arabella)
   Exec: Friend, Richard C. Holmes
   Wit: John Fowler, Anna M. Rayner

PECK, Louis F. - D. July 1, 1814
   Wife: Sally Peck
   Dau: Ann Eliza Peck
   Exec: Wife, Sally Peck, Colin Shaw
   Wit: John Shaw, Susan C. Wright

POPE, Mary M. - D. September 1, 1897
   Daus: Lucy E. Daughtry, Sally Ann Pope, Virginia F.
                 Gautier, Mollie Parsons
   Granddau: Millie Jane Lee
   Exec: G. W. Highsmith
   Wit: William A. Barbrey, W. B. Jones

POPE, Robert - D. September 13, 1813
   Wife: Elizabeth Pope
   Grandchildren: Rebecckah Powel, Sarah Tucker, Mary
                 Pearson, Selah Pearson, Patience Pearson,
                 Elizabeth Pearson, Jonathan Pearson, Isabel
                 Pearson, Jason Pearson
   Friend: John Carrell (son of Jesse Carrell)
   Exec: John Carrell
   Wit: Thomas Carrell, Hansel Ezzell

PRICE, Josiah - D. January 11, 1791
   Wife: Jemima Price
   Sons: Richard, Samuel, Joseph Price
   Daus: Dorothy, Susannah, Judith Price
   Exec: Wife, Jemima Price
   Wit: Fleet Cooper, Owen Holmes, Arthur Brown

PUGH, Crecy - D. March 21, 1884
   Son: Peter Holmes
   Dau: Olive Faison
   Exec: Son-in-law, Washington Faison
   Wit: Roman Bennett, Lewis Williams

REAVES, Catharine - D. March 10, 1843
  Sons: Jonas, John, William, Edmund, David Reaves
  Dau: Civil Craddock
  Grandson: Walter I. Craddock
  Exec: Daughter, Civil Craddock
  Wit: A. Monk, W. H. Craddock

REGISTER, Benjamin - D. April 5, 1811
  Sons: John, Silas (dec'd), Thomas, Benjamin,
             Joseph Register
  Dau: Mary Cook
  Exec: Son, John Register, Friend, John Bryan
  Wit: John Bryan, Burrel Register. John Register,
             Elias Sutton

RICHE, Lewis - D. Feb. 13, 1824
  Wife: Sabry Riche
  Dau: Marry Jane Riche
  Brother: Owen Riche, Lott Riche
  Exec: Owen Riche
  Wit: Hardy Spell, James Spell

ROBINSON, Alice - D. November 14, 1811
  Sons: Samuel, John, James, George Robinson
  Daus: Susannah, Elizabeth, Ann (dec'd) Robinson,
             Dorcas Robeson
  Granddaus: Margret Robeson, Alice Canon
  Heir: Larry Freeman
  Exec: William Robinson
  Wit: Richard McLemore, William Robinson

ROBINSON, Hannah Caroline - D. Feb. 15, 1896
  Husband: Daniel Robinson
  Father: Isaac Lamb
  Sons: Duncan T. Robinson, J. W. Scott Robinson
  Dau: Mary Graham Shaw
  Granddau: Carrie Shaw
  Sis: Thankful Miller (deceased)
  Wit: A. L. Hubbard, D. T. Robinson

ROYAL, Reason - D. August, 1849
  Wife: Catharine Royal
  Father: Young Royal (dec'd)
  Grandsons: John D. Carver, Alexander Carver, Josiah
             Carver

```
Sons:           Young, Josiah, John Royal
Dau:            Edith, wife of David Carver
Exec:           Wife, Catharine Royal, Relative, John Royal,
                Esquire
Wit:            Thomas J. Morrisey, Frank A. Roberts
```

SANDEFUN, Joseph - D. August 10, 1812 (SANDEFUR - FER)
```
Daus:           Dolly, wife of William Westbrook; Elisabeth,
                wife of John Livingston; Mary, wife of James
                Westbrook
Grandson:       James Kenard
Exec:           Friends, Josiah Blackman, Alexander Fleming
Wit:            Peter Lee, Robert Lassiter, Starling Lee
Preacher to conduct funeral - Benjamin Rose
```

SCOTT, Jonathan - D. February 25, 1781
```
County:         Duplin
Sis:            Mary Scott, Jenny Chesnutt, Jerusha Murphrey,
                Peggy Ades, Ashe Scott
Exec:           Mother (not named)
Wit:            David James, Jacob Fryer, Winaford Fryer
```

SESSIONS, Richard - D. April 7, 1816
```
Wife:           Esther Sessions
Sons:           Joseph, Richard, Jesse, Philip (dec'd),
                David, Boon, William, Uriah Sessions
Daus:           Bathshaba Herring, Mary Dodd, Winifred Ses-
                sions, Sarah Cromartie
Exec:           Sons, William, Uriah Sessions, Peter Cromartie
Wit:            James Williamson, Hiram Blackburn, Laban
                Tatom, John Wright, Jr.
```

SHAW, Catherine - D. September 15, 1877 - P. May 12, 1897
```
Granddau:       Martha Ann Stephens
Wit:            Anney Stephens, Daniel McKinnon
```

SHIP, Michael - D. April 26, 1816
```
Mother:         Ann Ship
Wit:            Rainey McIlwinn, Charity Millard
```

SIKES, Daniel M. - D. Sept. 11, 1893
```
Son:            George H. B. Sikes
Bro:            Murdock Sikes (dec'd)
Daus:           Laura L. Martin, Mattie D. Register
Exec:           Son, George H. B. Sikes
```

Wit: J. O. Herring, W. T. Devane

Land conveyed to D. M. Sikes by: Anna and Matthew Monce, William and Tom Devane, C. M. Sikes, Dorcas Melvin, Elva J. Sikes

SIMMONS, John, Sr. - D. January 22, 1807
Sons: Sherwood Simmons, Jeremiah Simmons, John Simmons
Son-in-law: Joel Horn
Exec: Sons, Jeremiah, John Simmons
Wit: Nicholas Parker, Thomas Frazier, Samuel Fowler

SMITH, William - D. October 29, 1895
Wife: Martha Smith (dec'd)
Son: James A. Smith
Dau: Rebecca E., wife of Henry Carter
Grandsons: Oliver Carter, William Henry Carter, Charlie Carter
Granddau: Minnie A., wife of Charlie Holland
Exec: Henry Carter
Wit: J. D. Johnson, J. W. Green

SPEARMAN, Edward - D. Nov. 1, 1818
Wife: Ann Spearman
Children mentioned but not named.
Exec: Enoch Herring, William Robinson
Wit: Gabriel Herring, Thomas Vann, William Stevens

STEVENS, Alice - D. October 20, 1802
Mother: Mildred Stevens
Sister: Suckey Herring
Brother: Charles Stevens
Exec: Brother, Charles Stevens, Mother, Mildred Stevens
Wit: D. Williamson, Henry Dewitt

STEVENS, Barnabas - D. Sept. 16, 1800
Wife: Lydda Stevens
Sons: William Stevens, Oates Stevens
Daus: Susanna, Arteasha, Elizabeth, Nancy Laruhamah, Lydda
Exec: Wife, Lydda Stevens, Friends, John Oates, Stephen King

Wit: James McLendon, Barnabas Standley

STEVENS, John - Undated - Proven in court Dec., 1784
  County: Duplin
  Sons: John, Isaac, Hardy, Richard Stevens
  Daus: Elizabeth Rogers, Mary Rogers, Maryan Carr
  Exec: John Stevens, Hardy Stevens, Joshua Sikes
  Wit: Fleet Cooper, Cager Stevens, John Stevens

STEWART, Dugald - D. July 22, 1805
  Sons: John, Daniel, Alexander, Allan Stewart
  Dau: Sarah Stewart
  Exec: Son, John Stewart
  Wit: Daniel McIntyre, James Stewart

SUTTON, Ann M. - D. December 30, 1885
  Father: Abel Sutton (dec'd)
  Sis: Argane C., Louisa Sutton
  Nephews: Isham C., Samuel A. Sutton
  Exec: John E. Chesnutt
  Wit: Thomas L. Mathews, Marshal B. Chesnutt

SUTTON, Argane C. - D. December 30, 1885
  Father: Abel Sutton
  Sis: Ann M., Louisa Sutton
  Nephews: Isham C., Samuel A. Sutton
  Exec: John E. Chesnutt
  Wit: Thomas L. Mathews, Marshal B. Chesnutt

SUTTON, Edmund - D. May 22, 1863
  Wife: Nancy Sutton
  Son: Oswin Sutton
  Exec: Son, Oswin Sutton
  Wit: L. C. King, Daniel C. King

SUTTON, Louisa - D. December 30, 1885
  Father: Abel Sutton
  Sis: Ann M., Argane C. Sutton

```
Nephews:        Isham C., Samuel A. Sutton
Exec:           Friend, John E. Chesnutt
Wit:            Thomas L. Mathews, Marshal B. Chesnutt
```

SYKES, Needam - D. December 13, 1806
```
  Wife:         Sarah Sykes
  Sons:         William, Duncan Sykes
  Exec:         Wife, Sarah Sykes, William Robinson
  Wit:          William Robinson, Naaman Carty
```

TARRINGTON (TURLINGTON), Southey - D. Sept. 24, 1810
```
  Children:     Israel, Elisha, James (dec'd), Polly
                Turlington
  Exec:         Son, Israel Turlington, Michael Sampson
  Wit:          John Chesnutt, Joshua Bass
```

TATOM, Love A. - D. April 8, 1865
```
  Wife:         Rebear Tatom
  Heir:         George M. Tatom
  Exec:         George M. Tatom
  Wit:          Hardy Spell, James Underwood
```

TATOM, William - D. Sept. 17, 1815
```
  Exec:         Daniel L. Kenan, William Waddill
  Wit:          J. Frederick, Peter Frederick, William K.
                Frederick
```

TEW, Alexander - D. February 13, 1868
```
  Sons:         Hawley, Robert, Osburn Tew
  Daus:         Mary, Morning Tew
  Exec:         Son, Osburn Tew
  Wit:          P. A. Tew, Thomas Williams
```

THOMAS, Luke - D. April 12, 1801
```
  Wife:         Susanna Thomas
  Sons:         William Thomas, Darden Thomas
  Heir:         Hardy Snell
  Exec:         Wife, Susanna Thomas, William Darden,
                Joseph Darden
  Wit:          Stephen King, Ann Darden, Tempey Darden
```

TOOLE, Edward - D. March 5, 1785
```
  Wife:         Judith Toole
  Son:          Geraldus Toole
  Daus:         Elisabethan, Matilda, Unity Toole
```

```
Exec:        Gabriel Holmes, Jonathan Tayloe
Wit:         Arthur Brown, Sherod Brown, John Stevens,
             Norman McQuinn
```

TORRANS, Elizabeth, Sr. - D. Nov. 15, 1826
```
  Sons:        Kenan, Alexander, Samuel Torrans
  Daus:        Martha Torrans, Ann Shine, Margaret Stanford,
               Elizabeth Morgan, Elenor Bryan (wife of John
               Bryan)
  Grandson:    Richard Nixon Torrans
  Exec:        Col. Thomas Kenan, Son-in-law, John Bryan
  Wit:         Kedar Bryan, Dickson Sloan
```

TURBEVILL
  (Turbyville, properly D'Urbeville)
TURBEVILL, Joseph - D. Sept. 16, 1794
```
  Wife:        Mary Turbevill
  Sons:        Joseph, Sampson Turbevill
  Daus:        Rhoda Turbevill, Milley Turbevill
  Sons-in-law: Samuel Trigs, William Blunt
  Heirs:       Isom Turbevill
  Exec:        Wife, Mary Turbevill, Sons, Sampson, Joseph
               Turbevill
  Wit:         Stephen King, Stephen Slocumb
```

TURBEVILL, Sampson - D. Jan. 18, 1797
```
  Wife:        Tempie
  Son:         Alfred
  Exec:        Wife, Tempie Turbevill, Friend, Stephen King
  Wit:         R. McKinne, Luke Moore, Thomas Musgrave, J.
               Morrisey, Joseph Turbevill
```

TURNAGE, William - D. Sept. 8, 1848
```
  Wife:        Sarah Turnage
  Sons:        Zackariah, Charles, James Turnage
  Dau:         Bede, wife of Willis Williamson
  Exec:        J. L. Clifton
  Wit:         J. L. Clifton, William T. Beaman
```

TURNER, John - D. September 25, 1883
```
  Wife:        Ruth Turner
  Heir:        Zilphah Cooper
  Exec:        Jonathan Carr, John Stephens
  Wit:         Jacob Cooper, Richard Clinton, John Marshburn
```

VANN, Kedar - D. May 6, 1893
  Wife: Louisa Vann
  Son: Preston S. Vann
  Daus: Seven unnamed
  Exec: Son, Preston S. Vann, Son-in-law, D. J.
               Elkins
  Wit: Josiah Robinson, Billie Robinson

WARWICK, Benjamin - D. Oct. 25, 1797
  Wife: Mary Warwick
  Sons: Sharod, Reubin, Elijah, Harrod, John Warwick
  Grandson: Henry Warwick
  Daus: -hevia Cammerain, Dicy Wadkins, Penellepee
               Warwick, Thereby Warwick
  Exec: Wife, Mary Warwick, Sharod Warwick, son
  Wit: William Caraway, James Sessions, John House

WEEKS, Mary - D. August 10, 1891
  Husband: A. M. Weeks (dec'd)
  Sons: Thomas Weeks, John A. Weeks
  Dau: Sarah F. Bell
  Grandson: Mikel H. Weeks
  Granddau: Annie F. Bell
  Exec: Son-in-law, Thomas C. Bell
  Wit: A. H. King, T. C. Bell

WELLS, Mary - D. Jan. 10, 1868
  County:.   New Hanover
  Sons: David James Wells, Daniel White Wells
  Daus: Mary C., Susan A., Martha P., Ellen F.,
               Rebecca A. Wells
  Wit: Jacob Wells, Samuel Newton

WEST, John - D. September 26, 1894
  Wife: Margaret L. West
  Nephews: William Julius, Samuel Thomas West
  Exec: Claudius E. Daniel
  Wit: E. Mainer (or Manuel), N. A. Daniel

WESTBROOK, James - D. April 18, 1816
  Wife: Mary Westbrook
  Sons: William, Charles, Moses, James, Uriah,
               Joseph (dec'd)
  Daus: Mary Westbrook, Judith Lee, Persis Westbrook
  Dau.-in-law: Polly Westbrook
  Grandsons: John James, William Henry, Uriah Westbrook
  Granddaus: Eliza, Charity, Sallyann Westbrook
  Exec: Joab Blackman, Sons, Moses, Charles, Uriah
  Wit: George Lassiter, Thinchen Adams

WESTBROOK, James - D. Dec. 12, 1817
  Wife: Isabell Westbrook
  Bro: Moses, Uriah, Charles, Joseph (dec'd)
  Mother: Mary Westbrook
  Sis: Judith Lee, Persis Westbrook
  Nephew: Uriah Westbrook
  Exec: Bro., Uriah Westbrook
  Wit: George Lassiter, Peter Lee

WESTBROOK, William - D. March 20, 1816
  Wife: Elizabeth Westbrook
  Son: Uriah Westbrook
  Exec: Bros., Uriah, James Westbrook
  Wit: George Lassiter, Thinchen Adams

WESTBROOK, William - D. March 23, 1809
  Wife: Mary Westbrook
  Sons: William, Furney Westbrook
  Grandson: William
  Exec: Sons, William, Furney Westbrook
  Wit: Willerba Creel, Jonathan Daniel
  Lends slave to Isaac Lankston

WHITE, Luke - D. June 15, 1804
  Wife: Martha White
  Sons: George White, John White, William White,
               James White, Matthew White
  Daus: Judy Fennell, Fameriah Jackson, Martha White
  Exec: Wife, Martha, Friend, William Robinson
  Wit: W. Robinson, Thomas Robinson

WHITLEY, Elijah, Sr. - D. May 17, 1825
  Sons: Elijah Whitley, Josiah Whitley
  Daus: Susanna Kenneday, Julianna King

```
Exec:           Son, Josiah Whitley
Wit:            Polly Gotierre, Samuel J. Pope
```

WIGGS, Ralph - D. May 26, 1801
  Wife and children not named
```
Wit:            A. Holmes, Feribee Holmes
```

WILLIAMS, Alexander - D. July 25, 1887
```
  Wife:           Francis L. Williams
  Exec:           Wife, Francis L. Williams
  Wit:            J. S. Bizzell, Henry E. Faison
```

WILLIAMS, Jacob - D. Oct. 19, 1757
```
  Wife:           Mary Williams
  Sons:           Jesse, Elias, (One illegible name)
  Daus:           Rachel, Leusay, Pashent, Elizabeth Williams
  Exec:           Wife, Mary Williams, Joseph Williams
  Wit:            William Odom, Joel Williams, Elisabeth Wil-
                  liams
```

WILLIAMS, Joseph - D. October 16, 1808
```
  Wife:           Winnifred Williams
  Son:            Nasa Williams
  Dau:            Rebecca Andres
  Exec:           Friend, Hardy Holmes, Son, Nasa Williams
  Wit:            H. Holmes, Dugald Duncan, Feriby Holmes
```

WILLIAMS, William - D. Jan. 11, 1826
```
  Sons:           Arther, Nathan, William, Reding Williams
  Dau:            Mary Byrd (dec'd)
  Exec:           Sons, Arther, Nathan, William Williams
  Wit:            Robert Bell, Sr., David Bell
```

WILLIAMS, William - D. July 3, 1827
```
  Wife:           Betsey Williams
  Daus:           A. Nancy Williams, Polly Holder, Patsey Wil-
                  liams
  Exec:           Charles Butler
  Wit:            Milly Doughfield, Robert Williamson
```

WILLIAMSON, Nathaniel - D. June 14, 1807
```
  Daus:           Anne, Elizabeth Williamson
  Exec:           Nathan Williamson, Nicholas Parker
  Wit:            Daniel Williams, James Williamson, Timothy
                  Williamson
```

WILLIAMSON, James - D. Sept. 24, 1822
  Wife: Mary Williamson
  Sons: Willie, James Munrow Williamson
  Dau: Jane Morgan
  Exec: Sampson Bennett, Alexander Killet
  Wit: Henry C. Bennett, Jonathan Cooper

WILLIAMSON, William - D. Aug. 20, 1797
  Wife: Esther Williamson
  Sons: Timothy, Nathaniel, James, William, Loroba-
             bel, Stephen, Anthony, Samuel, Nathan
  Daus: Mary, Winney, Elsey Williamson
  Exec: Sons, Nathaniel, James Williamson
  Wit: Daniel Williams, William Stevens, Joshua
             Tatum

WILLIFORD, Sion - D. March 14, 1803
  Wife: Sally Williford
  Children not named - estate divided between wife and
             children.
  Exec: Wife, Sally Williford, Micajah Williford
  Wit: Aaron Godwin, Nathan Godwin, John McClenney

WILSON, John Dickson - D. Dec. 29, 1882
  Sis: Elizabeth C. Wilson
  Grandfather: J. D. Wilson
  Exec: Sister, Elizabeth C. Wilson
  Wit: A. Robinson, George W. Robinson

WOOD, William - D. Sept. 2, 1813
  Wife: Elisabeth (disobedient, left one dollar)
  Sons: Jesse, Moore, William, Jonathan Wood
  Daus: Susanna (wife of Isaiah Warren), Happy Brown,
             Nancy (wife of William Smith), Kinney Best
             (wife of Thomas Best), Penny (wife of John
             Ingram), Kiddey (wife of Abram Ganey), Phere-
             by (wife of Abner Ingram)
  Exec: Sons, William, John Wood, Friend, Joab Black-
             man
  Wit: William Westbrook, Sr., Uriah Westbrook

WRENCH, John & Sophia (wife) - D. Dec. 10, 1900
             Hawley's Store
  Daus: Arabella Wrench, Novele Wrench
  Wit: M. Hall, E. J. Hollingsworth

SAMPSON, Col. James - D. --- 6, 1787
    Wife: Mary Sampson
    Son: John Lyon Sampson
    Exec: Wife, Mary Sampson
    Wit: General James Kenan, George Morisey,
                    R. Clinton

Olds' N. C. Wills

(Fred A. Olds, 1760-1800)

These wills copied as they appeared in book.
They are not on record.

1786 BASS, CHARLES, Elizabeth, William, Burell.

1792 BULLARD, JEREMIAH. G. S., James, Jason, Simmons, John.

1791 COOPER, JOHN, Scott, Jonathan, Raphael, Hester, Betsey,
Zylphia, Patience, Elizabeth.

1791 GAINEY, EDMUND, Edney, Beatty, Martha, Elias, Abram,
Noel, William, Reddick; Willis West; Lee Westbrook.

1770 HERRING, ABRAHAM, Abraham, Martha (wife).

1800 HILL, FRANCIS, Hill, B. H.; Martha, John Thornton;
William, Aley Westbrook; Hester, Simon Hobbs.

1797 McQUINN, NORMAN, Catherine, (wife).

1798 PORTIVENT, SAMUEL, Mary (wife), John, Isaac, James,
Susanna Larkins; Ann Bloodworth.

1780 SELLARS, SAMUEL, Hannah (wife), Abraham, Zilpha; Unity,
Rhoda Cooke; Elizabeth Pridgen; Alice, Sarah, Pearl
Register.

1795 TART, JOHN, Patty (wife), Mason, Charlotte, Sarah,
Janet, John, Turner, Mildred.

1795 WILLIAMSON, JACOB, Mary, Theophilus, Elias, Rachel,
Lucy, Patience, Elizabeth.

1793 YOUNGER, DAVID LEE, Jessie Lee, Joel Lee, Aaron Lee,
Nancy, Farby, (Pheraba).

Index

Names of testators are capitalized.

ADAMS, MARY, 1
  Colon, 1
  Edwin, 1
  Lewis, 1
  Rebekah, 1
  Sentha, 1
  Thinchen, 1, 115
Ades, Peggy, 109
ALDERMAN, AMARIAH BIGGS, 14
ALDERMAN, DANIEL W., 14
ALDERMAN, DAVID B., 104
  Amariah Enoch, 14
  Barella, 19
  Catherine E., 14
  Catie F., 14
  David E., 47, 104
  Ella Jane, 14
  Enoch W., 75
  Estella, 47
  F. P., 79
  Frank P., 14
  Franklin P., 47, 104
  Haywood, 19
  Henry Sampson, 19
  Ira D., 47, 104
  Jacob Oliver, 14
  James Edwin, 14
  John Thomas, 14
  Julian, 14
  Lena May, 14
  Leroy Walton, 14
  Lillean Isabella, 14
  Livingston W., 14
  Luther J., 47,104
  Mary P., 28
  Owen, 19, 44

Alderman, Palmer, 14
  Pennie Ann, 14
  Pennie Eliza, 14
  Sarah C., 47
  John E., 104
  Sarah, 104
Allen, Ethan, 62
  F. F., 30
Alston, John R., 71
AMMONS, THOMAS, 1
  Elizabeth, 1
  Joshua, 1
  Nowell, 1
  Vaughn, 1
ANDERS, NANCY C., 14
  James, 58
  James K., 14
  Nancy, 81
  Susan, 87
  Sophia A., 22
  W. A., 14, 22, 81
  W. K., 43
Anderson, Rev. N. L., 36
  Nannie H., 36
  John, Jr., 97
Andres, Rebecca, 116
ANDREWS, PETER, 14
  Elizabeth, 14
  James, 90
  Martin, 93
Armstrong, Fleet H., 78
  James, 83
  Jerusha, 20
Ashe, (Col.) Samuel, 46
ASHFORD, ELIZABETH A., 14
ASHFORD, THOMAS, 15, 18

Ashford, Isabella, 15
 Kate Pender, 15
 John, 14, 15
 Thomas B., 15, 77
 William, 18
Ashly, David, 92
Aswell, James, 10
Atkins, G. W., 41
 J. W., 44
Atkinson, John, 104
 Joseph, 104
 William, 104
AUGHTRY, DRURY, 1
 Archibald, 1
 Charity, 1
 Charlotte, 1
 Raiford, 1
 Sarah, 1
AUTREY, MARY, 15
 George W., 15, 66
AUTRY, EDNEY, 15
AUTRY, GEORGE, 15
 Archibald, 15
 Blackman, 15
 C. G., 77, 80
 Charity, 24, 27
 Frances, 15
 Isham, 15
 James, 42
 John, 15
 Lucy A., 24, 27
 Mary, 13
 Mary F., 80
 W., 15
 William H., 42, 92
Averitt, Martha J., 24

Baggat, John, 49
 Josiah, 49
 Silas, 49
Baggett, Autry, 78
 Bronson, 94
Bain, Daniel, 81
 George, 4
Bailey, Louisa, 39
BALKCUM, HESTER, 15
BALKCUM, NANCY, 15
 Eliza, 15

 Harmon, 15
 James Lucien, 15
 John, 15, 51
 Lemuel B., 15
 Margaret, 15
 Mariah, 15
 Mary, 15
Ballard, Nancy, 45
BARBARY, ALLEN, 8, 16
 A. B., 86
 Allen B., 16
 Elizabeth, 86
 Gabriel, 16
 Nanny, 16
 Ollen, 16
 Peter, 16
 William, 16
Barbray, W. A., 30
BARBREY, A. B., 16, 62
 A. G., 16
 Edgar, 16
 Jesse, 16
 L., 16
 Mamie, 16
 Mary A., 30
 Thaddeus, 16
 William, 16
 William A., 107
BARDEN, EPHRAIM, 16
BARDEN, JOHN, 16
BARDEN, WOODWARD, 16
 Allen S., 16
 Elizabeth C., 16
 Elizabeth, 16
 Everitt G., 16
 Fanny Meriah, 16
 Frances, 16
 Ida C., 16
 James J., 16
 Jane, 16
 J. E., 43
 Jesse, 16
 Jesse E., 16
 Killbee, 16
 Lena A., 69
 Levi, 18
 Margaret E., 16
 Martha P., 16

Mary J., 16
Nancy, 16, 29
Nancy Jane, 87
Patience, 16
Polly, 16
Sally A., 16
Sherwood, 16
W. E., 23
Zilpha Ann, 16
Zilphy, 16
BAREFOOT, ISABEL, 1
John Robert, 49
Kinon, 49
N. B., 94
Nancy Green, 49
Nathan, 56
Wiley B., 11
E., 105
BARFIELD, GEORGE, 17
BARFIELD, GRANGER G., 17
BARFIELD, RICHARD, 96
Blake, 17
Boswell, 17
John F., 17
Sarah, 17
Virginia, 17
Henry, 96
Isaac, 96
James, 96
Jesse, 96
Mary, 96
Solomon, 96
Tebeth, 96
BARKS, JOSEPH, 1
Henderson, 1
Littleton, 1
Tamer, 1
BARKSDALE, SHEROD, 17
Hattie, 17
Barnes, John, 12
Lucy, 104
James, 104
Barringer, Wm., 50
Barton, Watson, 38
BASS, ANDREW, 1, 2
BASS, FELIX, 2, 17
BASS, JOHN, 17
BASS, JOSHUA, 17

BASS, RHODA, 18
BASS, WILLIAM, (2 wills), 1,
2, 18
BASS, CHARLES, 119
Amma, 177
Ann, 1
Betty, 8
Bright, 50
Burrell, 1, 119
Caroline, 54, 55
Cela, 2
Drucilla, 2
Edney, 68
Elizabeth, 1, 119
Everitt, 17
Everett S., 24
Everett T., 37
Fanny, 45
Henderson, 17
Hillory, 17
John I., 17
Kiddy, 17
Lewis, 1
Nancy Jane, 17
Priscilla, 17
Rebecca, 17
Rebecca E., 48
Robert, 17
Roxy, 17
Shepard, 68
Sophia, 2
Sophiah, 17
Traven, 17
Uriah, 17
Wm. Everett, 17
Willis M., 2
Joshua, 112
William, 119
BEAMAN, J. R., 18, 19, 26,
28, 33, 37, 41, 44, 60,
67, 72, 87
Bedreaden Carraway, 26
Charlotte, 18
J. A., 89
Lovic Worth, 18
Mariah Ruth, 18
Mary, 181
R. H., 89

Rhoda A., 16
Susan J., 18
W. K., 28
Wm. K., 18
William T., 113
Beard, C. E., 78
Beck, Jas. P., 65
John, 104
Margaret, 104
BELL, MICHAEL, 18
BELL, ROBERT, 18
BELL, WILLIAM W., 18
BELL, MARY, 104
Augusta J., 33
C. C., 44
Cathran, 21
Charley, 18
E., 18
James, 18, 55
Jefferson, 18
John, 18, 91
Katharine, 18
Luther, 18
Luther S., 81
Mary, 8
Micajah, Sr., 18
Peggy, 94
R. J., 62
R. R., 21, 54, 79, 80
Sally, 18, 19
Sally Eliza, 68
Sarah Jane, 19
Shug, 19
Susey, 94
William James, 18, 19
Annie F., 114
David, 116
Robert, Sr., 116
Sarah F., 114
Thomas C., 114
George, 98
Jesse, 98
BENNETT, FLEET S., 19
BENNETT, JAMES, 19, 21
BENNETT, SAMPSON, 19, 27
BENNETT, HARDY, 19, 33
Fleet, 19
George W., 19

Hardy K., 19
Henry, 19
Nancy, 19
Penny, 19
Robert Henry, 19
S. E., 19
T. G., 83
Thomas K., 19
Henry C., 117
Roman, 107
Sampson, 117
BENTON, ALEXANDER, 8, 19,
24, 34, 38, 45, 84, 104
Alex N., 1
Alexander, Jr., 19, 38
J. H., 62
John, 19, 37
Polly, 19
Virginia A., 65
Best, Clarisa, 82
Sarah, 82
T. H., 70
Kinney, 117
Thomas, 117
Bevely, Anthony, 98
BEVERET, BENJAMIN, 96
Bird, Dicey L., 71
BIZZELL, JAMES A., 19, 35,
41, 53
BIZZELL, REPSEY, 20
Asher, 34
Celestial P., 19
David A., 32, 57
Dorcas, 26
E. A., 94
Henry, 19
Henry A., 34, 44, 57
James S., 19
L., 57
Patsey, 55
Polly, 20, 56, 57
Sarah Elizabeth, 27
J. S., 116
Black, Archibald R., 64
Elizabeth Jane, 63, 64
BLACKBURN, BURRELL, 20
BLACKBURN, HIRAM, 3, 7, 20
BLACKBURN, WILLIAM, 20

Allen M., 20, 42, 51
Elizabeth, 89, 114
Nancy, 20
Sion, 20
Hiram, 109
BLACKMAN, ABIGAIL, 20
BLACKMAN, SUSANNAH, 20
BLACKMAN, WILLIAM, 21
BLACKMAN, JOAB, 104, 105,
    115, 117
Annie, 19
Cader, 21, 48, 57
Calvin, 20
Elizabeth, 57
Joseph, 57
Josiah, 5
Powel, 48, 56, 57
William G., 20, 21
Josiah, 109
Susanna, 104
BLACKMON, WILLIAM, 2
Blanchard, J. M., 33
Minnie D., 16
BLAND, ISAAC N., 21
Adeline, 89
Esther, 31
James F., 21
John G., 21
L. F., 43
Mary E., 21
Mary J., 70
Milton, 21
Rebecca Susan, 44
Timothy, 89
William, 21
Blanks, Edith, 38
James, 24, 38
William, 38
Bloodworth, Fanny, 38
BLOUNT, JOHN, 21
BLOUNT, JOHN W., 21
BLOUNT, M. C., 21, 35, 79
BLOUNT, PENELOPE, 21
Catharine Ann, 18
Louisa, 21
Malcom Colan, 21
Margaret, 21
Mary Jane, 18

Sherman, 18
W. C., 15
Worthy, 21
Blunt, (Mrs.) Mary, 100
William, 100, 113
Boney, Elizabeth, 87
Boon, Dorcas, 28
Eliza, 29
Margaret, 87
Boone, Mary J., 59
BORDEAUX, WILLIAM W., 21
A. D., 21
Dicey A., 21
Ira F., 21
Elizabeth, 50
J. C., 21
L. H., 21
Luther H., 21
M. E., 21
Rebecca P., 56
W. F., 21
Bowden, Anna Jane, 41
B. C., 21
Daniel, 26
John C., 26
Lewis, 11
Mary T., 79
Bowen, Lewis, 106
Margaret, 106
BOYETT, JOHN, 18, 22
BOYETT, MARY J., 22
C. F., 22
C. T., 22
Frank, 58
John E., 22
Nathan, 6
Susan, 22
BOYETTE, WILLIAM H., 104
C. T., 105
Francis A., 104
John K., 104
Steven J., 104
Tempie Estella, 104
Boyt, Nathan, 5
BOYKIN, BYUS, 2
BOYKIN, JOSEPH, 2
BOYKIN, SARAH, 2, 22
BOYKIN, WILLIAM, 2

Ann E., 94, 95
Barberry, 2
Cherry, 2
Cynthia Ann, 44
Edith, 2
Edy, 2
Elizabeth C., 44
J. L., 19
Jeany, 2
John, 2, 92
John C., 22
Nancy, 2
Nicey, 2
Norma, 2
Rhoda, 2
Robinson, 19
Solomon, 2
Thomas, 2, 93
Thomas W., 22
Tobias, 2
Wm. H., 22, 26
Bracher, Moses, 69
Sion, 69
BRADSHAW, JESSE, 22
BRADSHAW, JOHN, 22
BRADSHAW, THOMAS, 22, 24
Alfred, 22
Betsy, 22
Charley, 22
Dicy, 22
Dorcas, 71
Edmund, 22
Guilford, 22
Henry, 22, 24
Jessy, 22
Jno. Eliot, 22
P----- E., 22
Sion, 22
Sophia, 5
Thomas, Jr., 22
BRANCH, JESSE, 22
Alpha, 86
Elizabeth, 22
Jonas, 22
Kenan, 22
Nancy, 22
Rhoda, 22
William, 22

Zilpha, 31
BREWER, HENRY, 23
Catharine C., 23
Edward, 23
Harry, 77
Herring, 23
Mary, 23
Nancy, 23
Sally, 23
Wiley, 88
Brewington, Nancy, 85
Bridges, Phanney, 3
Brinkley, G. W., 32
BRITT, JAMES, 23, 30
BRITT, SARAH A., 23
BRITT, SARAH A., 23
Catharine, 22
C. E., 82
Edwin T., 82
Joel, 3, 18
Tempy, 23
Thomas, 23
William A., 104, 105
Zilphia A., 104
Broadhurst, Hettan, 41
Brocas, Richard, 103
BROCK, LOUISA, 23
Daniel L., 66
Margaret J., 66
William L., 23
Bronson, G. S., 42
Brooks, Job, 98
Brothers, Sarah W., 62
BROWN, ARTHUR, 23, 95, 107, 113
A. L., 6
Ann, 46
Arthur, Sr., 23, 95
Caleb, 23
Edward, 23
Fanny, 65
James D., 46, 78
James I., 65
John, 6, 23, 65, 82
John W., 19
Lucy, 23
Lusia, 24
Margaret Ann, 36

Mary Lou, 63
Mary P., 61
M----, 65
Peggy, 23
Penny, 95
Polly, 65
Robert, 23
Sabra, 76
Thomas, 74
Happy, 117
Sherod, 113
Bruce, George, 97
BRYAN, JOHN, 11, 13, 23, 27,
  50, 61, 69, 70, 85, 108,
  113
BRYAN, SUSANA, 24
  Elcy Ann, 57
  Eleanor, 23, 85
  Elenor, 113
  Eliza Jane, 23
  Harry, 30
  James, 31
  Jemima, 23
  John A., 23, 85
  John, Sr., 1
  John D., 24
  Josiah H., 24, 30
  Kedar, 13, 23, 85, 113
  Needham, 85
  Sally, 1
  Sarah A., 24
  Susan Mary, 23, 85
  Thomas K., 23
  Wm. H., 24, 64
Bryant, Georgianna, 82
  Granger, 82
  John, 82
  Lela, 82
  Nancy, 82
  Sarah, 25
BUCHANAN, SAMUEL, 32
  Rachel, 2
Bulla, Thomas I., 64
BULLARD, JAMES, 24
BULLARD, WILLIAM, 24, 42
BULLARD, JEREMIAH, 119
  Amos, 24
  Carrie E., 24

David L., 24
Elizabeth Ann, 24
Giles M., 24
Henry, 24
Henry G., 24
James L., 24
John, 24
Mary L., 24
N. Matilda, 24
Sabery, 24
Thomas F., 24
G. S., 119
James, 119
Jason, 119
John, 119
Simmons, 119
Bullerd, Charles, 106
BUNCE, CHARITY, 24
  Anna Eliza, 24
BUNTING, DAVID, 24
  Mildred H., 61
  Owen, 24
  Richard C., 24
  Samuel, 24
  Samuel A., 17
  Thomas (Dr.), 15, 24, 25,
    26, 46, 53, 61, 86
Burnett, Adaline, 49
Burks, John, 86
Burten, Percilla, 36
Burton, R. C., 50
BUTLAR, ROBERT, 24
  Betsy, 24
  Cherrywine, 24
  Delilah, 24
  Gabriel, 24
  John, 24
  Patience, 24
  Sally, 24
  Travis, 24
BUTLER, CHARLES, SR., 2
BUTLER, GABRIEL, 25
BUTLER, HARTWELL, 25
BUTLER, MARY, 25, 29
BUTLER, ROBERT, 2, 24, 25,
  76
BUTLER, STEPHEN, 25
BUTLER, TRAVIS, 25, 76

BUTLER, WILEY, 26
  Adam, 25
  Ann Eliza, 25
Butler, Annamariah, 86
  Betsey, 25
  Brazel, 25
  Elizabeth, 2, 92
  Elizabeth A., 25
  Emma Jane, 25
  Ezekiel, 25
  Haywood, 86
  Jacob, 25
  Jane, 25
  Janetty, 83
  Joanah, 32
  John, 25
  John R., 37
  Lucinda, 25
  Margaret, 25
  Marion, 61
  Mary Jane, 42
  Miles C., 25
  Nancy, 25, 76
  Owen, 86
  Peggy, 25
  Poley, 25
  Raiford, 25, 92
  Rebecca, 25, 91
  Rebecca A., 86
  Rebecca Eliza, 25
  Reddin, 25
  Redman, 25
  Romelia, 26
  S. M., 37
  Sabra Jane, 25
  Sallie, 76
  Sally, 25
  Sally Jane, 87
  Sarah, 25
  Sophia, 25
  Susan, 25
  William, 24, 25
  Zilpha, 75
  Arabella, 107
  Charles, 116
  Reddin Egbert, 107
  William Martin, 107
BYRD, ROBERT, 26

Byrd, Hennant, 21
  Nancy, 26, 82
  Penny, 82
  Sarah, 83
  Thomas, 18, 44, 91
  Mary, 116

Cain, M. T., 88
CAISON, CANNON, 26
CAISON, JACOB, 26
  Fannie M., 26
  Lewis, 26
  Lucinda, 26
  Matilda, 26
  Polly, 26
  William, 26
Calhoun, James, 12, 106
Calter, Henry, 96
Cammerain, -hevia, 114
Cammeron, Sarah, 6
Campbell, John H., 95
  L. S., 50
  Neal, 66
Canady, John, 98
CANNADY, PATRICK, 53
  George, 53
  Hardy, 53
  James, 53
  John, 53
  Kisiah, 53
  Patrick, 53
  Samuel, 53
  Susannah, 53
  Nancy, 53
Canon, Alice, 108
Caraway, William, 114
Carathers, Kiziah, 39
  Redick, 39
Carlton, James K., 79
  John, 58, 70
  Nancy, 89
  Sally J., 79
CARR, PATIENCE, 3
CARR, PATRICK, 3
CARR, THOMAS, 3
CARR, WILLIAM, 96
  Amos E., 75
  B. G., 45

Benj., 1
Betsey, 3, 75
Charity, 7
Enoch, 3
Ferebee, 17
Jesse, 3
Jonathan, 1, 3, 7, 17, 113
Joseph, 3
Lewis F., 91
Mary, 3
Mary C., 75
Milly Jane, 17
Moab, 3

T. T., 48
Reddin, 3
Reddin T., 42
Susanna E., 75
Tabitha, 3
Tabitha Lewis, 50
Thamer, 3
Theophilus, 3
Turner, 3
Virginia, 91
William, 3
Archibald, 96
Hannah, 96
Jane, 96
Maryan, 111

CARRAWAY, BEDREADEN, 26
Gatsey Mage, 26
Susannah Duprey, 26
Theophilus, 26
CARRELL, ALEXANDER, 3
CARRELL, JESSE, 3, 107
CARRELL, JOHN, 3, 107
Hardy, 3
Joseph, 3
Lucey, 3
Priscilla, 3
Rachel, 3
Raeford, 3
Raiford, 3

Carrell, Rashel, 3
Reason, 3
Rebekah, 3
Thomas, 3, 107
Wylie, 3

CARROLL, LEWIS, 26, 28, 29,
46, 67
CARROLL, SARAH, 26
Alexander, 10
Amma B., 26
Benajah V., 87
C. Tate, 26
Cathrine E., 56, 87
Charlotte, 87
Demcy, 6
Edward, 27
Eliza, 26
Frank W., 26
Franklin M., 26
George W., 26
J. C., 63, 68, 85, 92
James L., 26
John C., 19, 34, 35, 47
L. R., 41, 79
Lucy, 74
Macy, 87
Mary E., 67
Nancy, 47
Raiford, 95
Sally, 87
Sally Ann, 87
W. C., 32
William, 26
Wm. J., 26
CARTER, JOHN, 105
CARTER, NAAMAN, 4
Catherine, 50, 60
Celia N., 60
Daniel, 4
Elizabeth, 4
Margaret M., 50
Sarahon, 4
Seeney, 4
Susana, 9
Sylvester, 74
Carter, W. R., 58
William, 50
A. J., 105
Charlie, 110
Edward, 98
H. J., 105
Henry, 110
John M., 105

Joseph D., 105
King S., 105
Oliver, 110
Rebecca E., 110
Sarah, 105
William Henry, 110
Carty, Naaman, 112
Sarah, 52
Carver, Alexander, 75, 108
Edith, 75, 109
John D., 75, 108
Josiah, 75, 108
David, 109
CASHWELL, HERRING, 27
Ann Pender, 27
Gaston B., 27
Lettie D., 27
M. C., 58
M., 78
Susan, 27
Wm. H., 27
Chambers, Elizabeth, 97
CHESNUTT, AMMA B. (A. B.),
15, 28, 60, 63, 65, 68,
71, 72, 73, 75, 86, 92, 93
CHESNUTT, CHARLES, 27, 28
CHESNUTT, DAVID, 3, 4
CHESNUTT, DAVID, 27
CHESNUTT, DRIVER, 27
CHESNUTT, ELIZABETH, 13, 27
CHESNUTT, JOSHUA, 28
CHESNUTT, JOSHUA J., 28
CHESNUTT, NICHOLAS P., 28
CHESNUTT, ROBERT, 27, 28
Absolem, 27
Albert P., 28
Alexander, 3, 77

Chesnutt, Alfred, 27
A. M., 28
Amelia, 53
Anna, 27
Anny, 4
Anney Jane, 4
Avah, 27
Becky Jane, 27
Charlotte, 72
Cornelius T., 28
Daniel, 4

Chesnutt, Nehemiah, 26, 62,
78
Nicholas, 27, 28
Paten C., 27
Peggy, 4
Peyton, 28
Polly, 4
Polly Ann, 27
Rebecca Jane, 28
Richard C., 28
Robert Driver, 27
Tabitha Lewis, 50
Thomas, 24
Unity, 27
William, 4
William K., 27, 72
Dorcas, 27
Edward T., 28
Fanny, 63
H. B., 27, 61
Harriet, 72
Henry, 4
Izzabell, 27
J. M., 61
Jacob S., 27
James, 4, 17
James A., 28
James Averet, 27
Jane, 3
Jenny, 109
John, 6, 112
John E., 34, 111, 112
Jonathan, 27
Joseph, 27
Josephine, 28
Joshua James, 27
Julia, 27
Kilbee, 74
Kitty Eliza, 27
Lemuel, 38
Mariah A., 56
Marshal B., 111, 112
Martha, 29
Martha A., 28
Martha Caroline, 50
Mary, 6, 27
Mary A., 28
Mary A. N., 59

Mitchel, 4
Nancy, 28
Clarkson, Thomas M., 78
Clifton, J. L., 54, 113
Jesse, 22
Clinton, R. C., 6
Ann, 102
Penelope, 102
Richard, 101, 102, 103,
113, 118
Coats, Jordan, 12
Cobb, Sarah E., 67
Cock, Ann, 98
Charles, 98
Francis Sena, 98
Cockburn, Richard, 97
Cogdell, Anny, 55
COGGINS, THOMAS, 4
Martha, 4
Mary, 4
Colbraith, Archibald, 106
COLE, WILLIAM, 4
Betsey Ann, 82
Jennett, 16
Martha, 4
Sary, 4
Joseph John, 104
COLWELL, ELIZABETH, 28, 29
COLWELL, JOHN, 28,29,43,60
COLWELL, RICHARD, 28, 29
A. E., 44
Colwell, Ann Julia, 44
Caty, 28, 29
E. J., 60
Edward J., 29
Henry, 29
Jane, 29
Peggy, 28, 29
Conoly, Malcom C., 46
COOK, JAMES, 4
COOK, PERIGREEN, 29
Caroline, 33
Charity, 29
Charles A., 29
Cornelius, 4
Hariet, 29
Jean, 4
John, 4

Matilda, 29
William R., 29
Mary, 108
Cooke, Rhoda, 119
Unity, 119
Cooley, Giden M., 56
James F., 56
COOPER, FLEET, 2, 9, 24, 29
COOPER, JOHN, 105
COOPER, JOHN S., 29
Abner G., 64
Amos J., 19, 29
Ann M., 50
Daniel, 29
Daniel A., 29
Daniel J., 29
Dicey, 29
Drusilla, 80
Druzilla, 80
Elizabeth N., 29, 50
Emma H., 14
Fleet J., 23
Fleet R., 58
Harriet, 19
H. J., 14
Hiram J., 29
Jacob, 29
John, 29
Cooper, John R., 47
Marthy, 86
Nancy, 29
Penelope, 29
Rhoda, 29
Sarah, 7, 29
Spicey, 47
William Thomas, 47
Wilson, 29
Zilpah, 80
Abner T., 104
Betsey, 119
Elizabeth, 119
F. R., 105
Fleet, 107, 111
Hester, 119
Jacob, 113
Jonathan, 117, 119
Patience, 119
Raphael, 119

Scott, 119
Zylphia, 119
Zilphah, 113
Coor, Dan., 12
Raiford, 7
Jemima, 13
Arthur, 5
Daniel, 5, 106
Corbett, J. M., 64
James M., 42
Mittie G., 42
Cotten, Jesey, 10
COX, JAMES ANDREW, 29
COX, MOSES, 30, 42
COX, SERENA, 30
COX, WILLIAM, 30, 33
Ann, 30, 104
Blackman, 30, 104
Betsey Ann, 104
D. H., 56
Daniel, 30
Flora J., 29
James D., 33
James P. N., 30
Joab B., 30
Cox, Nixon, 30
R. E., 33
Rebecca E., 33
Robert G., 33
Susan, 23
Susan J., 33
Susanna, 30, 104
Uz W., 30
Wm., Jr., 30
William, 104
Craddoc, Joshua, 21
CRADDOCK, CIVIL, 30, 108
Ann B., 30
John T., 30
Joshua, 36
Robert A., 30
Walter J., 30
William H., 30
W. H., 108
W. J., 105
Walter I., 108
Crawford, Alexander F., 20
Ann, 20

Ashley R., 20
Betsey, 20
Eveline, 20
Isaac, 20
Nathan G., 20
Olive, 20
William, 20
Creel, Barney, 82
Willerba, 115
Cromartie, Alexander, 5
Eleanor I., 34
Narcissa E., 34
P. L., 53
Peter, 109
Sarah, 109
Croom, Mary E., 26
CRUMPLER, JACOB, 4, 5
CRUMPLER, JOHN, 4, 5
Amos, 25
Barbary, 25
Betsy, 83
Blackman, 4, 29
Crumpler, Cajiah, 5
Colin, 4
Elizabeth, 5
Evan, 4
G. W., 19
Grace, 5
John H., 47
John S., 19
Letty N., 80
Micajah, 25
Micajer, 87
Nancy, 5
Owens, 4
Rachel, 5
Red., 85
Redman, 4
Sarah, 5
Sarah E., 79
Sarah J., 86
Treacy, 83
Cruse, William, 49
Crusenberry, James, 83
Culbraith, Neill, 2
Culbrath, Desia, 24
Culbreth, D. A., 58, 63,
75, 84

J. O., 26
John, 91
Daniel M., 91
Mabel, 62
Sarah A., 62
W. F., 67

Dameron, Daniel P., 39
  Mary, 89
DANIEL, JONATHAN, 5, 115
  Edney, 22
  Isaac, 5
  Lenny, 5
  Lydia, 5
  Polly, 5
  Raiford, 5
  Susanna, 5
  Willis, 81
  N. A., 114
Daniel, Claudius, 114
DARDEN, BILLY, JR., 5
DARDEN, JOSEPH, 30, 112
  Ann, 55, 112
  Betsey, 30
  David, 5
  Elizabeth H., 30
  Elizabeth M., 44
  Henry, 5
  James H., 30
  J. K., 54
  John, 5
  Nancy C., 30
  O. H., 52
  Peggy, 5
  Percy, 82
  Reddick, 5
  Sarah E., 30
  Simeon J., 30
  Thomas B., 30
  W. B., 52
  W. H., 90
  William H., 30
  William Jackson, 5
  Tempey, 112
  William, 112
Daughterry, Bryan, 82
Daughtery, Sallie, 23
DAUGHTRY, BRYANT, 30

DAUGHTRY, HARDY, 31, 38
DAUGHTRY, LYDDA, 5
DAUGHTRY, S. R., 31
DAUGHTRY, ALLEY, 105
  Lucy E., 107
  Aden, 45
  Adin, 31
  Ed Howard, 31
  George Allman, 58
  G. H., 38, 45
  Geo. H., 30, 31
  Geo. L., 31
  James Bryan, 31
  Jarrot, 31
  Lillie M., 31
  Patsey, 31
  Solomon Eugene, 31
  Tempia A., 31
  William, 31
  Zilphia A., 31
Dautrey, Sarah (Ward), 89
Davis, Stanley, 11
  Therebee, 106
  Thomas, 96
DAWSON, DAVID, 31, 76
DAWSON, JOSEPH, 31, 69
  Burrell, 31
  Celia Gene, 31
  Edith, 31
  Edithlizar, 31
  Henry M., 31
  Holley Gene, 31
  Joel, 31
  Martha, 31
  Mary Elizabeth, 31
  Morning, 84
  William, 31
Dawtry, Solomon, 30
  Zilpha, 30
DENNING, GEORGE W., 31
DENNING, JONAS, 32
DENNING, NANCY, 32, 83
DENNING, ROBERT, 32
  James W., 31, 32
  Jessy W., 31
  M----, 31
  Mary, 32
  Mary A., 41

Nathan, 32, 57
Pearcey, 32
Phebe, 32
Susan C., 31
Thomas, 32
Thomas J., 32
DEVANE, ELIZA A., 32
DEVANE, GEORGE, 5
DEVANE, MILTON K., 32
  Catharine, 5
  Cornelius, 5, 52
  Elizabeth, 5
  Felix, 5
Devane, H. S., 76
  John T., 5
  M. M., 32
  Mary Ann, 5
  Miriam, 5, 85
  Nancy, 73
  Preston R., 32
  Robert Harvey, 32
  Tabitha, 5

  William Thomas, 32
  Tom, 110
  W. T., 110
  William, 110
Dewitt, Henry, 110
Dickson, John, 96, 97, 98
DINKINS, JOSEPH JOHN, 5
  Ann Lewisar, 5
  Elanah, 5
  Lelah, 41
  Lettie Lucinder, 5
  Sally Surreney, 5
  Seley, 5
Dobbin, James C., 14
DODD, DAVID, 32
  Abner, 32
  Benajah, 32
  Daniel, 32
  David P., 32
  Eliza, 32
  Elizabeth, 32
  John, 32
  John Bolen, 32
  Mary, 109
  Willie, 32
Dollar, Louisa, 40

Dorman, Benjamin, 49
  Clarkey, 49
  James, 49
  John Allen, 49
Doughfield, Milley, 116
DRAUGHON, ELIZABETH R., 33
DRAUGHON, GEORGE, 33
  Augusta Jane, 33
  Betty H., 55
  Frances A., 33
Draughon, Gary, 57
  Garry, 30, 33
  George T., 33
  George W., 33
  James R., 19, 33
  James Walter, 33
  Martha Elizabeth, 33
  Martha Jane, 33
  Mary Berilla, 33
  Miles Sampson, 19, 33, 53
  Narcissa Bright, 33
  Pearcy, 70
  Rebecca Eliza, 33
  Robert Taylor, 33
  Walter, 33
  W. B., 75
  William C., 33
  William G., 33
DREW, ALCY, 6
DREW, JOHN, 33
  Ann M., 33
  Askew S., 33
  Christopher H., 33
  David W., 33
  Dilliard L., 33
  Feriby, 7
  Huey, 6
  Josiah, 6
  Julia A., 33
  Luisa, 34
  Luther R., 33
  Margaret P., 33
  Sary, 6
  William, 6
  William M., 33
  Willis, 6
  Wilson, 6
DRIVER, WILLIAM D., 33, 68

134

Ann E., 33
Eliza J., 33
George T., 33
Mary C., 33
DUACH, MAGDALENE, 6
Bettsy, 6
Caleb, 6
Duach, Henry, 6
Onece, 6
Phoebe, 6
Selah, 6
William, 6
DUDLEY, LABEN, 33, 34
DUDLEY, LEVI, 6
Catharine, 34
Eden, 6
Elam, 6, 10
Ely, 6
Enoch, 6
Hepzibak, 6
James, 34
Jenet, 6
John, 6, 34, 94
Lilly, 6
Lydia, 6
Mary A., 34
Nanney, 6
Nedham, 6
Viney, 33
Dudly, John, 50
Duffie, Ann, 9
DUNCAN, ALFRED, 34
Dugald, 116
Edith, 34
Henry J., 34
J. F., 34
Dunn, John, 97
Michael, 103

Eason, J. C., 94
John, 21
John V., 105
Julius C., 17
Edwards, Nathan, 57
Eldridge, Elizabeth, 70
Delaney, 105
Jos., 104
L., 105
Samuel, 105

Eliot, John, 5
John, Jr., 92
Mary B., 77
Elliott, Mary B., 14
ELLIS, GORMAN, 34
Edith, 34
Evan, 97
John Gorman, 34
Mary, 20
Samuel, 34
William N., 34
Elkins, D. J., 114
Elmore, J. H., 40, 93
John H., 56, 93
Elwell, Joseph B., 78
EVANS, MARTHA, 34
David, 34
Nancy Jane, 89
Samuel, 34
Everts, J. H., 91
Evritt, Muriel H., 56
EZZELL, JOHN R., 34
A. L., 88
Catherine, 34
Charles W., 34
David, 34
J. D., 31
J. R., 72
John B., 34
John D., 67
Joshua R., 27, 28, 40
M. J., 34
Margaret, 71
Sarah, 29
Hansel, 107

Faircloth, Asha, 66
Caleb, 1
Elizabeth, 10
Hannah, 10
Isham, 10
James, 10
Mary, 10
Milly, 1, 10
Priscilla, 47
Solomon, 36
Susannah, 10
FAISON, ELIAS, 34, 74

FAISON, JAMES, 35
FAISON, KILBEE, 35
FAISON, MARY A., 35
FAISON, SOLOMON J., 35
FAISON, THOMAS I., 35,80,86
FAISON, WILLIAM, 35, 62, 85
FAISON, WILLIAM H., 36
FAISON, W. L., 36, 63
  Abner M., 35
  Amelia Elizabeth, 35
  Ann Rebecca, 35
  Edward L., 35
  Elias Kilbee, 34
  Elizabeth, 35
  Franklin J., 35
  Helen J., 35
  Henry, 6, 52, 55
  Henry E., 22, 36, 63
  Isham R., 48
  John Haywood, 35
  John M., 35
  Julian P., 35
  Madge C., 36
  Margaret, 34, 35
  Margaret K., 34
  Maria Louisa, 35
  Mary Ann, 35, 65
  Mary E., 36
  Mary Jane, 74
  Mary Susan, 35
  Mary Virginia, 35
  Matthew J., 35
  N. C., 35
  Nehemiah C., 35
  Preston K., 35
  Sarah J., 36
  Susan, 35
  Thomas Kilbee, 35
  Virginia, 35
  William A., 35
  W. A., 15
  William Elias, 35
  William, 35
  William Lucien, 34, 35
  William S., 36
  William W., 35
Faison, Henry E., 116
  Olive, 107

  Washington, 107
Farrier, Sarah, 30
Fellow, John, Jr., 36
Fellows, Susanna, 2
  William, 2
FENNELL, MARGARET, 36
  John M., 35, 36
  John Walis, 36
  Judy, 115
  Nicholas, 36
  Owen, 36
Ferrell, J. A., 17, 26
  Thomas M., 26
FISHER, JOHN, 36

FISHER, THOMAS, 36
  Brother Worthy, 36
  Catharine, 36
  Elijah, 36
  Jane, 36
  Jinny, 71
  Penney, 36
  Phebe, 36
  Ralph, 36
  Sally, 36
  Sandars, 36
  Southy, 36
  William T., 36
FLEMING, ALEXANDER, 36, 104, 109

FLEMING, JOHN, 4, 36, 37, 45, 57
  David, 36
  Elizabeth, 37
  Felix, 36
  Hiram, 37
  James, 36
  James Allen, 37
  Jiney, 36
  Kitsey Alen, 37
  Nancy, 37
  Susannah, 37
  William J. F., 36
Flemming, Alexander, 84
Flemming, John, 19
Flowers, Jacob, 11
FORT, JOHN T., 37
FORT, MILLY, 37

FORT, SARAH, 37
  Hardy, 86, 24, 37
  John Jack Turner, 86
  John Turner, 37
  Mason, 86
  Milly, 86
  Sally, 86
  Emma J., 37
  John A., 37
  Laura J., 37
  Mary E., 37
FORTNER, JOHN E., 37
  John Everett, 37
  Nancy, 37
  Serena, 41
  Sureany, 37
  William, 37
FOWLER, CASSA, 36, 37
FOWLER, ELIZABETH, 37
  Ellen C., 37
  John, 19, 36, 107
  Lavony Crosby, 60
  Leonard C., 37
  Margaret R., 37
  Mary N., 37
  Mary V., 42
  Miles B., 37
  O. J., 37
  R. B., 37
  Sally A., 37
  Samuel, 110
  W. S., 31
  William, 66
FRAZIER, HOUSTON R., 38
FRAZIER, JOHN, 38
  Elsey, 38
  Elizabeth, 38
  Houston, 38
  Nancy, 38
  Sarah, 32, 38
  Thomas, 110
FREDERICK, JAMES, 7, 38
  Betsey, 38
  Henry F., 38
  Nancy, 38
  William, 38
  William K., 38, 112
  J., 112

  Peter, 112
Freeman, Larry, 108
FRYAR, JACOB, 6
FRYAR, JOHN, 38, 51
FRYAR, JONATHAN, 6, 38
FRYAR, WILLIAM, 4, 38, 51
  A------ Blackman, 38
  Celestia Ann, 39
  Charity, 38
  Daniel, 38
  Edy, 6
  Elizabeth, 6
  Emily Idella, 39
  George, 38
  H. B., 88
  James, 38
  J. M., 88
  Malisa Electa, 39
  Margaret, 38
  Martin Luther, 38
  Mary, 6
  Mary Ann, 38, 51
  Mary Cornelia, 39
  Molsey, 41
  Nancy Jean, 9
  Rachel, 38
  Sarah, 38
  William Jefferson, 38
  Winneford, 6,
Fryer, Jacob, 109
  Winaford, 109
Fussall, Benjamin, 96
  Jacob, 96
Fussell, John D., 89, 114
Futrell, Mary F., 31
F----, M. Elizabeth, 58

GAINEY, BARTHOLOMEW, 39
GAINEY, EDMUND, 119
GAINEY, MARTHA, 39, 119
GAINEY, THADDEUS G., 39
GAINEY, WM. G., 39
  Abram, 39, 119
  Beatty, 119
  Blackman, 39
  Blackman L., 39
  Bodie, 39
  Cenora, 39

Claudius, 39
Edney, 119
Elias, 39, 119
Franklin, 39
H. G., 32
Hinton M., 39
Hiram M., 39
Josiah, 39
L. G., 39
Mary A., 59
Nancy J., 39
Noel, 39, 119
Reals, 39
Redick, 39
Reddick, 119
Roy, 39
Sena A., 39
Vina B., 39
William, 39, 119
Wm. H., 39
Wilton F., 39
Gamford, William, 8
Ganey, Abram, 117
　Kiddey, 117
Garris, Albert C., 17, 71
Gautier, Virginia F., 107
GAVIN, EDWARD C., 1, 5, 6,
　16, 28, 29, 39, 44, 46
GAVIN, SAMUEL, 6
　Asha, 4
　Charity, 39
　Lewis, 8
　Samuel I., 27
　Samuel James, 39
Gavin, Sarah, 6
　W. A., 67
GENKINS, THOMAS, 6
　Jonathan, 6
　Sealey, 9
　Tabitha, 6
Giddens, H. B., 77
　Margaret Louize, 48
　Mitchel, 54
　N. C., 105
Glessen, L-------, 82
GODWIN, ELIZABETH, 40, 84
GODWIN, JOHN, 40, 69, 93
GODWIN, NATHAN, 1, 40

GODWIN, NATHAN, 40
　Aaron, 117
　Artie M., 40
　Bowdoin, 17
　Bud, 40
　David, 40
　Easter, 20
　Edmon, 45
　Elizabeth, Jr., 40
　Handy, 40
　Henry, 40
　Isham D., 88
　Jacob, 53
　Jerusha, 40
　Joel, 40
　Joel N., 88
　Jonathan, 12, 40
　Lucinda E., 40
　M. -. -. Elizabeth, 40
　Nathan, 117
　Penny, 40
　Polly, 40
　Rachel, 40
　Ransom, 93
　Royal, 40
　Silvania, 40
　Sophoronia J., 40
　William A., 40
　William David, 40
Goff, Catharine, 34
　J. M., 51
Goff, Luther Franklin, 51
　Milton Henry, 51
　Robert Charles, 51
　Thomas, 7
Gotierre, Polly, 116
Gow, Blen, 93
Gowry, Elizabeth, 3
Grady, Ann, 96
Grainger, Caleb, 100
GRANTHAM, NEEDHAM, 40
　Allen B., 17
　Barfield, 40
　Hiram, 40
　Needham J., 40
Gray, Mary, 30
　Rebecca Ellen, 20
Green, J. W., 110

GREGORY, LOTT, 41
GREGORY, LOTT, 41
GREGORY, ASA, 40, 69, 41
GREGORY, ELISHA, 6, 41
GREGORY, ELIJAH, 6, 41, 46
GREGORY, JANE, 41
GREGORY, WRIGHT, 41, 62
  Ann G., 69
  Anny, 41
  Asia, 6
  Beck, 41
  Eliza, 41
  Elizabeth C., 41
  Henry, 41
  Hubert Francis, 41
  James, 41
  James William, 41
  John T., 41, 42, 82
  Laney, 41
  Lewis, 41
  Lott, 6
  Louisa, 87, 41
  Marshal, 41
  Monk, 41
  Nancy, 41, 87
  Owen, 40, 41
  Polly Ann, 87
  Sally Jane, 41
Gregory, Sarah, 87
  Sarenia, 41
  Surrene, 6
  Sydney Forest, 41
  Thomas, 41
  William, 41, 54, 83
  Lena Simpler, 41
  Molsey, 41
Grice, John W., 44
  Robert, 10
  Susan Ann, 65
Griffith, Dollie, 14
  Flora, 14
Grozier, Jemima, 66
  William, 66
GUY, WILLIAM, 42
  Mary Ann, 42

Hailes, L--------, 76
HAIR, JOHN, 7, 106

HAIR, WILLIAM, 7
  Arthur, 7
  Delila, 13
  Eady, 7
  Elizabeth, 7, 8
  Felix, 7
  Guilford, 7
  Isaac, 7
  Letha, 7
  Raiford, 106
  Sarah, 7
  Thomas, 7, 106
  Zilpha, 7
Haise, Elizabeth, 94
HALL, ARMAGER, 7
HALL, ELIZABETH, 42
HALL, HENRY, 105
  A. Herring, 72
  Ann, 36
  Asia J., 28
  Charles H., 42
  Eliza E., 72
  Enoch, 76
  Feby, 7
  Ferebe, 42
  H. L., 80
Hall, Hizziah, 7
  M., 117
  M. M., 23, 79
  Mary, 10
  Nancy, 105
  Nanney, 49
  Thomas B., 29
  William, 7, 76
  William S., 42
  Zilper, 7
HANEY, SARAH, 7
  Gabriel, 7
  Joseph John, 7
  Joshua, 7
  Lalon, 7
Hanes, Sarrah, 83
Hare, Blackman, 37
  Blueford, 7
  William, Sr., 2
HARGROVE, ANN W., 42
HARGROVE, ARTHUR, 7
HARGROVE, SALLIE, 42

Aaron, 3, 7
Alvin, 42
Ben, 23, 55
Benjamin, 18, 54, 55, 77
Benjamin F., 42
Eady A., 48
George W., 63
Harper, Amey Ann, 94
  Eugenia A., 94
Harris, Bethany, 13
Harrison, Edward, Jr., 97
Harvard, W. H., 29
Harvel, Hariet, 52
  J. J., 72
Harvell, Joseph J., 50
Hatche, B. H., 80
HAWKINS, JOHN, 96
  Ann, 96
  Lettess, 96
  Mary, 96
Hawley, Jesse H., 84
  S. L., 93
  Samson, 50
Hawley, Susan C., 93
  W. D., 78
  William, 90
HAY, CHARLES, 7
  John, 103
  Mary Rice, 7
  Peter, 7
  Sarah, 7
  Solomon, 7
  Winny, 7
Hayard, John, 12
Hayes, James T., 53
  Penny, 7
  William H., 53
Hays, John H., 49
  Sally, 49
Heath, Fanny M., 46
Henry, Sarah Caroline, 59
HERRING, ABRAHAM, 119
HERRING, B. M., 8, 47
HERRING, G. W., 42
HERRING, GABRIEL, 42, 43
HERRING, JACOB, 8
HERRING, JOEL, 42
HERRING, NATHAN, 8, 42

HERRING, NEHEMIAH, 43
HERRING, STEPHEN, 5, 8, 43
HERRING, THOMAS W., 43
HERRING, UZZILL, 8
  A. H., 58
  Abram, 98
  Adolphus, 43
  Amos M., 43
  Ann, 8
  Ann Matilda, 26
  Bathshaba, 109
  Benajah, 42
  Benjamin, 8
  Betsy, 8
  Bright Middleton, 8
  Bright S., 18
  Dallas, 43
  Dicey, 43
  E., 52, 83
  Edger C., 42
Herring, Eleanor, 8
  Eliza, 8, 42
  Elizabeth, 42, 43, 64
  Elvira C., 42
  Emily, 43
  Enoch, 86, 110
  Gabriel, 110
  George Washington, 43
  Hanson W., 83
  Hardy, 43, 52, 73
  Isaac W., 43, 67
  J. O., 110
  Janet, 42
  John, 2, 5, 8, 32, 43
  John Octice, 43
  Joseph, 3, 25, 36, 64, 71
  Kitty, 8
  Lewis, 42
  Lewis H., 25
  Luther W., 43
  Lucien, 43, 51
  Margaret, 73
  Martha, 119
  Martha I., 28
  Mary, 8, 42, 64
  Mary I., 43
  Mary Jane, 36
  Mary Victor, 20

Herring, Sallyan, 8
  Sara, 42
  Sarah, 8, 27, 43
  Sarah A., 43
  Sarah Catharine, 27
  Sarah E., 43
  Silas, 67
  Solomon, 42
  Stephen B., 8, 43
  Suckey, 110
  Thomas I., 43
  Thomas J., 32
  W. E., 43, 51
  Wm. H., 62
  W. W., 79
  William, 8, 43
  William James, 42
  Murdock, 42
  Nancy, 8, 73
  Nancy I., 43
  O. F., 45
  Phebe Eleanor, 43
  Poidres, 42
  Polly, 8
  R. K., 52
  R. N., 37
  Rachel V., 16
  Rebecca, 98
  Richard, 43
  Robert N., 52, 94
  Robert Nixon, 8
  Rufus, 62
  Rufus I., 42
  Sally, 43
Hicks, Albert R., 74
  Athanasia, 74
  Isham F., 35
  Mary, 99
  William S., 61
HIGHSMITH, JACOB, 43
HIGHSMITH, LEWIS, 43
HIGHSMITH, NOAH, 43
HIGHSMITH, WILLIAM L., 44
  A. S., 44
  Ann Julia, 58
  Anna, 60
  C. C., 44
  Caroline, 60

Highsmith, Margaret E., 94
  Mariam Elizabeth, 53
  Miriam, 43
  N. F., 43
  Noah F., 43
  Owen E., 43
  Richard A., 43
  Robert, 43, 69
  Sarah, 72
  Sarah A., 60
  Susan, 43
  William R., 71
  W. R., 43, 44
  Charity, 53
  Elizabeth, 43
  G. W., 37, 58, 107
  George, 43, 69
  George Washington, 43
  Helen, 72
  Isaac M., 43
  James B., 73
  James H., 43
  John J., 15, 67
  Joseph Sydney, 43
  Lewis D., 43
  Luther R., 43
  M. E., 44
HILL, EDWARD, 44
HILL, FRANCIS, 119
  B., 64
  J. K., 38
  Mary E., 44
  May C., 44
  B. H., 119
  Frederick J., 103
HINES, JAMES, 44
  Albert, 44
  Felix, 13
  J. S., 44
  Joel, 18
  John, 61
  Margaret Ann, 40, 44
  Rebecca E., 15
  Stephen, 85
  William, 44
  William F., 78
  Wm. S., 94
Hinson, Ann, 13

HOBBS, ABRAM, SR., 44
HOBBS, GABRIEL, 44
HOBBS, MARY A. R., 45
HOBBS, SIMON P., 44, 45
HOBBS, WILLIAM, 44, 45
HOBBS, WILLIAM, 44, 45
  Abram, 44, 45
  Annie, 13
  Charles M., 45
  David W., 45
  Edwin H., 45
Hobbs, G. W., 27
  Gaston Mears, 44, 45
  George, 4, 53
  George W., 44
  Henry A., 45
  Hester, 7, 119
  Hosea J., 44, 66
  Isaac, 44
  Isaac M., 37, 45
  J. M., 27
  Judson, 44
  Lewis, 45
  Margaret Jane, 16
  Mary, 44
  Mary A., 66
  Mary Ann Rebecca, 44, 45
  Mary E. Stevens, 45
  Mortimer E., 45
  Nancy, 47
  Nanney, 45
  Phanna, 45
  Pleasant, 45
  Rebecca Eliza, 45
  Rebecca Eliza (Trouble-
  field), 16
  Redn., 90
  Reddin, 45
  Simon, 7, 119
  Susanna, 45
  William P., 44
Hodge, Rachel, 8
HOLDER, GEORGE, 8
HOLDER, JESSE, 8, 45
HOLDER, JOHN, 8, 45
  Abel, 45
  Ann, 8
  Anna, 8

Holder, Mary, 8
  Mary Jane, 68
  Nathan, 8, 45
  Polly, 116
  Sally, 68
  Sampson, 68
  Thomas, 8
  William, 8
  Zachariah, 45
  Elizabeth, 45
  Ezrael, 45
  George Vincent, 8
  Glada, 8
  Jennett, 68
  Joel Nicholas, 45
  Lilla, 8
  Martha, 8
HOLLAND, THOMAS, 9
  Daniel, 9
  Charlie, 110
  Elizabeth, 76, 80
  Henry, 6, 9
  John, 9
  Lou, 87
  Mary, 53
  Mary Charity, 4
  Milly, 9
  Minnie A., 110
  Nancy Orpha, 9
  Thomas James, 9
  Willis Daniel, 9
HOLLEY, JAMES, 45
  John, 57
  Nancy, 31
HOLLINGSWORTH, HENRY, 16,
  42, 46
HOLLINGSWORTH, JACOB, 46, 62
  Catherine E., 46
  E. J., 117
  Elizabeth, 29, 45, 46
  Guilford, 45
  H., 27, 29, 41
  James, 46
  Julia, 82
  Mary, 3
  Peggy Ann, 46
  Thomas, 4
  Zebulon, 45

Holly, Anna, 8
  James, 1, 49
  John, 8, 13
  Sherwood, 10
HOLMES, ANN, 46
HOLMES, JAMES C., 46
HOLMES, HARDY, 8, 9, 11,
  41, 46, 116
HOLMES, OWEN, 25, 46, 55,
  86, 107
  A., 116
  Archibald, 25, 37, 65
  Eliza J., 46
  F., 41
  Feribee, 116
  Feriby, 9
  Gabriel, 2, 8, 14, 25,
  26, 46, 72, 86, 101, 113
  Hardy Lucien, 46
  Hepsey M., 75
  Mary, 46
  R. C., 18, 22, 25, 27,
  36, 37, 46, 67, 71, 76,
  77, 86, 92
  Richard C., 46, 86, 107
  Thomas H., 70
HONEYCUTT, W. B., 46
HONEYCUTT, WILLIAM, 46
  B. A., 46, 47
  Blackman, 47
  Charles, 47
  Chillin, 47
  John, 47
  John G., 47
  M. C., 47
  Malsis, 46, 47
  Mary Ann, 64
  Molsey, 4
  Redin A., 47
  Sarah J., 46
  Susan, 64
  William A., 47
  William B., 47
  Willie, 4
Hooks, Franklin, 20
  John, 20
  Mary, 20
  William, 20

Horn, Daniel, 66
  Joel, 110
HOUSE, DOLLIE S., 47
HOUSE, JOHN, 47, 114
HOUSE, JOHN C., 47
  Betsey Ann, 61
  Caroline, 47
  Francis Elizabeth, 47
  Franklin, 47
  H., 64
  Hardy, 45, 47, 61
  J. H., 64
  Polley Jane, 47
  Susan Ann, 47
  William, 42, 47
Houston, Catharine, 38
  James, 38
  William, 97
HOWARD, MARY, 47
HOWARD, MINSON, 47
HOWARD, THOMAS M., 9
  Fleet H., 9
  Henry, 36
  J. C., 9, 66
  John, 99
  Laura, 67
  Mary E., 9
  Mary P., 78
  Penelope J., 86
  Sarah A., 9, 89
  Thomas A., 9
Howell, E. E., 26
  L. Francis, 88

Hubbard, A. L., 108
  Langdon C., 37, 46, 60,85
  T. L., 17
  Thomas L., 16, 17
  W. G., 93
HUDSON, HOLLEY, 48
HUDSON, SARAH M., 48
HUDSON, THOMAS I., 48
HUDSON, WILLIAM, 48
  Ann, 70
  Anna, 48
  Benajah, 48
  C. J., 39
  D-----, 48

Hudson, Dicy, 48
  Elizabeth, 32
  Hawley, 48
  J. H., 48
  J. J., 49
  Jane, 48
  Joel, 48
  John T., 41
  Nancy, 34
  Nanna, 48
  Pherabe A., 57
  R. Benjamin, 48
  Rebecca, 68
  Samuel, 48
  Spicey J., 57
  William H., 48
  William W., 48
Hufham, Sarah S., 36
Huggins, James J., 23, 81
Humphrey, Morgan, 98
Hunter, Marjorie Jane
  Lockamy, 11

INGRAM, ABNER, 48, 117
  Abner, Jr., 48
  Elizabeth, 49, 57
  Elizabeth Ann, 48
  Jesse Martin, 50
  John, 11, 61, 77, 117
  Pherebe, 48
  William R., 48
  Penny, 117
  Phereby, 117
Inman, Josiah, 104
  Robert, 104
IRELAND, SAMUEL,R., 48, 65
  Eliza, 48
  Henry Bizzell, 48
  James Daniel, 48
  Octavie Josephine, 48
ISHAM, JAMES, 97
  Charles, 97
  Jane, 97
  Margaret, 97
IVEY, THOMAS, 12, 48
Ivey, C., 103
  Charlotte, 48
  Claburn, 48

  Elizabeth, 48
  Murtilda, 1
  Rebecca, 48
  Thomas, Jr., 12
  Thomas Routledge, 48

JACKSON, EDEN, 49
JACKSON, HENRY, 49
JACKSON, IRVIN, 49
JACKSON, JAMES, 9, 49
JACKSON, JOHN, 9, 49
JACKSON, LEMMON, 49
JACKSON, RICHARD, 49
JACKSON, WILLIAM, 49
JACKSON, WILLIE B., 48,49,50
  Allen, 9
  Amy, 9
  Aney, 9
  Anna, 49
  B. B., 48
  Bennett, Sr., 9
  Blackman, 81
  C. C., 48, 59
  Charity Jane, 49
  D. M., 84
  Dickson, 15
  Dicy, 75
  Drew, 9
  Eden, 49
  Elizabeth, 49
  Fameriah, 115
  Fredrick, 49
  Hezekiah, 49
  James, 49
  James T., 49
  Jennet, 49
  John N., 49
  John Wiley, 49
  Joel, 9, 15, 94
  Josiah, 31
  Julius E., 49
Jackson, Kezziah, 50
  Leanna, 49
  Lewis, 49, 80
  M. O., 46
  Martha, 49
  Mary, 49
  Mary Adline, 50

Matthew E., 5C
Nancy, 49, 90
Nancy Queen, 81
Nathan, 49
Needham, 49
O. M., 50
Ollen, 50
Patty, 9
Phebe, 48, 50
Rachel, 49
Raiford, 49
Sampson D., 50, 59, 79
Samson B., 50
Susan Jerusha, 49
Thomas N., 49
William C., 15
Willis B., 90
JACOB, ABRAHAM, 9
JAMES, THOMAS, 50, 85
O. P., 59
Robinson, 88
Sabry, 50
David, 109
Richard, 97
JERNIGAN, FERNEY, 50
H. W., 49, 79
Harriet, 56
Martha, 33, 50
Susah, 57
William, 57
Jocelyn, Mary Ann, 103
JOHNSON, AMOS, 50, 52
JOHNSON, BRIGHT, 50, 52, 73
JOHNSON, EPHRIAN, 9
JOHNSON, JOAB, 9, 51
JOHNSON, JOHN, 9, 51
JOHNSON, JOHN, 51
JOHNSON, MATTHEW, 51
JOHNSON, NANCY, 9, 57
JOHNSON, NATHAN, 9, 16, 51
JOHNSON, SOASBE, 52
JOHNSON, SOLOMON, 9, 52
JOHNSON, WARREN, 52, 81
JOHNSON, WILLIAM, 9, 20
JOHNSON, WM. C., 52
A., 92
A. F., 17, 36, 63, 74, 77,
84, 93

Johnson, Helen P., 50
Ira J., 89, 114
J. D., 110
Jese, 9
Joel, 9
Kezziah, 51
Keziah Katharine, 51
King, 52
Kitty, 9
Laura A., 14
Margaret Ann, 34
Margarett M., 51
Martha Jane, 27
Mariah, 52
Mary, 51, 83
Mary E., 52
Mary Ellen, 15
Maurrisy, 9
Molsy Chappell, 9
Nancy Elizabeth, 9
Nancy J., 89, 114
Nathan Washington, 34, 51
Owen H., 50
Robert Calvin, 51
S. W., 39
Samuel, 50, 52
Samuel K., 50
A. J., 44, 72, 75
A. M., 38
A. N., 21
Aaron, 9, 51
Alexander, 58
Alfred, 53, 37, 75
Alice R., 50
Allen, 9, 51, 52
Allen Chatham, 51
Alpheus Marshal, 52
Amos J., 50
Ann M., 50
Ann N., 51
A., 89
Betsey, 9, 57
Bizzell, 34, 51, 73
C. C., 14, 39
C. P., 18
Charity, 51
Charles P., 66
Charlotte M., 50

D. F., 44
Daniel T., 73, 74
David Clark, 52
Dorcas, 9
E. E., 19, 63, 64
Electy, 51
Eliza, 50
Eliza J., 61
Elizabeth, 38, 50
Enoch, 52
Everrett, 51
Frances Marion, 52
G. M., 51
George, 9, 51
Sarah, 52
Sarah Jane, 50
Stephen, 50, 52
Stephen W., 50
Susan J., 60
Taylor, 9
Thomas, 50
Warren, 111
William A., 74
William L., 72
William Samuel, 52
Winney, 26
JOHNSTON, JOHN, 10, 11, 59
  Angus, 68
  Charity, 68
  Elizabeth, 10
  Mark, 10
  Mathew, 10
JONES, JOHN, 10, 31
JONES, JOHN, 97
JONES, LANCELOT, 52, 94
JONES, THADRICK, 10
  Ann, 52, 97
  Benjamin, 10
  Charity, 61
  F. P., 34
  Gaston, 89
  George, 56
  Harriett, 19
  J. F., 47
  Katie, 89
  Mary, 10
  Milcoh, 10
  Nathan, 70

Noel, 52
Philip, 10
Polly, 10
Rachel, 10
Reddick, 10
Sally, 10
Sophiah Helen, 52
Thomas Isaac, 61
Treacy, 82
Catherine, 97
Charley D., 105
Elizabeth, 97
Elizabeth A., 105
James M-----, 105
Jeromey, 105
Mary Ann, 97
Patte, 97
Samuel, 98
Sarah, 97
T. D., 105
W. B., 107
William, 97
JORDEN, RICHARD, 52
  Elizabeth, 52
  James, 25
  Mary Ann, 52
  Mary Jane, 52
  Mary Susan, 52
JOYNER, JAMES, 10
Joyner, Benjamin, 10
  Daniel, 27
  Joel, Jr., 21
  Worthy, 21

KEEN, JAMES R., 53
KEEN, JOHN, SR., 10
  Elizabeth, 10
  Ema Hattie, 53
  Franklin, 53
  Gardner, 12
  George, 53, 89
  Henry, 53
  Jennett, 89
  Jim, 53
  John, 10, 53
  Marion, 53
  Mary J., 53
  Sally J., 53

William, 10
Willie, 31
Young, 6
KELLY, FELIX, 53
KELLY, JOSEPH, 10
  Edith M., 53
  Elizabeth, 10
  Gemimy, 10
  Isaiah I., 53
  Jacob, 10
  Julia, 43
  Marshal M., 53
  Mary, 10
  Minney Ellen, 53
  Sylvester R., 53
  Thomas O., 53
  William, 10
Kenan, Daniel L., 112
  (Gen.) James, 118
  (Col.) Thomas, 113
  Thomas, 96
  William, 97
  Michael J., 46
  Thomas, 85
Kenard, James, 109
Kenneday, Susanna, 115
KERR, JACOB, 53
KERR, JAMES, 53
  Andrew D., 53
  Catherine, 53
  Charles S., 53
  Daniel, 53
  Edwin W., 17, 54, 74
  Hatter L., 53
  Hayes B., 53
  Henry R., 53
  Jacob D., 53
  Jane Ellen, 53
  John, 53
  John D., 52
  John T., 53
  Noah T., 53
  Robert Gales, 53
Killet, Alexander, 117
KILLETT, ALEXANDER, 53
KILLETT, JULIAN A., 54
  Dixon, 27
  Herodias, 20, 53

J. A., 92
M. M., 54, 92
Rebecca, 50, 54
Sihon, 87
Sinon B., 57
Sion, 53
Killen, William, 10
KING, BRYAN, 54
KING, DAVID C., 54
KING, EDMUND, 54
KING, HENRY, 54, 55
KING, JENNY, 54
KING, JETHRO, 54, 55
KING, RICHARD J., 54, 55
KING, SENEY, 55
KING, WILLIAM, SR., 104
  A. H., 14, 114
  Allen, 54, 55
  Alvin, 54
  Alvin H., 62
  Alvin Houstin, 54
  Alworth, 55, 77, 62
  Amy, 55
King, Arkansas, 54
  Barney, 54
  Benajah, 54
  Charles, 54, 55
  Cherry Catharine, 18
  Clarrisa, 18
  Clarisey, 54
  Daniel C., 81, 111
  D. C., 30, 82
  Dolly, 54
  Edmond, 54
  Edy, 57
  Eliza R., 54
  Flora I., 77
  George, 91
  George Thomas, 77
  George W., 54
  H. H., 14
  Harrett, 55
  Harriett, 54
  Irvin, 54
  J. W., 54, 65
  James, 55
  Joel, 57
  John, 54, 55, 98

King, Nathan J., 54
  Oates S., 91
  Polly, 18, 54, 55
  R. H., 16
  Rebecca Eliza, 18
  Rhoda E., 54
  Robert T., 54
  Rosa A. A., 54
  Sallie, 54
  Sally, 54, 55
  John B., 54, 55
  John G., 31
  John William, 18
  Josiah, 57
  Julia, 54
  Julius S., 54, 82
  L. C., 23, 24, 30, 42,
  48, 54, 81, 82, 83, 90, 111
  Laura C., 54
  Lenny, 65
  Louis D., 18
  Margaret E., 77
  Marion D., 54
  Martha E., 81
  Mary Ann, 93
  Mary Jane, 18, 54
  Michael, 54, 55, 98
  Michael Everett, 18
  Nathan, 55
  Sally Ann, 18
  Sarah Ann, 54
  Sarah C., 54, 55
  Serena Catharine, 54
  Stephen James, 18
  Stephen, 55, 110, 112, 113
  Steven S., 54
  T. W., 65
  Thomas, 55
  Thomas William, 18
  Virginia, 54
  W. R., 20
  Walter M., 54
  William B., 54
  Ann, 98, 104
  Devane, 104
  Helen, 104
  Julianna, 115
  Margaret, 104

  Mary, 98
  Thomas D., 104
  William R., 104
Kinsey, Daniel, 4
KIRBY, WILLIAM, 55
  Elizabeth, 55
  George L., 55
  John C., 55
  William Turner, 55
Knowles, D. J., 74
  Mary M., 47
KORNEGAY, DAVID, 55, 85
  George O., 55
  James F., 55
  Margaret, 55
  Sarah, 55
Kornegay, Tabitha, 104
  Zilpha, 55

LAMB, J. H., 55
LAMB, REBECCA, 17, 56
  Allen W., 55
  Anna E., 55
  Colin T., 55
  Eliza, 17
  George W., 56
  Isaac, 108
  James C., 55
  John, 17
  John D., 55
  Nancy C., 55
  Rachel C., 59
  Thomas C., 56
  William B., 55
Lane, Isaac W., 30, 90
  J. W., 77
  John B., 77
Langston, Nancy, 20
LANIER, JOHN, 58
  Betsey, 58
  Esther, 58
  Killery, 58
  Killy Jane, 58
  Nancy, 58
  Thomas, 58
Lankston, Isaac, 115
Larkins, Susanna, 119
LASSITER, KILBY, 56

LASSITER, PATIENCE, 23, 105
LASSITER, ROBERT, 105, 109
  Charley, 105
  Charlie, 39
  George, 12, 39, 105, 115
  Kilbee, 40, 62
  Louisa, 56
  Euphemia, 105
  John T., 105
  Joseph W., 105
  Susanna, 105
Laton, Demey, 40
  Edna, 40
Laton, Hillery, 10
  Lalon, 7
Lawhon, A. F., 43
  Harriet D., 71
  Serena D., 37
LEE, BATT, 50, 56
LEE, BATT, 56
LEE, BETHANY, 56, 57
LEE, BLACKMAN, 20, 56, 57
LEE, BURCHET, 56
LEE, CURTIS, 57
LEE, GARDNER, 57
LEE, JESSE, SR., 57
LEE, JOAB, 57
LEE, JOSEPH, 105
LEE, PETER, 57
LEE, PHAROAH, 58
LEE, THOMAS M., 58
LEE, WILLIAM, 57, 58
  Algernon M., 19, 47, 52,
  58, 63, 78, 92
  Amanda A., 39
  Appy, 57
  Bethany, Jr., 57
  Boyet, 58
  Calvin, 58
  Catharine, 56
  David, 32, 56, 57
  Delilah, 56
  Dicey, 39
  Dorcas, 51
  Edney, 39
  Edy, 57
  Elem, 8
  Emmer, 60

Lee, John, 57, 58, 105
  John Thomas, 58
  Jonathan, 57, 85
  Joseph, 57
  Joseph Gardner, 57
  Josiah, 57
  Kezia, 56
  Keziah, 56
  Laura A., 56
  Lemuel H., 50, 56
  Lovett James, 58
  L., 39, 79
  Major D., 56
  Marshall, 56
  Martha, 56, 57
  Mary, 34
  Mary A., 39
  Matthew L., 58
  Milly Jane, 58, 107
  Nancy, 56, 57
  Nancy Jane, 58
  Peter R., 57
  Pharaba, 57
  Pharabee, 85
  Polly, 57
  R. C., 8
  R. R., 42
  Richard Henry, 58
  Robert E., 56
  Samuel, 57, 85
  Samuel B., 56
  Sarah, 85
  Simon H., 57
  Susan, 56
  Susan Ann, 58
  Susan C., 56
  Susan S., 56
  Susannah, 57
  Thomas J., 58, 66
  Tilley Catherine, 58
  Troy, 56
  Ulissis, 56
  Vianna, 57
  Westbrook, 39, 57, 90
  William Henry, 58
  Erasmus B., 56, 57
  Fox, 58
  George, 58

Lee, William R., 94
  Arthur, 105
  Eliza, 205
  George R., 105
  Jos., 104
  Judith, 115
  Media, 105
  Peter, 105, 109, 115
  Starling, 109
  Guard, 58
  H. N., 56
  Henry, 45, 58, 92
  James B., 56
  James W., 20, 57
  Jesse, 56, 57
  Joel, 32, 57, 105
Lester, Jane, 38
LEWIS, OLLEN M., 52, 58
LEWIS, TABITHA, 58
  A., 59
  Alford, 59
  Anderson, 59
  Charles Tate, 58
  Cherry, 59
  J. C., 58
  Julian Franklin, 58
  Mary, 34
  Mary S., 69
  Oates, 26
  R. L., 74
  Susan, 58
  Susannah C., 37
Lindsay, Altha, 56, 57
  John, 57
  Sarah, 81
Linsey, J. D., 88
Livingston, Elizabeth, 109
  John, 109
Lockaman, Civil, 34
  Martha J., 67
  Rachel, 40
Lockamay, Martha Jane, 88
LOCKAMY, ELI, 11
  Joseph, 7
  Martha, 15
  Mary, 94
  Odom, 7
  Sarah, 13

LOCKERMAN, JACOB, 13, 106
LOCKERMAN, JAMES, 106
  Aaron, 106
  Betsey Ann, 106
Lockerman, Catherine, 106
  Dennis, 106
  James, Jr., 106
  Mary, 106
  Odam, 106
  Ruth, 106
  Sarah, 106
  Suviah, 106
LOVE, DANIEL, 85, 97
  Cathrine, 97
  James, 97
  Sarah, 97
Lowell, Elizabeth, 55
LUCAS, GEORGE A., 58
LUCAS, LEWIS, 106
  Sophia A., 58
  Mary B., 60
  Charles, 106
  Elizabeth, 106
  John, 106
  Priscilla, 106
  Raiford, 106
  Sherod, 106
Lusso, William, 104
MACKLEMORE, WEST, 12
  Redick, 13
  Seley, 12
Magee, Wyatt, 26
Mainer, E., 114
MAINOR, F. D., 59
  William Ottis, 59
MANUEL, ISHMAEL, 59
  Alpha Jane, 59
  C------, 59
  Martha, 59
  Rebecca Eliza, 59
Marable, B. F., 15
MARLEY, FRANCES, 11
MARLEY, ROBERT, 11,12,59, 89
  Eliza, 11, 59
  Fanny, 12
  H. J., 77
  Horatio, 11
  James, 10, 12

Marley, Rolland, 11
  Sally Ann, 11
  W. M., 34
  Willie, 11
Marly, Arabella, 73
Marshburn, John, 113
MARTIN, RICHARD, 11
  Lewis, 11
  Laura L., 109
  Mary, 11
  Mary Jane, 22
  Rebecca E., 69
  Sally, 11
Massengill, Henry, 83
  Nelly, 83
Mate, Abel, 7
MATHIS, FREDERICK, 59
MATHIS, MARY, 60
MATHIS, JAMES, 59
MATHIS, MARY, 60
  Abram N., 59
  Albert, 60
  Caroline, 73
  David S., 59
  Edmond, 59
  Elizabeth, 59
  Elizabeth A., 60
  Fleet C., 59, 60
  Henry, 60
  James, 59
  Lavina Jane, 59
  Lazarus, 60
  Luther Rice, 59
  Margaret Jane, 59
  Marshal, 60
  Mary Ann, 59
  Miriam, 87
  Nancy, 59
  Penney, 59
  Rhoda Catharine, 77
  Sabra, 59
  Silvester R., 60
  Sloan, 59
  Thomas B., 59, 60, 87, 89
MATTHEWS, JOEL, 59
Matthews, Archibald, 56
  Elizabeth C., 94
  J. T., 80

John M., 87
John W., 15, 66
Katharine, 59
Polly, 29
R. D., 36
William I., 36
William S., 28, 41, 47,
  56, 69, 71, 78, 79, 104
Wellington L., 41
Thomas L., 111, 112
MATTHIS, A. N., 59, 67
MATTHIS, JOEL, 11
MATTHIS, MARSHAL H., 60
MATTHIS, ZACHEOUS, 11
  Abraham N., 67
  Abram N., 60, 67
  Archibald, 16, 26, 28
  Asa V., 60
  Ellen E., 60
  Elizabeth A., 60, 72
  Elizabeth C., 60, 94
  Eliza Jane, 89
  George E., 60
  Harmon, 63, 68
  Henry, 11
  J. B., 59
  James T., 63
  Jenetty, 11
  John C., 11
  John O., 60
  J. Tate, 59
  Kathern, 11
  Liza, 11
  Marshall, 11
  Marshall M., 60
  Mary, 11
  Mary T., 60
  Milton, 11
  O. M., 22
  Perry C., 60
  Rachel Caroline, 67
  Rice P., 63, 77
Matthis, Susan C., 59
  Susannah, 13
  T. J., 59
  Thomas, 11
  Thomas B., 87
  W. A., 59

Wm. S., 16, 26, 33, 41, 47, 56, 69, 71, 78, 79
Willie L., 60
Mawbley, Olin, 12
Maxwell, Daniel, 64
  J. R., 9, 59, 91
  Nancy Jane, 24
  Rebecca M., 9
  Thomas, 1, 3
  William, 24
Meares, William, 98
  William B., 55, 103
MELVIN, DANIEL, 60
  Daniel H., 60
  Dorcas, 77, 110
  Elizabeth L., 60
  James H., 60
  John F., 60
  Lucinda, 60
  Robert G., 60
  Stephen B., 60
  Stephen H., 60
  W. A., 35
  William C., 60
MERADITH, JOSEPH, 97
  Ann, 97
  Elizabeth, 97
  Hannah, 97
  Nathan, 97
  Sarah, 97
Merriman, Rebecca P., 26
MERRITT, BENAJAH C., 60
MERRITT, ELIZABETH, 61
MERRITT, GABRIEL, 11, 61
MERRITT, NATHANIEL, 11
MERRITT, UNITY, 11
MERRITT, DANIEL, 106
MERRITT, MARY, 106
  Alexander H., 60, 106
  Ann, 11
  Anna, 28
  Bryant, 60
  David, 11, 61
  Eliza Matilda, 89
  Felix, 58
  Gibson, 65
  Haywood, 61
  James, 11

Kilby, 11, 51
Killbee, 51, 60
Lewis L., 60, 106
Nancy, 34
Patrick, 11, 12, 61
Rachel A., 60
Robert, 58, 61
Sally, 61
Temperance, 11
Tempy Jane, 61
Teresy, 11
Treecy, 11
William Henry, 59
William Nicholas, 61
Wright, 61
Molsey, 106
Merret, Bradly, 106
  Catherine, 106
Merrett, Haywood, 106
MICKS, ELIZA J., 61
MICKS, WM. G., (Dr.), 61
  Sarah Rowena, 58
Middleton, Elizabeth A., 79
MILLARD, BITHANA, 61
MILLARD, FELIX B., 61
  Betsey Ann, 61
  Charity, 109
  David S., 61
  Eleanor, 61
  F. B., 35
  Hepsey Jane, 61
  Junius M., 61
  L. B., 21
  Luther R., 61
  Richard W., 61
  Sallie, 61
Millard, T. B., 94
Miller, Thinkful, 108
  Wm., 52
MOBLEY, BIGGERS, 12
MOBLEY, OLLEN, 7, 11, 12, 61, 75
  Betsey, 12
  Elizabeth, 12, 84
  Fanny A., 61
  J. W., 31
  James, 1
  Jessie Martin, 84

Lucinda, 31
Middleton, 31, 63
O., 7
Ollen, 31
Susan, 61
Walas, 10
Wiley O., 61
Willie, 12
Wallis, 1
Zilpha, 31
MOLTON, JOHN T., 62, 77, 86
Ann, 62
Monce, Anna, 110
Matthew, 110
MONK, ARCHIBALD, 16, 21, 30,
45, 62, 70, 82, 83, 84,
85, 89, 108
MONK, B. R., 62
MONK, JOHN C., 16, 17, 41,
62, 89
Anna, 62
Benjamin, 86
C., 40
C. H., 55
Claudius B., 62
Flora, 62
H. C., 41, 62
Henry, 62
Henry C., 41, 62
James M., 62
Julius Alexander, 62
Lizzie N., 62
Mary, 62
Monk, Rufus, 62
W. H., 30
Waneta E., 62
MOORE, JAMES, 11,18,62,77
MOORE, MARY, 62
MOORE, W. H., 62
Ann, 62
Eugenia F., 76
George D., 88
H. W., 64
Harriet O., 62
Henry W., 62
I., 23
J., 41
James A., 81, 111

Jane, 62
John, 62
John W., 60
Joseph, 38
Lewis, 103
Luke, 113
Mariah O., 62
Polly, 38
Thomas, 62
Walter O., 62
William, 62
More, Lucrecia, 88
Morgan, Elizabeth, 113
Giney, 92
Jane, 74, 117
Susannah, 80
MORISEY, J. K., 63
MORISEY, RICHARD B., 63
MORISEY, WILLIAM H., 63
Ann B., 63
Ann E., 63
Carrie, 63
David, 24
Eliza J., 63
Elizabeth C., 63
James K., 27, 63, 65
Mary P., 63
Penelope, 24
Robert G., 63
Thomas J., 75
Morisey, Thomas K., 73
William, 85
William G., 63
Morris, Allen, 55
H. G., 7
John, 96
Morrisey, George, 118
J., 113
Thomas J., 109
Ann, 24
Richard, 24
Owen, 24
Moseley, Geo. W., 70, 88
J., 38
J. W., 42
James, 45
Jonathan, 26
R. A., 70

R. D., 85
Sarah Eliza, 44
MOSELY, ROBERT A., 63, 75
  James M., 66
  Mary A., 63
Mosley, Horatio J., 75
  Mary K., 74
Moulton, Abraham, 86
  John T., 75
  Zilpah, 85, 86
Murphy, Archibald, 83
  Charles, 6
  C. T., 15
  C. Tole, 68
  David, 23, 59, 106
  Eliza A., 35
  Henry, 14
  Jerusha, 109
  Kate E., 94
  Kesiah R., 32
  Matt, 47
  Matthew, 32
  Patrick, 23, 35, 59, 61
  Phebe, 32
  Preston, 32
  Robert Henry, 64
  Robert J., 85
Murphy, Sarah Jane, 32
  Thomas J., 32
Murray, Jenette, 34
Murry, Mary C., 16
Musgrave, Thomas, 113
Myhand, Silas, 2

MacKay, John, 63
McAlexander, Sarah, 97
  Susannah, 96
McAlster, A. M., 12
McARTHUR, JOHN A., 63
  James O., 63
  John Thomas, 63
  Margaret A., 63, 77
  Mary E., 63
  William A., 63
McCaleb, T. D., 29
  M. S., 29
McCanne, Hugh, 96
McClam, Lewis, 48

McClenney, John, 117
McCorcudale, Sarah, 12
McCullen, Calvin J., 64
McCullin, Bryan, 82
McDaniel, Elizabeth, 55
McDONALD, SARAH, 63
  Catharine, 63
  Daniel, 63
  Kenneth (Rev.), 64
  Mary Ann, 63
McDUFFIE, CATHARINE J., 63
McDUFFIE, WILLIAM ARCHIBALD,
  63, 64
  Anna Cornelia, 63, 64
  Laura Electa, 63, 64
  Susan Alice, 63, 64
McDugald, Margaret J., 72
  Mary A., 35
  Neill, 72
McGEE, BETSEY ANN, 107
  Hardy W., 107
McILWINER, (McILWIN), JOHN,
  12
  Fannie, 12
McIlwinn, Rainey, 109
McIntyre, Daniel, 111
McKay, William (Dr.), 73
McKee, William, 97
McKeen, James, 97
McKense, Barnabas, 20
  Betsey, 20
  John S., 20
  Olive, 20
  Sarah, 20
  Sarah Ann, 20
  Susy, 20
  William, 20
McKenzie, Sophiah, 92
McKinne, R., 113
McKinnen, Polly, 12
McKinnon, S. Addelaid, 58
  Daniel, 109
McKinsie, Frances A., 37
  J. T., 37
  W. R., Jr., 37
McKOY, ALLMAND A., 15, 35,
  47, 61, 62, 63, 64, 58,
  78, 85, 87, 95

Lydia A., 64
W., 53, 55
Wm. H., 53
McLAMB, PERCY, 64
  Civil, 47
  Della, 23
  Elizabeth, 83
  Isham, 47
  Isham T., 87
  J. C., 53
  John, 64
  Julia, 23
  Nathan, 87
  Pharebee, 83
  Susy, 70
McLane, William, 52
McLemore, Elizabeth A., 24
  Lofton H., 76
  Matilda I., 37
  Richard, 108
  Susan, 71
McLENDON, LEWIS, 12
  Burrel, 12
  Denes, 12
  Dunnes, 12
  James, 12, 111
  Jesse, 12
  John, 12
  Jule, 12
  L. W., 12
  Mary, 12
  Patsy, 12
  Sally, 12
  Shadrick, 12
  Simon, 12
  Zilpha, 12
McLEOD, NEILL, 12
  Angus, 12
  Elizabeth, 72
  John, 12
  Malcom, 12
  Neill, Jr., 12
  Sarah, 12
McMillan, Daniel, 81
  Sarah, 16
McPHAIL, DUNCAN, 8, 64
  A. A., 15
  Ann Eliza, 64

Catharine, 64
Duncan C., 26, 64
Ellen S., 67
Isaiah, 64, 90
Phereba, 90
P. W., 105
Thereby, 64
McQueen, Daniel, 12
  Susannah, 77
McQUINN, NORMAN, 113, 119
  Catherine, 119
McRae, Alexander, 83
McREE, WILLIAM, 96, 97
  James, 97
  John, 97
  Robert, 97
  Samuel, 97
  Susanna, 97

Nance, Sally, 29
Naylor, Abraham, 2, 81
  Abraham, Sr., 15, 17, 81
Newbern, Tearsy, 2
NEWMAN, JACOB, 64
  Archibald, 64
  Elizabeth A., 64
  Margaret E., 67
  Mary Ann, 64
  Nancy, 23
Newsom, Micager, 13
Newton, D. B.,
  Samuel, 114
  Trecy, 51
Nicholson, D. B., 51
Noles, Mary, 57
Norris, Betsy, 78
  Penny, 49
  Robert, 50

OATES, DAVID, 54, 64
OATES, ELIZABETH, 65, 77
OATES, JAMES, 5,30,62,65,70
OATES, JETHRO, 18, 54, 65
OATES, MARY ANN, 65
OATES, STEPHEN, 5, 65
  Ann E., 65
  D. A., 15
  Calvin, 65

Catharine, 18
Curtis C., 28, 35, 65
Curtis Caraway, 65
Claiburn I., 65
Claborn Ivey, 65
Eliza, 65
Jesse O., 65
Jethro W., 64
John, 12, 65
John A., 48, 55
John Olen, 65
Joth., 55
Lewis C., 35
Louetta W., 65
Malinda J., 64
Mary B., 65
Oates, Michael, 65
  Mildred J., 65
  Samuel, 6
  Susan, 64
  Thomas, 65
  Thomas I., 65
OATS, STEPHEN, 12
  Catharine, 5
  Fanny, 12
  Jesse, 5
  John Olin, 12
Odam, Andrew, 93
ODOM, SARAH, 13
  Cozzen Jacob, 13
  Dicy, 23
  Jacob, 13
  James, 10
  John, 13
  Richard, 13
  Sylva, 82
  William, 13, 116
ODUM, DICEY, 65
  Sopheah, 81
Oliver, Jacob, 14
  Sarah, 55
O'Quinn, Eliza, 22
Orrell, Virginia T., 16
Overton, Elizabeth, 22
OWEN, JOHN, 65, 66, 67, 73
OWEN, MILES P., 29, 60, 65, 66, 95, 105
OWEN, OWEN, 66

OWEN, REDDIN, 66
  Ann E., 66
  Benson S., 65, 66, 67
  Bernice B., 66
  Caroline, 50, 66
  David C., 66
  Edward J., 66
  Edmund B., 65
  Elizabeth, 66
  Elizabeth Ann, 67
  Gabriel, 66
  George P., 66
  Harmon, 88
  Helan C., 69
Owen, Henry L., 66, 95
  Irvin, 66
  Jennetta, 66
  J. C., 22
  John, 110
  John, Sr., 66
  John W., 65, 66
  Junius P., 66
  Leonidas C., 66
  Letetia, 66
  Martha, 66
  Martha A., 66
  Martha Jane, 66
  Mary, 66
  Mary Allia, 66
  Millard F., 66
  Patsey, 66
  Reden, 66
  Rody, 66
  Samuel W., 66
  Sarah, 65
  Thomas I., 65
  Thomas L., 67
  William, 66
  William B., 60
  William J., 66
  William T., 65
  Zilpha, 88
Owens, Nancy, 88

Packer, Ira Ann, 42
Paddison, John, 32
Page, John Richard, 19
  Mary, 19

Rebecca M., 16
Richard, 33
Sarah E., 19
PARKER, ANN, 66
PARKER, CHARITY M., 67
PARKER, HARRIET, 67
PARKER, JEMIMA, 13, 67
PARKER, JOHN, 67
PARKER, JONATHAN, 13
PARKER, JOSEPH D., 25, 67
PARKER, THOMAS, 67
Parker, Annie F., 30
  Bathsheba, 13, 67
  Cathrine, 67
  Charles K., 67
  Daniel, 36
  David B., 67
  David F., 67
  Denis, 66
  Edney, 67
  Elisha, 69
  Gabriel, 67
  James C., 67
  James M., 67
  James W., 67
  Joel, 74
  John B., 67
  John W., 67
  Jon, 4
  Joseph, 67
  Joseph D., Jr., 67
  Joseph L., 67
  Lucien E., 67
  Mary J., 67
  Molsey, 67
  Nancy E., 31
  Nanny, 7
  Nicholas, 4, 13, 110, 116
  Payton A., 4
  Peyton, 13
  Peyton R., 40, 69
  Rachel C., 67
  Richard, 4, 13, 25
  Robert A., 67
  Sabra, 66
  Samuel J., 67
  Sarah E., 66
  Sarah L., 67

Sophia, 66
Susan A., 67
Timothy S., 67
William W., 67
Zachariah, 69
Parish, Richard, 51
Parrish, Ollie C., 32
  R., 23
Parrish, Catharine M., 104
Parsons, G., 61
  Gardner, 37
  Mollie, 107
  Sydney, 37
Pass, Mary Elenor, 48
Paxton, James, 97
Pearce, Stephen, 51
Pearsall, J. Dickson, 70
PEARSON, THOMAS EDWARD RAN-
  DOLF, 68, 69
  Jonathan, 67, 68, 69,
  88, 107
  Elizabeth, 107
  Isabel, 107
  Jason, 107
  Mary, 107
  Patience, 107
  Selah, 107
PECK, LOUIS F., 41, 107
  Ann Eliza, 107
  Louis, 18
  Sally, 107
Pender, Ann, 27
Perkins, E. L., 84
Perry, Richard, 96
PETERS, SAMUEL, 12, 68
  Barbary, 68
  Clarkey, 45
  Eleas, 6
  Elias, 105
  Jesse, 68
  Josiah, 68
  Lucretia, 68
  Polly, 105
  Sally, 39
  Samuel, Jr., 68
  Zilpha, 12
PETERSON, AARON, 68
PETERSON, CHARLES, 68

PETERSON, ELISHA, 28, 68
PETERSON, ELIZABETH, 68, 69
PETERSON, HIRAM, 68
PETERSON, ROSS, 69
PETERSON, STEPHEN, 69
PETERSON, THOMAS, 69
PETERSON, WILLIAM D., 69
  A. C., 69
  Adonisam, 68
  Allen, 68
  Anna, 51, 68
  Babel, 4
  Becky, 71
  Bryant, 69
  Catharine, 28, 34, 87
  David T., 69
  Dicy, 68
  Dilcy, 68
  Enock, 68
  Everett, 22
  Fleet, 68
  Francis, 69
  Gabriel, 68
  George, 69
  Hariet, 68
  Haywood, 105
  Henry B., 69
  Howard J., 77
  Isaac, 17
  James, 33
  John, 93
  Kitty Ann, 50
  Laban, 68
  Larkin, 68
  Lewis, 69
  Lucy, 69
  Marsden C:, 17
  Martha A., 51
  Milton, 69
  Miriam, 69, 87
  Nancy, 4, 83
  Nixon, 68
  Patrick, 68
  Polley Ann, 40
  Priscilla, 88
  Rachel, 69
  Raiford, 68
  Richard, 69

  Robinson, 69
  Rosa, 69
Peterson, Sabrah A., 69
  Sarah, 20, 68
  Sarah Jane, 69
  Susan, 88
  Susannah, 53
  William, 69
  William F., 69
  William L., 68
  Winslow, 69
Philips, Ben, 2
PHILLIPS, SAMUEL, 69
  Ben, 4
  David, 69, 76
  Eley E., 40
  Hannah, 69
  James J., 69
  Jane, 34
  Samuel J., 69
Pierce, Stephen, 52
Pigford, Elizabeth A., 36
  J. L., 21
  James B., 40
  Sarah E., 21
  Susan Matilda, 40
  Virginia, 18
Pipkin, Sarah C., 73
  Stephen, 73
Pool, Adelia Ann, 33
  Delia A., 33
POPE, MARY M., 107
POPE, ROBERT, 107
  Elizabeth, 29, 107
  Jerusha, 2
  Joshua, 2
  Milton, 63
  Sally Ann, 107
  Samuel J., 26, 65, 116
  Samuel S., 83, 90
PORTER, JOHN, 13
  Absolom, 13
  Alen, 11, 59
  Elesabeth, 13
  Mark, 7, 13
  Nancy, 25
  Samuel, 13

Porter, Sarah, 1

S., 13
Susy, 29
William, 1, 13
Portevint, Elizabeth, 85
PORTIVENT, SAMUEL, 119
  Isaac, 119
  James, 119
  John, 119
  Mary, 119
POWELL, LUKE, 69, 70
POWELL, MARK, 70
  Amos S. C., 70
  Anne, 70
  Anom L., 70
  Arcada, 70
  Benj. J., 70
  Cader, 98
  Cora N., 70
  Duella, 47
  Elizabeth, 34
  James M., 33, 47, 71, 104
  John G., 68, 70
  Josiah, 5
  Luke A., 22, 70
  Mary, 70, 98
  Milton, 68
  Molsey, 88
  Moses, 98
  Nancy, 69
  Patience, 70
  Payton M., 70
  Polly Ann, 87
  Rebeckah, 69, 107
  Sherod C., 70
  Susan R., 50
  Zilpha, 70
Precythe, Nancy, 82
PRICE, JOSIAH, 107
  Dorothy, 107
  Joseph, 107
  Judith, 107
  Richard, 107
  Susanna, 105
  Jemima, 107
Price, Samuel, 107
  William, 7
PRIDGEN, WILLIAM E., 70
  Emily J., 70

Elizabeth, 119
PRIDGEON, MATTHEW, 70
  Ann Jane, 70
  Deborah, 70
  Jemima, 70
  Luke, 70
  Peggy, 70
  Rebecca, 70
PUGH, CRECY, 107
  Peter Holmes, 107
  Mary Ann, 55
  Thomas L., 37
Purvis, Sophia, 68
  Stephen, 68

RACKLEY, NANCY, 40, 70
  Arabella, 72
  Catherine E., 33
  C. J., 21
  Joshua, 16
  Mary E., 62
  Sarah R., 69
  Virginia J., 74
  Zilpha J., 50
  Elizabeth, 106
  Elizabeth Emeline, 106
  James S., 106
  Molsey Swan, 106
Rainer, John, 70
  Jarris J., 70
  Harriett Elizabeth, 50
RAINOR, AMEY, 70
  Joab, 70
  John, 69
  Matthew, 70
  Richard, 70
  Samuel, 70
  William, 70
Raynor, Festus F., 83
  Sarah Mariah, 83
Rayner, Anna M., 107
REAVES, CATHARINE, 108
  David, 108
  Edmund, 108
  John, 108
  Jonas, 108
  William, 108
REGISTER, BENJAMIN, 108

REGISTER, GIBSON, 70
REGISTER, HARMON H., 71
REGISTER, JOHN, 71
REGISTER, JOSEPH, 71
REGISTER, WILLIAM, 71
  Alice, 119
  Burrell, 71, 108
  Edith, 71
  Edmond, 71
  Edward S., 70
  Elizabeth, 71
  H. H., 44, 87
  Henry H., 70
  Henry M., 71
  James H., 71
  John W., 71
  Kitty, 28
  Mary, 71
  Mellissa A., 71
  Nancy L., 70
  Newton Francis, 70
  Sally, 70
  Sarah E., 70
  Susan, 71
  William E., 71
  John, 108
  John L., 106
  Joseph, 108
  Mattie D., 109
  Pearl, 119
  Sarah, 119
  Silas, 108
  Thomas, 108
REID, DAVID, 71
  Alexander, 71
  Ambrose R., 71
  James, 50
  James W., 71
Reid, Sophia, 71
Reynolds, Anna Maria, 64
Rhodes, Reddick, 24
RICH, LOTT, 71, 72
RICH, LOTT, SR., 71
  Dicey, 71
  Eleazar, 94
  Harriet, 71
  Isaac, 78
  James O., 71

Lewis, 32
Lott Jasper, 71
Margaret M., 71
Mary Jane, 72
Owen, 71, 72
Owen R., 75
Polly, 72
Sarah A., 71
RICHE, LEWIS, 108
  Lott, 108, 2, 20, 32
  Marry Jane, 108
  Owen, 108
  Sabry, 108
  Mary, 2
Richardson, Milton C., 16,
  27, 58, 64
RIVENBARK, DAVID F., 43, 72
  Daniel J., 72
  Matthew J., 72
  Owen J., 72
  William J., 72
Robert, Frank N., 75
Roberts, Frank A., 109
Roberson, Janetta, 60
  Martha J., 65
Robertson, Ann, 77
Robeson, Dorcas, 108
  Margret, 108
ROBINSON, ALICE, 108
ROBINSON, HANNAH CAROLINE,
  108
ROBINSON, GEORGE, 72, 73
ROBINSON, GEORGE R., 72, 73
ROBINSON, GEORGE W., 11, 50,
  52, 72, 73
ROBINSON, J. W., 73
ROBINSON, JAMES, 72
ROBINSON, JOHN, 36, 73, 89
ROBINSON, OLIVER P., 72, 73
ROBINSON, WILLIAM, 4,9, 41,
  50, 53, 71, 73, 83, 85,
  95, 108, 110, 112, 115
ROBINSON, WILLIAM D., 68, 73
ROBINSON, WILLIAM L., 15,
  16, 28, 67, 68, 71, 72,
  73, 88, 105, 106
  A., 32, 117
  Abner, 15, 72, 73, 92

Robinson, Josiah, 17, 34, 50, 52, 58, 59, 60, 64, 63, 69, 72, 73, 74, 114
L. W., 72
Lucien W., 72
Margaret, 72
Marget, 73
Mary A., 34
Mary Catherine, 73
Mary Jane, 73
Missouri F., 72
Molcy Jane, 73
Nancy, 72
Otavey, 74
Polly, 68, 84
Rebecca, 52, 72
Sarah J., 34
Sophia Ann, 73
Susan M., 72
Tabitha, 72
Thaddeus, 74
Victoria E., 74
Wm. Henry, 73
Ann, 108
Billie, 114
D. T., 108
Duncan T., 108
Elizabeth, 105
George, 105
George W., 117
J. C., 105
J. W. Scott, 108
James, 105
John, 105
Samuel, 105
Susannah, 105
Thomas, 115
Annabella, 72
B. W., 69
Benjamin, 52
Burriess W., 60, 69, 74
Charlotte, 85
Columbus G., 42, 50
D. L., 73
Daniel, 55, 108
Dicey A., 73
Duncan Thomas, 73
Eleanor, 72

Elizabeth H., 72
Ferdinand, 74
G. N., 36
G. W., 83, 87, 88, 89
Harrieta C., 73
Ira, 69
Isaiah, 15
J. B., 51
J. H., 44
J. W. L., 55
J. W. S., 73
J. Monroe, 72
James C., 72
James M., 71
Jenetta, 74
John Bright, 72
John F., 73
John, Sr., 52
Joseph, 72
Julia B., 72
Katharine, 73
Rodgers, Charity P., 79
Rogers, Lucretia, 85
Mary, 34, 111
O. P., 76
Polly, 29
Elizabeth, 111
Rooks, Martha A., 21
Rose, R. F., 56
Rose, Benjamin, 109
Ross, Sarah Bertha, 73
Rouse, William, 21
ROYAL, A., 74
ROYAL, CATHARINE, 74, 75
ROYAL, HARDY E., 74
ROYAL, HARDY, SR., 74
ROYAL, ISHAM, 29, 64, 74, 75
ROYAL, JOHN, 74, 75, 80
ROYAL, REZIN, 75, 76
ROYAL, NOAH, 75
ROYAL, OLLEN, 64, 75
ROYAL, OWEN, 75
ROYAL, SARAH J., 74, 75
ROYAL, WHITNEY, 14, 61, 74, 75
ROYAL, WILLIAM, 75, 76
ROYAL, YOUNG, 75, 76, 108, 109

ROYAL, ZACHARIAH, 25, 76
ROYAL, REASON, 108
  A. E., 59
  Albert, 22, 76
  Albert B., 74
  Albert Bernard, 7, 75
  Alfred, 76
  Alexander, 74, 75
  Allen, 76
  Althenisa, 74
  Alvin, 75
  Amos, 74
  Apsilla, 84
  Betsey Ann, 3
  Biggers, 75
  C---, 74
  E. F., 47
  Edith, 76
  Elias F., 75
  Elias T., 75
  Elizabeth, 74, 76
  Elizabeth Maria, 75
  Emily, 76
  Gabriel H., 75
  H., 76
Royal, Hardy, 3
  Hardy Elverton, 74
  Sardy S., 74
  Ivey Adlas, 74, 75
  Tabitha, 76
  John Allen, 75
  Jonathan, 76
  Josiah, 75, 109
  Labon, 75
  Lizzie, 16
  Louisa, 22, 76
  Lucy, 75
  Margaret A., 78
  Mariah, 74
  Mary A., 74
  Mary Adeline, 74
  Miney N., 74
  Minnie Novelle, 75
  Moulton, 75
  Nancy, 75, 76
  Nellie, 75
  Ollen J. M., 75
  Oliver, 76

  Polly, 75, 76
  R., 25
  Rachel C., 26
  Raiford, 76
  Rice, 76
  Sarah, 75
  Susan A., 16
  Susanna A., 75
  Telitha, 8
  Thomas, 76
  Timothy L., 74, 75
  Vinson, 76
  W., 80
  Walter Dane, 25
  Whitney, Jr., 64
  W., Sr., 64
  Wm. R., 75
  William Rufus, 74
  Willis, 75
  Wilson, 76
  Zilpha A., 67
  Catharine, 108, 109
Royal, John, 109
Runnels, Amos, 8
  Lewis, 2
Russell, Wm. 54
  Francis, 91
Ryals, Suffer, 24

Sampson Hall, 101
SAMPSON, JAMES, 101, 102,
  103, 118
SAMPSON, JANE, 103
SAMPSON, JOHN, 96, 97, 100,
  103
  Eliza, 103
  John Lyon, 118
  Lucy, 103
  Mary, 118
  Michael, 112
SANDEFUN (FUR), JOSEPH, 109
Sanderlin, Eliza, 79
Sanders, E. W., 44
Sanderson, Jesse S., 82
  L. M., 23
  Susan T., 81
Saunders, Robert, 8
Saur, Jane, 57

Savage, William, 96
SCOTT, JONATHAN, 109
  Ashe, 109
  Mary, 109
SEAVEY, J. B., 76
  Ann J., 76
  Hannah W., 76
  Jeremiah B., 76
  Mary B., 76
Sellars, Amariah, 106
  Ann, 106
  Everitt, 106
  Jane, 106
  Jenny, 106
  Martha, 106
  Mary Jane, 106
  Nancy, 106
SELLERS, SAMUEL, 119
  Abraham, 119
  Hannah, 119
  Zilphia, 119
  Archibald, 64
  Edwin, 64
  John, 2, 3, 37
SESSIONS, RICHARD, 109
  Boon, 109
Sessions, David, 109
  Esther, 109
  James, 114
  Jesse, 109
  Joseph, 109
  Philip, 109
  Uriah, 109
  William, 109
  Winifred, 109
Sessoms, Eley, 73
  Leman, 36
  Salmon, 10
SESSUMS, BLAKE, 76
SESSUMS, SOLOMON, SR., 76
  Colan, 76
  Elizabeth Ann, 76
  Fanny A., 51
  Frances J., 37
  Gray, 76
  Guy, 76
  Irwin, 76
  John, 76

  John Nelson, 76
  Lemmon, 76
  Mary Ann, 76
  Miles, 76
  Nicholas, 76
  Owen, 76
  Polly Hanah, 76
  Rachel, 76
  Solomon, 76
  Sophia, 76
  Sophiniah, 76
Sewell, Thomas, 12, 48
Shaver, Ida May, 14
  Margaret Elizabeth, 14
  P. A., 14
SHAW CATHARINE, 109
  Carrie, 108
  Colin, 107
  John, 107
  Mary Graham, 108
  Elias F., 35
  Katharine, 81
  Susan A., 35
Sheffield, Nancy I., 46
Shelly, Samuel C. S., 70
Shepherd, Jesse G., 77
SHINE, FRANCIS, 77
  Alexander, 77
  Ann, 113
  Ellen Jane, 77
  James K., 77
  John, 77
  Margaret Ann, 77
  Sarah Green, 77
  Thomas T., 77
  William R., 77
SHIP, ANN, 77, 109
SHIP, MICHAEL, 109
  Isaac, 91
  Jane, 77
  Michael, 77
  Robert, 46, 77
Shipp, Robert, 18, 65
SIKES, DANIEL M., 77, 109,
  110
SIKES, JOHN, 77
SIKES, MURDOCK M., 76
  C. M., 110

George H. B., 109
Murdock, 109
Charles M., 77
Elva J., 76, 77, 110
James H., 77
Joshua, 10, 111
Sillars, Wm., 58
Simes, Ambrose, 10
SIMMONS, JOHN, SR., 106, 110
Jeremiah, 110
John, 110
Sherwood, 110
Miles C., 47
Sallie M., 24
Simpson, Fleet, 33
Sloan, David D., 73
Dickson, 11, 12, 27, 59, 67, 69, 113
Slocum, Rebecca, 15
SLOCUMB, MARTHA A., 77
SLOCUMB, STEPHEN, 12, 38, 77, 113
SLOCUMB, WILLIAM K., 77
Dolly, 77
Elizabeth, 77
Isabella, 77
J. C., 17
John C., 77
R. K., 77
Sivel, 77
William, 77
SMITH, DAVID, 25, 78, 95
SMITH, HENRY E., 28, 78
SMITH, JAMES M., 78
SMITH, JOHN, 78
SMITH, JOHN, 78
SMITH, JOHN, 78
SMITH, JOHN W., 79
SMITH, WILLIAM, 110, 117
SMITH, WILLIAM H., 40, 78, 79
Alexander, 78
Amos J., 78, 79
Andrew, 7, 78
Ann, 78
Anna C., 60, 78
Bennett, 78

Smith, George, 78, 98
George E., 78
George W., 79
Hannon, 78
J. B., 33
James, 78
James A., 110
James K., 79
Jane, 52, 78
Jefferson D., 78
Jesse T., 78
John, 97
John D., 79
John K., 29, 78
John R., 25
Julius R., 79
Marcellus, 78
Margaret, 78
Miriam, 20
Martha, 23, 110
Martha Jane, 93
Mary, 7
Mary Belenda, 40
Mary K., 67
Mary P., 79
Matilda, 78
M------- F., 78
Nancy, 117
P. B., 78
Rhody, 78
Richard, 78
Robert L., 78
Rufus, 78
Sally Shepherd, 40
Samuel, 57
Sarah A., 66
Sarah C., 79
Sarah McRee, 97
Susan S., 79
Susannah, 7, 57
Sydnia T., 93
Thomas, 78
William, 8
William Alfred, 81
William Haywood, 81
Betsey Van, 81
C. C., 67
Caledonia, 78

Catharine, 78
Clara, 78
Charity, 13
Charles H., 79
Charlotte R., 16
Christopher C., 78
Della, 78
E. C., 51, 79
Edward C., 78
Edward E., 79
Elizabeth, 11, 78
Elizabeth C., 78
Ella Jane, 79
Franklin, 78
Smith, Yancey B., 78
Snead, Agnes, 30
  Ann F., 30
  Catharine, 30
  Charles, 30
  Edward, 30
  Franklin, 30
  George, 30
  Laura, 30
  Nathan, 30
  Thomas D., 30
  Walter, 30
SNELL, ROGER, 98
  Ann, 98
  Hardy, 112
  James, 98
  Partheny, 98
SOUTHERLAND, ARKANSAS, 21,
  79
  Charley, 79
  Emma, 21
  J. B., 21, 61
  John, 21
  Kittie, 79
  Mack, 79
  Mariah A., 26
  Robert B., 79
  Swenee, 21
  W., 79
  Wallace, 21
SPEARMAN, DOLLY JANE, 27, 79
SPEARMAN, EDWARD, 96, 110
  Ann, 110
  Agnes Eldora, 79

Eliza, 28
J. H., 88
James E., 79
Mary Ann, 79
SPELL, JOHN, SR., 79
SPELL, MARGARET J., 79
SPELL, W. D., 79, 80
  Archie, 79
  B----, 80
  Betty, 79
  Burnice B., 80
Spell, Cora, 79
  David, 91
  David D., 80
  Elizabeth, 32
  Elizabeth Katherine, 79
  Hardy, 80, 108, 112
  Hardy A., 80
  Hardy L., 74
  Hariet, 79
  J. M., 80
  Jacob H., 79
  James, 108
  James M., 18
  John I., 59
  John J., 79
  Lewis, 4, 79
  Margaret Matilda, 79
  Mary M., 79
  Minnie, 79
  Olive, 80
  Polly E., 80
  Rachel, 4
  Sarah, 79
  Virginia D., 80
  Susannah, 72
Springs, Elizabeth, 26
Spyvea, Polly, 7
Stallings, Wiley, 106
Standley, A. C., 23
  Edny, 5
  Susan, 18
  Barnabas, 111
Stanford, Eleanor E., 85
  Margaret, 113
Stanly, Mary Ann, 40
  Penny, 81
Starling, Anna, 40

Stephens, Eliza, 20
  Eliza J., 74
  Joseph M., 55
  W. D., 74
  Anney, 109
  John, 113
  Martha Ann, 109
STEVENS, ALICE, 110
STEVENS, BARNABAS, 110
STEVENS, JOHN, 111, 113
STEVENS, JEMIMA, 80
STEVENS, JOHN, 80
STEVENS, MARY JANE, 80
STEVENS, WILLIAM J., 30
  Angelina, 80
  Barnaby, 80
  Charity, 4
  Charles, 80, 110
  Charles Thomas, 80
  Charlotte C., 88
  Eliza Jane, 80
  Elizabeth, 80, 110
  Hardy, 25, 74, 80, 111
  Jas. H., 21, 27, 73
  Marry, 6
  Mary, 80
  Mary Ann, 80
  Mary E., 45
  Nancy, 29
  Sabrah, 80
  Sally T., 80
  Sarah Jane, 80
  Serena F., 64
  Susan, 23, 64
  W. L., 14
  Whitley, 2
  Wilber D., 80
  William, 80, 110, 117
  Willy T., 19
  Arteasha, 110
  Cager, 111
  Isaac, 111
  Lydda, 110
  Mildred, 110
  Nancy Laruhamah, 110
  Oates, 110
  Richard, 111
  Susanna, 110

STEWART, DUGALD, 111
STEWART, DANIEL, 80
STEWART, JOHN, 80
  Christian, 81
  Dougal, 80
Stewart, James, 80, 111
  J. L., 15, 23, 37, 78, 90
  Jonathan L., 19, 45
  Mary Eliza, 80
  Nancy, 80
  Nancy Evaline, 80
  Neill, 12
  R. J., 11
  Will, 80
  Alexander, 111
  Allan, 111
  Daniel, 111
  John, 111
  Sarah, 111
Stith, B., 23, 77, 90
  Caroline, 52
  G. W., 94
Stokes, Mary C., 79
Stone, Louise A., 40
STRICKLAND, HOLLY, 81
  Alexander, 49
  Allen, 84
  Betsey, 81
  Isaac, 9, 31, 45, 49, 68,
    70, 81, 84, 90
  Jane, 83
  Jeremiah, 84
  John, 7, 81
  John A., 94
  Laura Ann, 24, 45
  Lilly J., 79
  Malinda, 49
  Martin, 81
  Redding, 84
  Samson, 45
STRONG, SALMON, 37, 61, 62,
    65, 81
  Catharine M., 81
  George V., 81
  Henry R., 81
  Michael I., 81
  Robert C., 81
  William A., 81

SUTTON, BARNABAS, 81, 82
SUTTON, EDMOND, 81
SUTTON, ELIZABETH, 30, 81, 82
SUTTON, JAMES, 81, 82
SUTTON, JOHN B., 82
SUTTON, JOSEPH, 82
SUTTON, LUKE W., 82
SUTTON, MATILDA, 82
SUTTON, THEOPHILUS, 82
SUTTON, ANN M., 111
SUTTON, ARGANE C., 111
SUTTON, LOUISA, 111
SUTTON, EDMUND, 111
  Abel, 111
  Elias, 108
  Isham C., 111, 112
  Mary E., 104
  Samuel A., 111, 112
  A. M., 81
  Ann Mariah, 81, 82
  Artesha, 82
  Benjamin, 82
  Bryant, 81
  Bryant McKoy, 81
  Buthsdela, 10
  Clarissa, 82
  Edmund, 82
  Elizabeth C., 82
  Ezekiel, 82
  George W., 81
  Hepsy A., 82
  J. B., 90
  J. H., 82
  John Brown, 82
  John H., 82
  Joseph R., 81, 82
  Josiah, 82
  Josiah, Jr., 81
  Julius, 82
  Lewis, 82
  Mary F., 82
  Mary Jane, 82
  Mattie, 23
  Nancy, 81, 111
  Nancy J., 81
  Oswin, 81, 111
  Penelope, 82

  Sally Ann, 82
  Sarah Ann, 81
  Sena C., 82
  Stephen, 82
  Stephen W., 81
  Susan, 81
  Susan Anna, 19
  Susannah, 32
  Sylvia, 82
  Thomas, 10
  Thomas H., 81
  Thomas J., 82
  Thomas W., 82
  Virginia S., 81
  William, 81
  William R., 81
  William Rufus, 82
  W. R., Jr., 81
  W. T., 31
  William T., 81, 82
Swann, Sally, 103
Swearingarne, Josiah, 2
SYKES, NEEDAM, 112
  Duncan, 112
  Sarah, 112
  William, 112

Taler, Catrrun, 96
  Tebeth, 96
TARRINGTON (TURLINGTON), SOUTHEY, 112
  Elisha, 112
  Israel, 112
  James, 112
  Polly, 112
TART, JOHN, 119
TART, THOMAS, 83
  G. A., 20
  J. W., 31
  Charlotte, 119
  Janet, 119
  Mason, 119
  Mildred, 119
  Patty, 119
Tart, Turner, 119
  James, 83
  John, 57, 83
  Kitsey, 57

Nathan, 83
Sarah, 83, 119
Susan, 57
Thomas, Jr., 83
Tate, Jenetta, 74
TATOM, JOSHUA, 83
TATOM, LABAN, 83, 109
TATOM, LOVE A., 20, 72, 83
TATOM, WILLIAM, 112
George M., 112
Rebear, 112
Beckky, 83
Dicey, 83
Dickson, 83
Elizabeth, 83
Marget, 83
Mary, 83
Molsey Jane, 83
Nancy C., 43
Richard, 83
Sally, 83
Sarah, 83
Sooky, 83
William, 48
Wm. R., 72, 83
Zilpah, 83
Tatum, Joshua, 117
Sarah, 72
Tayloe, Jonathan, 113
TAYLOR, RANSOM, 83
Elijah, 44
George, 4
L. K., 58
Laban, 3
Tedder, Mary Ann, 3
TEW, ALEXANDER, 112, 9, 84
TEW, DANIEL, 83
TEW, EMILY JANE, 84
TEW, HOLLEY, 84
TEW, LEWIS, 84
TEW, PHILIP, 84
Tew, Aley, 84
Hawley, 112
Morning, 112
P. A., 112
Alston, 84
Bedford, 84
Elcey, 84

Elisha, 70
Elizabeth, 84
Ephriam, 2
Huston Hobbs, 84
Jennet, 83
Joab, 70
Joel, 32
John, 59, 83, 84
John Holley, 84
Logan, 84
Luiza, 84
M. K., 40, 93
Mariah, 84
Mary, 84, 112
M., 84
Morning D., 79, 84
Nancy E., 50
Nancy Elizabeth, 70
Nanny, 12
Osburn, 84, 112
Patience, 83
Pleasant A., 70
Rachel, 84
Robert, 84, 112
Sarah, 83
Selesia Jewel, 85
Wiley, 83
THOMAS, LUKE, 112
Darden, 112
Evan, 98
John, 98
Susanna, 112
William, 112
Jonathan, 55
William, 22
Thompson, Jane, 62
Lucy, 48
Wm. I., 21, 35
Thomson, Dicey Ann, 42
Mary E., 41
W. J., 61
Walter O., 41
THORNTON, BENJAMIN, 84
THORNTON, BENJAMIN S., 84
THORNTON, NATHANIEL, 84, 85
THORNTON, SUSANNAH, 85
A., 17
Averitt, 84

Averitte, 94
Benjamin Sims, 85
Bershaby, 85
Christian, 85
David, 85
Eldridge, 84, 85, 105
Elizabeth, 84, 85, 89
Handy, 84
Joseph, 85
Martha, 1, 119
Millie, 84, 85
Phereba, 70
Polly, 39
Right, 84
Sally, 84
Samuel, 84
Samuel Sugs, 85
Sarah, 85
Susan, 89
Thomas, 85
Thomas, Sr., 84, 85
Uriah, 85
Whitfield, 84
Wright, 84
John, 119
Nathaniel, Sr., 105
TINDAL, JANNETTA, 85
TINDAL, JOSHUA, 85
Joshua Lawrence, 85
Nancy, 85
Rebecca Eliza, 85
Sarah, 85
Young, 85
TOOLE, EDWARD, 112
Elisabethan, 112
Toole, Geraldus, 112
Judith, 112
Matilda, 112
Unity, 112
Fanny, 80
G., 23, 80
Gary, 3
James R., 23
Willie M., 23
TORRANS, ELIZABETH, SR., 113
TORRANS, MARTHA, 85
TORRANS, THOMAS K., 85
Alexander, 113

Kenan, 113
Martha, 113
Richard Nixon, 113
Elizabeth, 85
Margaret, 85
Samuel, 85, 113
Thomas, 85
Torrence, Sally Jane, 40
TREADWELL, JAMES P., 85
TREADWELL, JOHN, 5, 85, 86
A. N., 42
Charlotte, 73
J. P., 105
J. T., 69
Nancy, 32
Trigs, Samuel, 113
TROUBLEFIELD, PETER B., 16, 86
Alexander, 86
Barbrey, 86
Lizzie, 86
Marshall, 86
Mary, 86
Nancy E., 86
P. B., 30
Peter S., 86
Sallie E., 86
S-- William, 86
Willie, 16
Troy, William W., 2
Tucker, Tobitha, 13
Sarah, 107
TURBEVILL, JOSEPH, 113
TURBEVILL, SAMPSON, 113
Alfred, 113
Isom, 113
Mary, 113
Milley, 113
Rhoda, 113
Tempie,
Turlington, Jas. H., 86
TURNAGE, WILLIAM, 113
Charles, 113
James, 113, 49
Sarah, 113
Zachariah, 113
Ann, 30
Nancy, 30

TURNER, JOHN, 113
TURNER, ELIZABETH, 86
TURNER, LYTTLETON, 86
  Alfred, 92
  David, 86
  Henry, 86
  John, 3
  Sprattiff, 86
  William, 55, 86
  Ruth, 113
Turns, Wm., 20
Tyson, John A., Jr., 71
Tyler, Eliza J., 14
  John, 14

UNDERWOOD, JOHN, 86, 88
UNDERWOOD, JOSIAH, 86
UNDERWOOD, SARAH, 86
UNDERWOOD, WRIGHT L., 87
  David, 86
  David D., 86
  Eli, 86
  Eliza Ann, 86
  Elizabeth, 77
  Elizabeth B., 87
  Emma Catharine, 87
  Jacob, 86, 87
  James, 112
  John P., 86
Underwood, John Walter, 87
  Joseph B., 86
  Julia Frances, 87
  Louisa A., 86
  Margaret Ann, 86
  Mary Ann, 75, 86
  Mary J., 67
  Sabra, 86
  Sabrey Swan, 86
  Sarah Ann, 86
  Sarah J., 86
  Theophilus, 86
  Thomas, 86
  Thomas R., 86
  Tobias, 22
  Uriah, 86

Vail, E., 60
  Edward, 11, 60

  Elizabeth, 60, 104
  Fleming, 104
  Harriett, 11
  Lorenza D., 60
  Mahala, 11
  Sarah, 60
  Thomas, 60
VANN, ENOCH, 87
VANN, HENRY, 87, 88
VANN, JAMES, 87, 89
VANN, JOHN, 60, 63, 87, 88
VANN, KEDAR, 10, 12, 71, 87,
  89, 114.
VANN, NEEDHAM, 88
VANN, OWEN, 88
VANN, SUSAN A., 88
VANN, THOMAS, 8, 87, 88,110
VANN, VALENTINE, 51, 87,
  88, 89
VANN, WILLIAM H., 51, 87,
  88
  A. D., 88
  Alia, 41
  Aaron, 71, 87
  Andrew C., 87
  Arthur, 87
Vann, Cader, 4
  Charity, 88
  Civil, 87
  Daniel, 88
  Dennis J., 87
  Dicey Ellen, 87
  Dolsey Ida, 87
  Elizabeth, 88
  Franklin, 87
  H. L., 88
  J. E., 88
  James H., 88
  Judith, 88
  King, 39, 104
  Lavinia, 21
  Lenora, 74
  Lewis F., 88
  Lott, 88
  Louisa, 72, 114
  Margaret, 88
  Margaret Ann, 87
  Marion M., 88

Mary, 72, 87
Mary Frances, 87
Mary Jane, 87
Nancy, 88
Phareby Elizabeth, 87
Polly, 29
Rebecca, 87
Robert, 87
Robert D., 88
Sally, 87
Susan C., 27
W. R., 87
William, 8, 88
Preston S., 114

Wade, Ira T., 50
Waddill, William, 112
Wadkins, Dicy, 114
Walker, Casper, 14
  Martha A., 33
  Sarah, 71
  Susan R., 14
Wall, Rebeckah, 1
WARD, MARY, 73, 89
WARD, NANCY, 89
WARD, WILLIAM, 89
WARD, THOMAS, 84, 89
  Alfred, 89
  Clarissa, 89
  Clifton, 58, 89
  E. G., 73
  Edbridge G., 89
  Elizabeth, 73
  George, 14
  George W., 38
  Isaac, 89
  Isabella, 72
  J. J., 38
  Jesse, 89
  John, 89
  Kezziah Jane, 51
  Mariam Elizabeth, 58
  Mary J., 50
  Mary P., 14
  Otis, 39, 59
  Patsey, 83
  Robert, 70, 89
  Robeson, 94

Robinson, 39, 40, 89, 91
Sally, 84
Samuel, 89
Sarah, 89
WARREN, BENNETT, 89
WARREN, ISAIAH, 31, 89, 90,
  117
WARREN, RICHARD, 90
  Angelina, 17
  Annie, 89
  Aquilla, 50
  Archy, 89
  Ashley, 89
  Blake, 89, 90
  Burrel, 31
  Camel, 89
  Elizabeth, 31
  H. F., 79
  Handy, 17, 90
  Henry M., 31
  Hester, 90
Warren, Isaiah, Jr., 90
  J. C., 89
  John, 89
  John Thomas, 75
  Joseph Isaiah, 31
  Lavina, 90
  Lovitt, 31, 89
  Mary, 90
  Miny Cindy, 90
  Nancy, 8, 89, 93
  Needham, 90, 93
  Rachel, 93
  Rachel Ann, 90
  Richard Townly, 90
  Right, 90
  Sally Jane, 31
  Samson, 89
  Sarah Jane, 31
  Susanna, 117
  William H., 8
  William Hawley, 90
Warters, Benjamin, 6, 8
WARWICK, BENJAMIN, 114
  Elijah, 114
  Harrod, 114
  Henry, 114
  John, 114

Mary, 114
Penellepee, 114
Reubin, 114
Sharod, 114
Thereby, 114
Waters, Adline A., 70
  Mary E., 44, 60
  Peggey, 16
Watkins, Ann, 4
  Nancy, 90
  Nancy Jane, 90
Watson, D. B., 27
  Neill, 19
  W. J., 60
Watters, Benjamin, 41
Webb, William, 46
WEEKS, BENAJAH, 90
WEEKS, JOHN, 90
WEEKS, KENON, 90, 94
WEEKS, MARY, 114
  A. M., 114
  John A., 114
  Mikel H., 114
  Arthur Moore, 90
  Benjamin, 90
  Della C., 31
  Eliza, 90
  Harriet, 90
  Henry, 90
  Hester, 90
  James, 90
  James H., 90
  Jasper, 90
  John Wright, 90
  Joshua, 90
  Laura A., 22
  Margaret, 90
  Mary I., 16
  Nancy, 90
  Nathan, 22, 91
  Susan, 22
  Thomas, 114
  Ula May, 90
  Wm. R., 14
  William Rufus, 90
  Willie, 90
WELLS, MARY, 114
  Daniel White, 114

David James, 114
Ellen F., 114
J. C., 51
Jacob, 44, 114
Martha P., 114
Mary C., 114
Rebecca A., 114
Sady, 34
Susan A., 114
WEST, JOHN, 40, 43, 46, 114
WEST, HARDY, 90
WEST, LOYED, SR., 39, 91
  Margaret L., 114
  Samuel Thomas, 114
  William Julius, 114
West, A., 76
  Allen, 39
  Annie C., 20
  Dorcas, 45
  Gainey, 91
  Handy, 39
  J. C., 93
  J. E., 83
  John E., 40, 56
  John H., 40, 34
  Kitsay, 20
  Lawed, 39
  Loyd, Jr., 91
  Mary, 23
  Mary M. W., 89, 114
  Matilda Ann, 90
  Meritta Ann, 90
  Nancy, 39
  Nancy E., 39, 114
  Noel, 39, 91
  Pennington, 39
  Ransom, 39, 40, 48, 90,91
  Uriah, 91
  W. J., 89
  Wm. H., 90
  Willis, 39, 119
WESTBROOK, JAMES, 109, 115
WESTBROOK, JAMES, 115
WESTBROOK, WILLIAM, 115, 117
WESTBROOK, WILLIAM, 115
  Aley, 119
  Charity, 115
  Charles, 115

Dolly, 109
Eliza, 115
Isabell, 115
John James, 115
Joseph, 115
Lee, 119
Mary, 109, 115
Persis, 115
Polly, 115
Sallyann, 115
Uriah, 115, 117
William, 83, 109
Westbrook, Betsy, 76
   William Henry, 115
Bartholomew, 39
Edney, 39
Elizabeth, 31, 115
F., 54
Furney, 5, 115
Gainey, 3
John, 83
Joseph B., 64
Joseph R., 20
Mary Miles, 83
Moses, 39, 115
R. S., 31
Uriah N., 30, 32, 64
Wm. T., 32
Wetherington, Ann, 42
WHITE, LUKE, 115
   George, 115
   James, 36, 115
   John, 115
   Martha, 115
   Matthew, 115
   William, 115, 119
   Elsey Ann, 38
   James, Jr., 38
   L. M., 67, 87
   Marthy, 36
   Murdock, 86
   Sophia, 89
Whitfield, Penelope, 46
   William, 97
WHITLEY, ELIJAH, SR., 115
   Josiah, 115, 116
Wiggins, Elisha, 5
   Willis, 93

WIGGS, RALPH, 116
   Martha, 34
   William, 5
WILKINS, SALLY ANN, 91
   Eliza, 54
   Eliza Jane, 91
   James, 91
   William Isaac, 91
Wilkinson, Polly, 38
WILLIAMS, ALEXANDER, 116
WILLIAMS, BARNABY, 91
WILLIAMS, BLANEY, 91
WILLIAMS, ELIZABETH, 91
WILLIAMS, JACOB, 116
WILLIAMS, JOEL, 91
WILLIAMS, JOSEPH, 116
WILLIAMS, ANTHONY, 98
WILLIAMS, JOYCE, 98
WILLIAMS, WILLIAM, 116
WILLIAMS, WILLIAM, 116
WILLIAMS, ROBERT, 11, 59
WILLIAMS, ROBERT, 91
   A. Nancy, 116
   Alace McRee, 97
   Arther, 116
   Benjamin, 98, 99
   Betsey, 116
   Daniel, 3, 59, 99, 116,
   117
   Easter, 98
   Elias, 116
   Elizabeth, 116
   Francis L., 116
   Hester, 99
   James C., 114
   Jesse, 116
   Joel, 116
   Joseph, 99
   Leusay, 116
   Lewis, 107
   Mary, 98, 99, 116
   Nasa, 116
   Pashent, 116
   Patsey, 116
   Penelope, 98
   Pherabe, 98
   Rachel, 116
   Reding, 116

Williams, Ann, 82, 97
  Anny, 65
  Asha, 29
  Dicey C., 43
  Edney, 15
  Edward S., 98
  Effy, 91
  Elizabeth Catharine, 92
  Frances Lee, 24
  Stephen, 98
  Thomas, 112
  William, 97
  William H., 103
  Winnifred, 116
  Abner, 7
  G. R., 17
  Hariet M., 52
  Harper, 92
  Isaac, 56
  J. R., 54
  James, 92
  James C., 20, 44, 75, 89, 94
  James Sessom, 92
  Jane, 25
  John, 91, 97, 98
  John A., 92
  John C., 91
  Louis F., 21, 91
  Margaret Jane, 91
  Margret, 91
  Mary Clarrilly, 92
  Mary E., 66
  Mary Jane, 33, 91
  Matilday, 59
  Molsey Mariah, 25
  Nathan, 3, 30, 116
  Noel, 19, 38
  R. J., 20
  Redin, 77
  Rosey, 91
  Sam R., 91
WILLIAMSON, JACOB, 119
WILLIAMSON, JAMES, 117
WILLIAMSON, ALLEN, 27, 92
WILLIAMSON, BURRELL, 92, 93
WILLIAMSON, H. G., 83, 92
WILLIAMSON, MARY, 92, 93

WILLIAMSON, OLLEN, 92, 93
WILLIAMSON, STEPHEN H., 92
WILLIAMSON, WRIGHT, 93
WILLIAMSON, NATHANIEL, 116, 117
WILLIAMSON, WILLIAM, 117
  Anne, 116
  Adolphus, 74, 75, 92
  Albert M., 93
  Alley D., 92
  Amanda, 93
  Ann J., 92
  Bartholomew, 39
  Benjamin, 92
  Charity, 93
  Charity Ann, 92
  David, 92
  David Ashly, 92
  Edward W., 93
  Elizabeth, 92, 116, 119
  Erskin, 92
  Euphenia, 92
  Frances, 28
  Francis Jane, 92
  Henry, 92
  Henry G., 92
  Henry Lee, 92
  Hepsey, 92
  James, 92, 93, 109, 116, 117
  Jerusha J., 92
  John A., 92
  John W., 93
  Julian, 92
  Katharine, 92
  Lucinda, 92
  Lucy Ann, 92
  Mary S., 93
  Meriah, 41
  Minnie, 92
  Owen, 93
  Page, 86
  Polly, 92
  Ritta, 92
  Sarah, 92
  Stella, 92
  Stephen, 74, 117
  Thomas, 27

Williamson, Virginia, 92
  William, 93
  William C., 74
  William M., 92
  William Wright, 92
  Z., 6
  Anthony, 117
  Bede, 113
  D., 110
  Elias, 119
  Elsey, 117
  Esther, 117
  James Munrow, 117
  Lorobabel, 117
  Lucy, 119
  Mary, 117, 119
  Nathan, 116, 117
  Patience, 119
  Rachel, 119
  Robert, 116
  Samuel, 117
  Theophilus, 119
  Timothy, 116, 117
  Willie, 117
  willis, 113
  Winney, 117
WILLIFORD, JASON, 93
WILLIFORD, MARY E., 93
WILLIFORD, MICAJAH, 93, 117
WILLIFORD, SION, 117
  Benton, 93
  James M., 93
  Jason C., 93
  John C., 56
  Margaret Ann, 93
  Marshal A., 93
  Martha J., 93
  Martin Andrew, 93
  Mary, 90
  Rebecca, 93
  S. W., 56, 93
  Sally, 117
  Susanna, 93
  Thomas, 93
  Warren, 93
Williford, William, 45, 93
WILSON, JOHN DICKSON, 117
WILSON, ISHAM, 93, 104

WILSON, JOSEPH, 58, 94
WILSON, ROBERT, 34, 94
  A. R., 94
  Abigail (Mrs.), 91
  Adolphus R., 94
  Calvin D., 94
  Catharine, 28
  Elinor, 93
  Elizabeth, 46
  Elizabeth Ann, 89, 94
  Elvira, 94
  James, 38
  Jesse, 34
  Jinny, 83
  John, 48
  John T., 88, 93
  Joseph J. F., 94
  Mary F., 94
  Robert B., 94
  Sarah Jane, 93
  Susan Ann, 93
  Susan C., 93
  Willie Elisha M., 93
  Willis, 72
  Young, 90
  Elizabeth C., 117
  J. C., 117
  Shadrack, 104
Windows, Nancy J., 16
Winslow, Warren, 86
Wise, Mary, 4
  Morris, 4
Wo--, Thomas, 10
WOLF, RICHARD, 18, 94
  Icey, 94
  Sally, 94
  Seaborn I., 94
WOOD, WILLIAM, 105, 117
  Alfred, 70
  Elizabeth, 117
  Jesse, 117
Wood, John, 117
  Jonathan, 117
  Linda, 105
  Moore, 117
WOODARD, ANY ANN, 94
WOODARD, JAMES, 94
  Amey, 94

Amey Ann, 94
Isaac, 94
Katherine, 94
Martha Jane, 94
Martha Jean, 94
Rachel, 94
William C., 94
Wooten, Crawford, 48
Daniel, 83
Lucinda, 48
Oliver, 21
Tabitha, 8
WRENCH, JOHN & SOPHIA, 117
WRENCH, JAMES, 94
Hugh L., 94
John, 94
Joseph, 94
Thomas E., 94
Arabella, 117
Novele, 117
WRIGHT, ELIZA J., 94, 95
WRIGHT, ISAAC C., 66, 94,
95

WRIGHT, JOHN, SR., 95, 109
A. B., 65
Betsy, 95
Catharine E., 95
Isaac 95
James, 97
James W., 75, 94, 95
John, 95
John C., 71, 94, 95
Margaret C., 94, 95
Nancy, 95
Penelope, 95
Polly, 95
Rebecca, 95
Susan C., 107
Wright, Thomas, 35, 65
Thomas B., 35
YOUNGER, DAVID LEE, 119
Aaron Lee, 119
Farby, 119
Jessie Lee, 119
Joel Lee, 119
Nancy, 119

(Note) The surname YOUNGER is in error. It should be David Lee, the younger.